an IISS strategic dossier

GW01513567

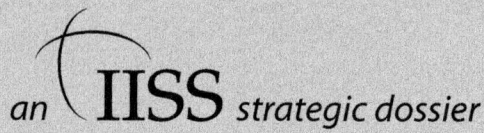

ASIA-PACIFIC REGIONAL SECURITY ASSESSMENT 2024

Key developments and trends

published by

The International Institute for Strategic Studies
ARUNDEL HOUSE | 6 TEMPLE PLACE | LONDON | WC2R 2PG | UK

an IISS strategic dossier

ASIA-PACIFIC REGIONAL SECURITY ASSESSMENT 2024

Key developments and trends

The International Institute for Strategic Studies
ARUNDEL HOUSE | 6 TEMPLE PLACE | LONDON | WC2R 2PG | UK

DIRECTOR-GENERAL AND CHIEF EXECUTIVE **Dr Bastian Giegerich**
EDITOR **Dr Evan A. Laksmana**
ASSOCIATE EDITOR **Gregory Brooks**
RESEARCH SUPPORT **Douglas Barrie, Henry Boyd, Nick Childs, Aaron Connelly, Paul Fraioli, James Hackett, Ithrana Lawrence, Antoine Levesques, Morgan Michaels, Meia Nouwens, Veerle Nouwens, Viraj Solanki, Ben Thornley, Julia Voo**
EDITORIAL **Aaron Chan, Nick Fargher, Jill Lally, Margaret Lin, Adam Walters**
GRAPHICS COORDINATOR **Nick Fargher**
DESIGN AND PRODUCTION **Alessandra Beluffi, Ravi Gopar, Jade Panganiban, James Parker, Kelly Verity, Jillian Williams**

This publication has been prepared by the Director-General and Chief Executive of the Institute and his staff. It incorporates commissioned contributions from recognised subject experts, which were reviewed by a range of experts in the field. The IISS would like to thank the various individuals who contributed their expertise to the compilation of this dossier. The responsibility for the contents is ours alone. The views expressed herein do not, and indeed cannot, represent a consensus of views among the worldwide membership of the Institute as a whole.

First published May 2024 by the International Institute for Strategic Studies.

© 2024 The International Institute for Strategic Studies

COVER IMAGES: (TOP) Sailors assigned to the forward-deployed amphibious transport dock ship USS *Green Bay* stand at parade rest on the ship's forecastle while transiting through Sydney Harbour during *Exercise Malabar 2023*, 11 August 2023 (Mass Communication Specialist 2nd Class Daniel Serianni/U.S. Navy). (MIDDLE L–R) Hundreds of Thai and US military personnel participate in a Strategic Airborne Operation exercise as a part of *Cobra Gold 2024*, in Lopburi, Thailand, 5 March 2024 (Matt Hunt/Anadolu/Getty Images). Vice Admiral Saito Akira (far l), Commander-in-chief of the Japan Maritime Self-Defense Force's Self Defense Fleet, talks with commanders from US, Indian and Australian naval forces before the annual *Exercise Malabar* joint drills begin on 10 August 2023 in Sydney (BJ Warnick/Newscom/Alamy Stock Photo). Thai and US military personnel participate in the *Cobra Gold 2024* exercise, in Lopburi, Thailand, 5 March 2024 (Matt Hunt/Anadolu/Getty Images). (BOTTOM) A mineman directs a French Navy H160 Airbus to land aboard USS *Charleston* during joint training exercise *La Pérouse 2023* in the Bay of Bengal, 14 March 2023 (Mass Communication Specialist 2nd Class Daniel Serianni/U.S. Navy).

Printed and bound in the UK by Hobbs the Printers Ltd.

All rights reserved. No part of this book may be reprinted or reproduced or utilised in any form or by any electronic, mechanical, or other means, now known or hereafter invented, including photocopying and recording, or in any information storage or retrieval system, without permission in writing from the publishers.

British Library Cataloguing in Publication Data
A catalogue record for this book is available from the British Library

Library of Congress Cataloging in Publication Data
A catalog record for this book has been requested

ISBN 978-1-032-86937-7 (Print)
ISBN 978-1-003-53006-0 (eBook)

About The International Institute for Strategic Studies

The International Institute for Strategic Studies is an independent centre for research, information and debate on the problems of conflict, however caused, that have, or potentially have, an important military content. The Council and Staff of the Institute are international and its membership is drawn from over 100 countries. The Institute is independent and it alone decides what activities to conduct. It owes no allegiance to any government, any group of governments or any political or other organisation. The IISS stresses rigorous research with a forward-looking policy orientation that can improve wider public understanding of international security problems and influence the development of sounder public policy.

CONTENTS

INTRODUCTION   6
Dr Evan A. Laksmana

CHAPTER 1: SPECIAL TOPIC
Scripted Order: Combined-military Exercises in the Asia-Pacific   14
Dr Evan A. Laksmana, Paul Fraioli, Veerle Nouwens and James Hackett

CHAPTER 2
Middling and Muddling Through? Managing Asia-Pacific Crises   50
Meia Nouwens

CHAPTER 3
Preferred Security Partner: Anchoring India in the Asia-Pacific   72
Antoine Levesques and Viraj Solanki

CHAPTER 4
Disparate Diplomacy: Managing the Post-coup Myanmar Conflict   92
Aaron Connelly and Morgan Michaels

CHAPTER 5
Driving Wedges: China's Disinformation Campaigns in the Asia-Pacific   108
Julia Voo

CHAPTER 6
Waiting in the Wings: The Asia-Pacific Air-to-air Challenge   124
Douglas Barrie and Ben Thornley

INDEX   140

COMMON ABBREVIATIONS

ADMM-Plus	ASEAN Defence Ministers' Meeting Plus
AI	artificial intelligence
ARF	ASEAN Regional Forum
ASEAN	Association of Southeast Asian Nations
ASW	anti-submarine warfare
AUKUS	Australia, the United Kingdom and the United States (trilateral security agreement)
BRI	Belt and Road Initiative
CCG	China Coast Guard
CCP	Chinese Communist Party
CPEC	China–Pakistan Economic Corridor
CPTPP	Comprehensive and Progressive Agreement for Trans-Pacific Partnership
EAOs	ethnic armed organisations (Myanmar)
EEZ	exclusive economic zone

FPDA	Five Power Defence Arrangements
HADR	humanitarian assistance and disaster relief
MoU	memorandum of understanding
NUG	National Unity Government (Myanmar)
PDF	People's Defence Force (Myanmar)
PLA	(Chinese) People's Liberation Army
PLAA	People's Liberation Army Army
PLAAF	PLA Air Force
PLAN	PLA Navy
PRC	People's Republic of China
RCEP	Regional Comprehensive Economic Partnership
SAC	State Administration Council (Myanmar)
UAV	uninhabited aerial vehicle

INTRODUCTION

The more things change, the more they stay the same. This phrase, coined by a French writer in the 1840s, interestingly captures the zeitgeist of the Asia-Pacific security landscape since the first edition of what was then called the *Regional Security Assessment* (RSA), published in 2014. That first Strategic Dossier analysed the key themes that had emerged from successive IISS Shangri-La Dialogues over the preceding decade. It focused on the role of major powers amid the rise of regional flashpoints – from the Korean Peninsula to the South China Sea – as well as internal and transnational challenges, ranging from armed conflict to energy and water security to emerging cyber threats.

Since then, the annual IISS Shangri-La Dialogues have sought to help defence policymakers from around the region to better understand emerging security trends and manage them peacefully. In that spirit, the *Asia-Pacific Regional Security Assessment* (APRSA) sought to reflect upon and deepen our understanding of those challenges. Over the past decade, after all, the competing impulses of great-power strategic competition and the often elusive quest for a stable regional order have become sharper and the stakes increasingly higher.

DRAINING DECADE

The Donald Trump presidency often sent the anxiety levels of Asia-Pacific leaders and policymakers through the roof during his tenure, a feat he will likely repeat if he returns in 2025. America has certainly shown a serious interest in dealing with China, even if the policymaking process had been incoherent and its credibility in question. President Joe Biden's Asia-Pacific policies expanded upon and refined Trump's impulsive approach, from the trade-war tariffs to technological controls. But the Asia-Pacific domain has also been overshadowed by the wars in Europe and the Middle East over the past two years. Being 'strong on China' is nevertheless now a litmus test in Washington, even as its geopolitical bandwidth increasingly looks overloaded.

Under President Xi Jinping, meanwhile, China has been more willing to throw its weight around. Its economic, diplomatic and security coercion has been uneasily felt by countries across the region, from India, Japan and South Korea to Malaysia, Vietnam, the Philippines, Indonesia and even across the South Pacific. Yet, while rhetorical assurances around 'peaceful rise' ring hollow, many regional policymakers still believe their economic prosperity is tied to China in one way or another. Managing the anxiety over China's coercion while being bullish over its economic prospects is now a constant preoccupation for many policymakers.

The pandemic years and their aftermath have sharpened the debate over economic interdependence. For many, deeper economic ties come with greater vulnerabilities, from supply-chain disruptions to geopolitical uncertainties. Competing geo-economic visions, from the Belt and Road Initiative to the Indo-Pacific Economic Framework, could encumber the region's already patchy economic integration and overlapping trade deals, which range from the Regional Comprehensive Economic Partnership to the Comprehensive and Progressive Agreement for Trans-Pacific Partnership and the upcoming ASEAN–China Free Trade Agreement 3.0.

Regional-security flashpoints have continued to proliferate as existing mechanisms struggle to manage them. The security situation around the Taiwan Strait and the South China Sea has only worsened in recent years. Incidents involving and coercive acts by China's military and maritime security assets in these waters have grown more frequent and dangerous. North Korea's missile development and threats have worsened the security environment in Northeast Asia and beyond. China's relationship with India has taken a nosedive since the 2020 border clash in the Galwan Valley.

Meanwhile, Asia-Pacific multilateral mechanisms anchored by the Association of Southeast Asian Nations (ASEAN), such as the East Asia Summit, the ASEAN Regional Forum or the ASEAN Defence Ministers' Meeting-Plus, are struggling to find a footing and make an impact. Senior ASEAN officials cling to established procedures – including

Figure 0.1: **Asia-Pacific: membership of selected minilateral and multilateral mechanisms**

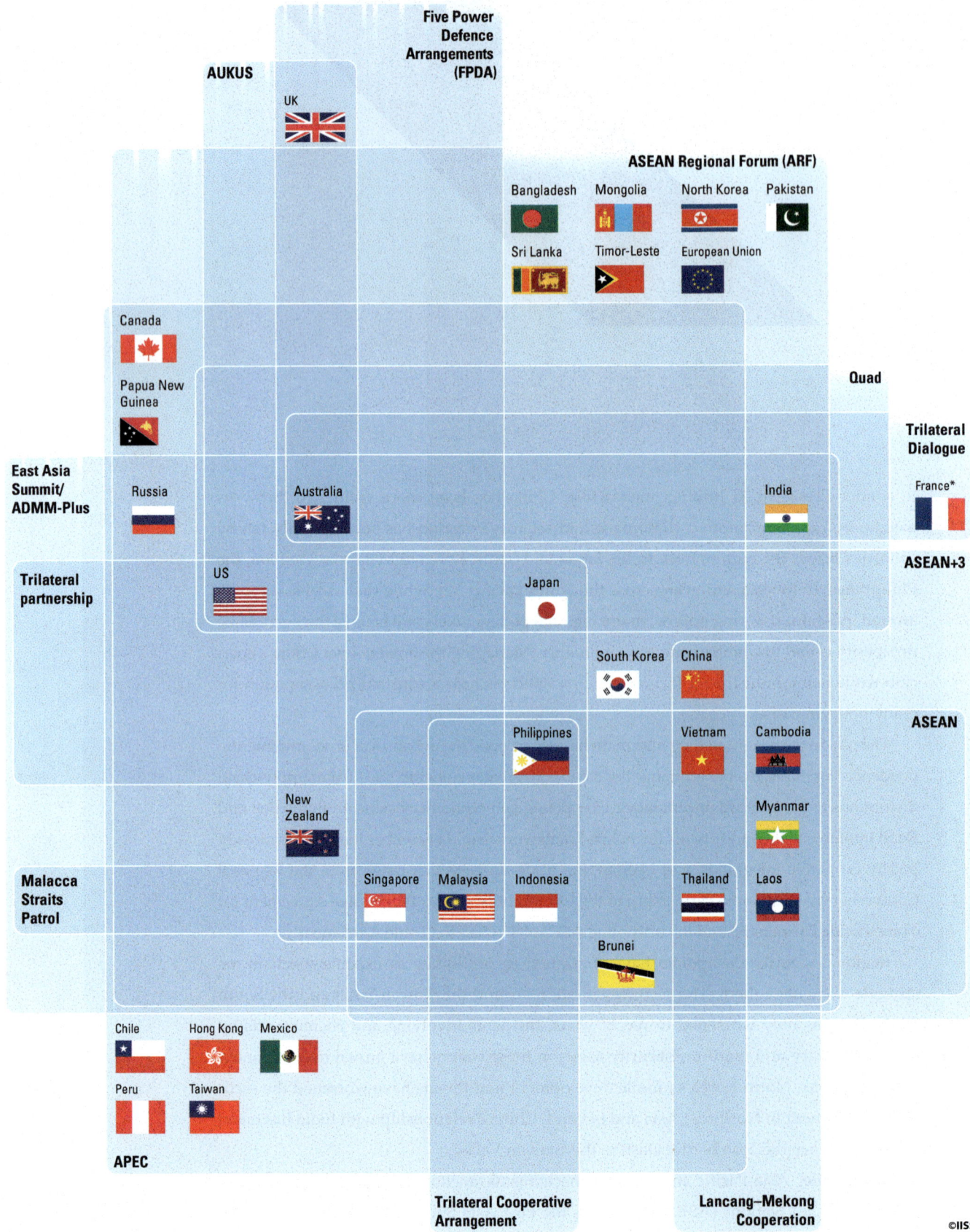

more than 1,200 meetings across all levels annually – while their leaders slowly try to understand each other amid region-wide generational political transitions. Without an energetic leadership, regardless of who the rotational chair is, ASEAN's attempt to shape the broader Asia-Pacific will likely fall short.

The mix of 'old and new' minilateral arrangements – as well as the growing interest of European powers – provides ASEAN with further competition for the attention of regional leaders and, by implication, the resources they can commit. The Asia-Pacific regional security architecture increasingly looks overcrowded (see Figure 0.1). Whether and how established mechanisms such as the Five Power Defence Arrangements, the Malacca Straits Patrol or the Trilateral Security Arrangement in the Sulu Sea complement or constrain the Quad or AUKUS and where ASEAN stands remain in question. The debate is not which will replace the other, but which platforms regional leaders will commit more of their limited resources to.

Displaced Pekon Township residents cut pods to retrieve opium resin at an illegal poppy field near the border between the Kayin and southern Shan states, Myanmar, 26 February 2024

(STR/AFP via Getty Images)

In the meantime, while some of these mechanisms have helped stem the tide of armed robbery and maritime terrorism, the challenges of illegal fishing and transnational crime at sea continue to proliferate and are increasingly tied to great-power politics and strategic competition. Further to this, armed conflict inside Myanmar since the 2021 coup continues to spill over and exacerbate a range of security challenges from human and drug trafficking to online-scam centres. The conflict has been a central concern among its neighbouring countries, particularly China, India and Thailand, as well as in the broader region. Armed conflict and transnational crime, in other words, remain key fixtures of the Asia-Pacific security landscape.

CIRCUMNAVIGATING COMPETITIVE CONSTRAINTS

The APRSA celebrates its first decade this year by reflecting on what has changed – and what has not – across key regional-security challenges since the RSA came out in 2014. The authors in each of the chapters reflect on how developments over the past decade have shaped specific security challenges and responses across the region. A dozen IISS research staff provide authoritative expert analysis of the underlying structural features of key security challenges – from military crisis management, to defence partnerships, to disinformation campaigns – and their prospects. Taken together, they also touch on three intersecting themes.

The first is the continued pressure and constraints emanating from the United States–China strategic competition. The competition is no longer limited to just being a 'security matter' occupying defence and military policymakers. Instead, economic, technological, social, diplomatic and other domains are all now increasingly connected and contested. This cross-domain competition comes with several features.

For one thing, networks formed around key hubs or nodes – that is, the US or China – are increasingly polarised and exclusionary. The more integrated a regional country is within the US-led security network, for example, the higher the cost for that country to expand or deepen its defence relationship with China, and vice versa. Such networks consist of overlapping layers of defence cooperation – from visiting-forces agreements, combined exercises, shared education and training to joint development and production of arms. Under Biden, the United States' alliances with Australia, Japan, the Philippines and South Korea have certainly been revived, tightening the 'latticework' of the system.

Chapter 1 explores the broad patterns of combined-military exercises in the Asia-Pacific over the past two decades and analyses why and how the US, China and key European powers conduct military exercises with regional allies and partners. Combined-military exercises across the region are more than the sum of their operational or tactical benefits, as strategic signalling – whether to deter or assure – remains another key motivation. The US has been the singular node in this exercise network, having conducted more than 1,100 exercises with regional countries from 2003–22. While China's combined-military exercises only amounted to around 10% of the United States' in the same period, it is seeking to catch up.

For another, with overlapping networks across different domains, challenging encounters and frictions driven by competitive impulses are growing. Operational interactions at sea between different coastguards patrolling their claimed exclusive economic zones, for example, become strategic problems when one side claims the other is being prodded into confrontation by their great-power patron. Even domestic political contestations are portrayed as extensions or proxies of great-power competition. We see this dynamic unfolding in Myanmar, with chapter 4 describing the disparate diplomatic approaches to managing the post-coup armed conflict.

Managing the US–China competition therefore is an imperative in any search for a stable regional order. Chapter 2 examines the nature of and challenges surrounding the US–China crisis-prevention and -management mechanisms as the rate of their military-to-military encounters has increased in recent years. Washington and Beijing arguably have asymmetrical assessments of the value of such channels, placing their effectiveness in doubt. More broadly, regional countries have also developed crisis-communication and -management mechanisms with either China or the US – and other platforms exist without both. Crisis management in the Asia-Pacific is nevertheless too important to be left only to Washington and Beijing.

FRIENDS WITH BENEFITS

But for all the constraints that come from the strategic competition unfolding in the Asia-Pacific, the value of alliances and strategic partnerships endures. How defence establishments work with each other across the region is the second theme present across all chapters this year. Chapter 1 certainly demonstrates that trend over the past two decades. When placed beyond combined-military exercises and alliance relationships, however, several key features of the emerging security architecture come to the fore.

Firstly, the polarising US–China strategic competition has created a partnership vacuum – there is a dearth of major powers whom the small and middle powers of the Asia-Pacific can work with and benefit from without the baggage of either Washington or

Beijing. The growth in 'partnership diversity' across the region is therefore a by-product of great-power competition. Australia, Japan and South Korea, while clearly US allies, have stronger and more nuanced approaches to regional engagement. They also have a more developed set of economic, diplomatic, political and security footprints than the US. These qualities make them appealing strategic partners and alternatives to the US and China for many in the region.

India falls into this category too. Chapter 3 examines India's role as a defence partner for Asia-Pacific countries, especially for those

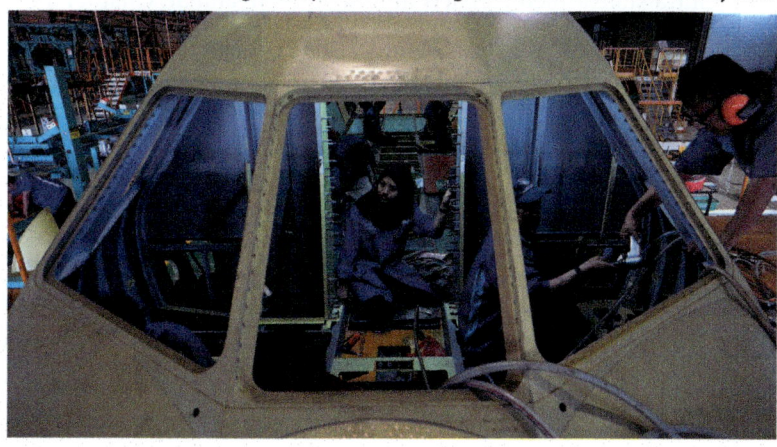

Employees of Indonesian defence supplier PT Dirgantara work on an aircraft inside a hangar at a plant in Bandung, West Java, Indonesia, 13 May 2019

(Dimas Ardian/Bloomberg via Getty Imagess)

in the Indian Ocean region and Southeast Asia. India has sought to become the 'preferred security partner' in recent years by raising the frequency and scope of its regional defence diplomacy, from military exercises and port calls to ministerial visits, arms sales and defence lines of credit. The goal for New Delhi has been to increase its regional presence and counter Beijing's regional influence. After all, China will continue to be India's primary defence and security challenge over the coming years.

Secondly, the competitive pressures of great-power competition also mean that the defence-partnership needs of small and middle powers in the Asia-Pacific are often 'limited' to specific areas, such as defence technology and industry development, training, education or exercises. Cambodia, Indonesia, Malaysia, Thailand, Vietnam and others have often instinctively 'compartmentalised' their defence partnerships with the US and other Western powers for fear of being left overly dependent – and therefore vulnerable – and their broader economic relationship with China being undermined.

In other words, it should not be assumed that more policy alignment on defence-specific areas will automatically result in broader cross-domain strategic alignment. The challenge is different, of course, for Australia, Japan, the Philippines and South Korea, where China's behaviour in recent years has led to a significant deterioration of their immediate security environment, from the Korean Peninsula to the Taiwan Strait and the South China Sea. For these countries, their worsening security environment means they will instinctively seek to double down on their alliance with the US.

Such patterns underlie perhaps an almost asymmetric set of strategic expectations surrounding defence partnerships by major powers and their allies and partners across the region. The US and China seek to expand and deepen their respective networks – from economic to defence and technology – seeking access and influence among regional countries while in competition with one another. Outside of the key US allies and partners, the rest of the region seeks to hedge their security partnerships while growing their economies – imperatives requiring simultaneous cooperation with both the US and China.

Thirdly, under such conditions, managing regional crises and flashpoints becomes even more challenging. Aside from the military-to-military encounters discussed in chapter 2, we can also see the difficulties of coordinating diplomatic management of intra-state armed conflicts unfolding in Myanmar. Chapter 4 examines the four different diplomatic tracks led by Western states and ASEAN as well as Myanmar's neighbours, especially China and Thailand. Given Myanmar's geopolitical centrality, the post-coup conflict since 2021 naturally attracts outside interest and exacerbates a wide range of transnational security challenges, from human trafficking to online-scam centres.

Taken together, alliances and defence partnerships continue to endure and are even set to expand in the years ahead. But the cross-domain pressure of strategic competition means that seeking friends with a specific set of benefits, without being fully committed to a broader strategic alignment or an exclusive group of partners, will also remain the strategic approach of many in the region. Different allies and partners will provide different values and benefits for different regional countries. A simple bifurcated world view, as if one major power can provide all the benefits the other cannot, is no longer persuasive.

TAMING TECHNOLOGICAL FRONTIERS

The final intersecting theme is the drive among regional countries to develop and deploy advanced and emerging technology to serve broader defence and strategic interests. Indeed, emerging technology in itself is a domain contested by the major powers. The expansion of the United States' efforts under Biden to limit China's ability to access advanced chip-making capabilities, for example, attests to this development. China has also increased its efforts to regulate and master emerging technology like artificial intelligence, quantum computing and biotech, among others.

In recent years, China has also deployed such technological capabilities to boost its information operations across the region. Chapter 5 describes how China uses disinformation operations to discredit political leaders abroad and deter the Taiwanese electorate, as well as using a range of cyber tools to push its positive image in the Philippines and drive a wedge in the US–Philippine alliance. While these challenges stem from the broader trend of strategic competition among states, the solutions rely significantly on whole-of-society and whole-of-government approaches which include commercial platforms and civilian experts.

Progress on emerging technology, especially on social media, continues to be quicker in the civilian domain than in the military one. Military organisations tend to be slower to innovate and adopt new technologies in general. But the pressure of strategic competition has certainly pushed regional militaries to try and experiment and adopt new and emerging technology as their security environment has deteriorated over the past decade.

Chapter 6 shows how the People's Liberation Army Air Force (PLAAF) has benefitted from sustained and substantial investment in tactical combat aircraft and air-to-air weapons. China seeks to be a credible – and, therefore, a best-avoided – adversary in any regional war with the US, most likely over Taiwan. The PLAAF has also been acquiring advanced air-to-air missiles that are equal to if not better than the weapons now fielded by the US and its allies. While the latter as a collective alliance remains qualitatively ahead of China, the skies over the Asia-Pacific will be more contested in the years ahead.

The almost tit-for-tat technological development around military capabilities between China and the US and its allies cannot be taken for granted. While the US and its allies retain a significant qualitative edge over China, the regional balance of military power might eventually tilt to the latter. The challenge for China, as chapter 1 demonstrates, is of course its lack of operational war-fighting experience since its war with Vietnam in 1979 and the fact that its combined-military exercises with regional countries remain underdeveloped and overly scripted for a regional contingency. It should be noted, however, that China likely does not define its military readiness the same way the US does in terms of needing to fight alongside allies.

For the time being, China's adoption of advanced and emerging technology might be more visible in the non-military domain, especially in the information space when paired with other toolkits, as chapter 5 shows. But the development around 'dual use' technology, America's expanding efforts to prevent China mastering the technological frontier and the growing complexity of any regional contingency mean that advanced and emerging technology will remain a significant and contested domain in the Asia-Pacific security architecture.

CLOSED FOR RENOVATIONS?

For the past decade, the APRSA Strategic Dossier series has helped provide deeper analyses and strategic insights of the key regional-security challenges as part of the IISS Shangri-La Dialogue process. While the series celebrates its tenth anniversary in 2024, it also enters its second decade with more geopolitical uncertainty and security challenges across the Asia-Pacific. The APRSA will continue to help defence and security policymakers and analysts to better understand the deeper contours and currents of the regional security order. It strives to provide rigorously researched facts, original data and authoritative insights that will remain relevant beyond its publication year.

Our objective has added relevance because the Asia-Pacific security architecture is undergoing renovations. Its key pillars – economic integration, defence partnerships and ASEAN-led multilateralism, among others – are being shaken by the worsening regional environment. The US–China strategic competition continues to exacerbate regional flashpoints and sharpen old and emerging fault lines. The wars in Ukraine and the Middle East reverberate as regional countries struggle with their post-pandemic recovery. Political transitions, from Pakistan to Indonesia, inject another dose of uncertainty. It is not clear how extensive the renovations will be, for how long and what the final structure will look like. But the post-Cold War regional-security architecture is slowly making way for a new, yet-to-be finished model.

DR EVAN A. LAKSMANA
Senior Fellow for Southeast Asia Military Modernisation, IISS; Editor, *Asia-Pacific Regional Security Assessment*

CHAPTER 1
SPECIAL TOPIC

SCRIPTED ORDER: COMBINED-MILITARY EXERCISES IN THE ASIA-PACIFIC

DR EVAN A. LAKSMANA

Senior Fellow for Southeast Asia Military Modernisation, IISS; Editor, *Asia-Pacific Regional Security Assessment*

PAUL FRAIOLI

Senior Fellow for Geopolitics and Strategy, IISS; Editor, *Strategic Comments* and *Strategic Signals*

VEERLE NOUWENS

Executive Director, IISS–Asia

JAMES HACKETT

Head of Defence and Military Analysis, IISS

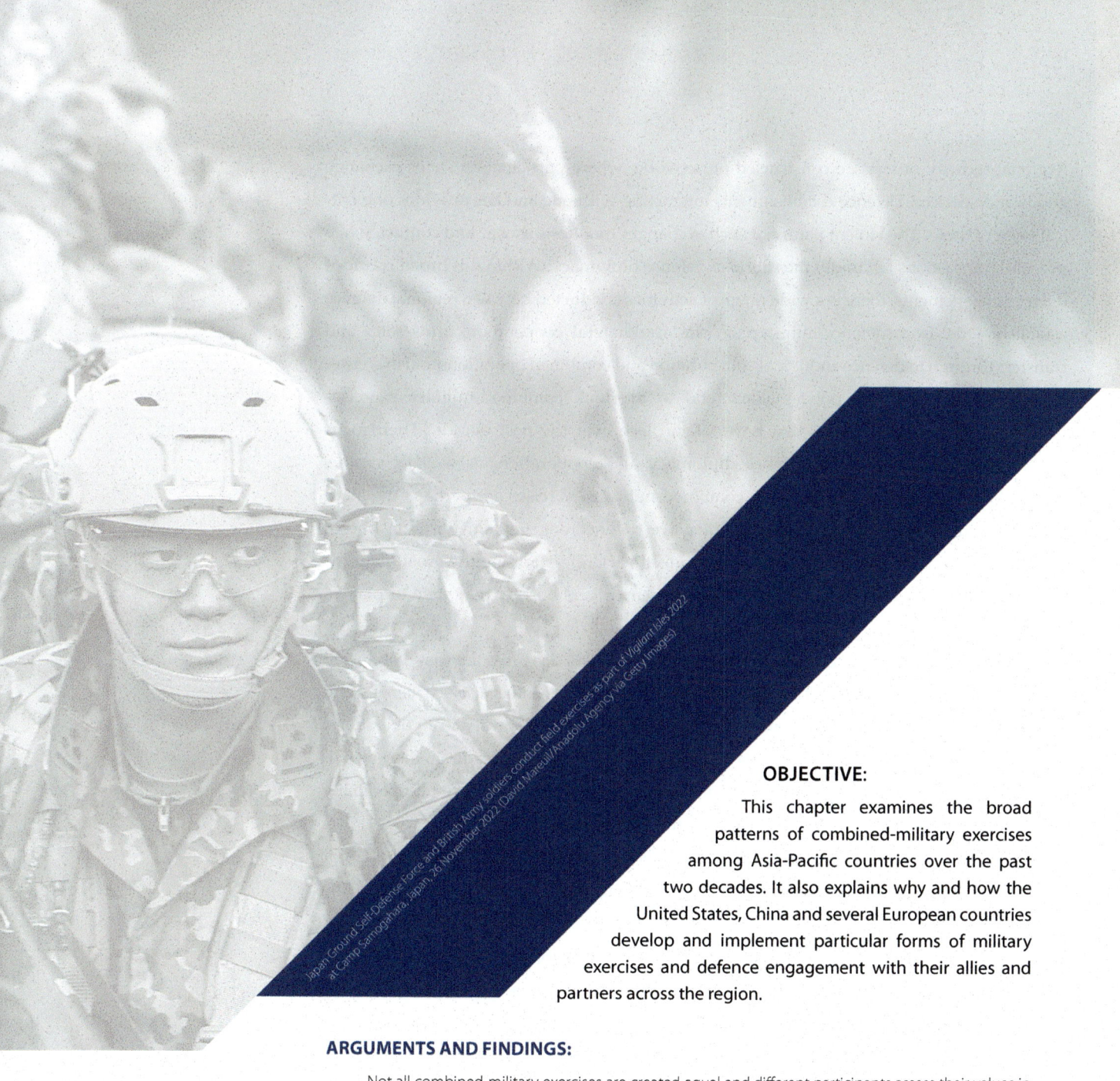

Japan Ground Self-Defense Force and British Army soldiers conduct field exercises as part of Vigilant Isles 2022 at Camp Samogahara, Japan, 26 November 2022 (David Mareuil/Anadolu Agency Via Getty Images)

OBJECTIVE:

This chapter examines the broad patterns of combined-military exercises among Asia-Pacific countries over the past two decades. It also explains why and how the United States, China and several European countries develop and implement particular forms of military exercises and defence engagement with their allies and partners across the region.

ARGUMENTS AND FINDINGS:

Not all combined-military exercises are created equal and different participants assess their values in different ways. Complexity, durability, utility and diversity of partners remain important benchmarks. The US continues to be the most significant exercise partner of choice for Asia-Pacific countries. It engaged in 1,113 exercises with regional countries from 2003 to 2022, whereas China executed nearly 130 in the same period. Most US exercises have been more complex and better tested, having been focused on joint warfare as well as naval and air-combat operations. China has been gradually catching up over the past decade, while also focusing on working with partners on ground operations, counter-terrorism and humanitarian assistance and disaster relief. Expectations for recent defence engagement with Europe remains high, even if perhaps the involved parties are less significant in strategic or operational terms than regional powers, such as Australia or India.

REGIONAL SECURITY IMPLICATIONS:

Combined-military exercises are one of the core pillars of the Asia-Pacific security order. Why and how regional countries develop and implement combined-military exercises can affect their ability to respond to a wide range of security challenges and contingencies and shape regional stability.

Regional security orders are constructed of networks where participating states exchange goods and services. Defence establishments interacting with one another provides one critical layer of these. The violent nature of such exchanges manifests as war and conflict, while peaceful transactions fall under the rubric of defence diplomacy. Within this broad rubric of defence engagements, there is a wide range of activities conducted between regional defence establishments, from defence-ministerial visits, multilateral cooperation, arms sales and transfers through to defence-industrial collaboration and combined operations and exercises.

Defence analysts and policymakers tend to overlook combined-military exercises between Asia-Pacific countries that have taken place over the past decade. Their focus instead has been on broader defence diplomacy and cooperation, as well as various regional security flashpoints. And yet, combined-military exercises are perhaps the more sophisticated, challenging and resource-intensive defence engagement, forming one of the core pillars of the Asia-Pacific security architecture. Understanding the broad patterns of regional military exercises and investigating their drivers and current state of play is, therefore, important.

The United States' 1,113 combined-military exercises from 2003 to 2022 were conducted with 14 regional counterparts. The US focused on almost a dozen security challenges and contingencies, even if the majority centred more on joint warfare than naval and air operations. The US has sought to maintain its role as the primary military-exercise leader to meet its alliance needs, to signal credible commitment, to deter adversaries, to practise inter-operability and to build the regional infrastructure for any future US war effort.

China, meanwhile, is increasing its efforts, even if it remains far behind the US; it conducted 128 regional exercises (around 10% of what the US had done) in the same period. But China has fewer institutionalised defence partnerships and its regional combined exercises focus on tightly scripted ground operations, counter-terrorism and humanitarian assistance and disaster relief (HADR). China's exercise objectives range broadly from operational self-assessments to building trust through to strategic signalling. But while it will still focus on the East and South China seas, it is increasingly developing sophisticated exercises with Indian Ocean partners like Pakistan.

Both the US and China have been and will remain the primary hubs for combined-military exercises across the Asia-Pacific. Other countries such as Australia, India and Indonesia will continue to be important exercise partners for many in the region, even if nowhere near the scale of what the US has done. However, within this established network, several European countries – France, Germany and the United Kingdom in particular – are seeking to enhance their defence engagements, including through combined-military exercises. While expectations have been high among European capitals, it remains unclear the extent to which European countries can become credible and sustainable military-exercise partners to regional countries given that, at times, rhetoric runs ahead of reality.

THINKING THROUGH TRAINING

Military exercises are more than training routines. When done in partnership with other nations, combined-military exercises serve broader goals beyond tactical or operational benefits alone.[1] For certain, such exercises have an underlying practical purpose of training personnel from

SCRIPTED ORDER: COMBINED-MILITARY EXERCISES IN THE ASIA-PACIFIC 17

Figure 1.1: **Asia-Pacific: number of selected bilateral exercises with China and the United States, 2003–22**

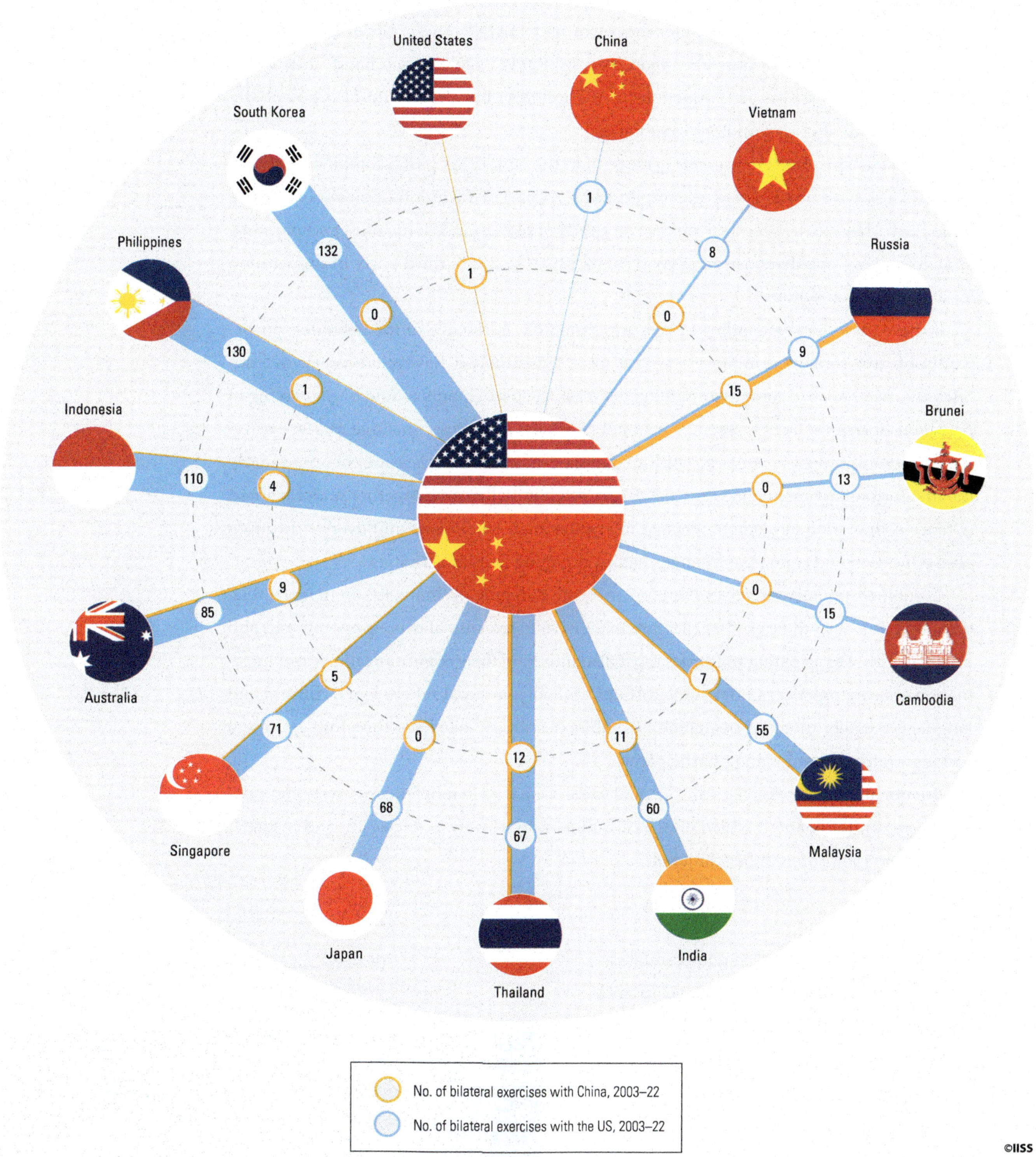

Source: IISS

different countries to work together. These include, for example, communications and logistics training, or the execution of tactics, techniques and procedures with new technology or concepts.[2] Inter-operability is perhaps the most often cited operational goal in this regard.

The old motto 'train as you fight' continues to resonate – and is why exercises are designed to mirror future wartime operations. During the Cold War, states primarily used combined-military exercises to improve their conventional war-fighting readiness.[3] Over time, however, such exercises have evolved to cover different 'non-conventional' operations such as peacekeeping, counter-terrorism and HADR. These fall under what are known as military operations other than war (MOOTW). On the one hand, they could entrench the domestic-security functions of the military, but they could also potentially improve overall offensive military capabilities.[4]

But just as any effective exercise is more than the sum of its parts, combined-military exercises also have broader strategic implications. As part of a wider framework of defence diplomacy, they can be seen as a 'defensive' signal of reassurance with allies and partners, as an 'offensive' one demonstrating coercive pressure against a third party in preparation for aggression, or as both.[5]

If these diplomatic-signalling effects are ultimately in the eye of the beholder, participants of any combined-military exercise must nevertheless have elementary defence relations. After all, in a combined-military exercise, the participants would be displaying in part their doctrines, tactics, assets, personnel readiness and other sensitive military activities or organisational features. Complex combined-military exercises are therefore rarely the first form of defence engagement. Partners often initially come together under a broad defence-cooperation agreement, engage in regular high-level visits and even institutionalise education and training exchanges before engaging in joint activities.

Combined-military exercises therefore indicate a degree of 'maturity' in defence relationships. It is also the case that they are expensive to execute and pose operational and political risks. Participating militaries must also integrate their communications and information-sharing practices under some form of unified command where legal, cultural and language barriers must be overcome.[6] Combined-military exercises therefore represent serious strategic intent among participants.

But not all military exercises are of equal value. One way that defence analysts and policymakers can think about which ones to examine more closely is to classify and measure them across four different benchmarks.

Complexity

How complex is the combined-military exercise for the participants to develop and execute? Different participants will have different answers. For countries such as Australia, Japan and the US, all of which have high operational readiness and frequent exercise mileage, major anti-submarine warfare (ASW) exercises will be less 'complex' than for countries like Indonesia, whose daily operational tasks and readiness are geared towards internal security.

Furthermore, the more complex the exercise, the more resources are needed to

US Navy Captain H.B. Le and Royal Thai Navy Captain Sanitwong Wongsanit discuss operations during the joint US–Thai ASW exercise *Guardian Sea* on the USS *Sterett* in the Andaman Sea, 27 May 2017

(PJF Military Collection via Alamy Stock Photos)

implement it well. The more resources that states are willing to commit towards the exercise, the more likely there is to be trust and commitment between the participants, and the more likely the exercise is a strategic signal. In other words, the more complex the exercises, the more significant the potential operational and strategic implications are likely to be. Some scenarios, after all, require the deployment of more sophisticated hardware, more highly trained personnel and more complicated operations.

Presumably, combined-military exercises around MOOTW will necessitate less military operational or tactical intensity compared to those involving conventional major military operations, such as ASW or amphibious assaults. Combined-military exercises involving a small, single unit are also likely to involve less operational intensity compared to those involving all three services. Finally, minilateral and multilateral exercises involving more than two participants should be more complex than bilateral ones.

Durability

How frequent and enduring are combined-military exercises? The level of institutionalisation of such exercises varies widely, as does how well integrated the planning and execution of those activities are with the participants' force development and strategic planning. But all else being equal, the more institutionalised and long-running the exercises, the better for the participants. A regular exercise that has been developed, implemented and expanded consistently for decades (e.g., *Cobra Gold*, discussed below) is also likely to be more advanced than an exercise only executed in recent years.

To be clear, the operational value, let alone the symbolic or strategic significance, of combined-military exercises is not determined solely by their durability. But their durability signifies the level of commitment, as well as the operational experience and proficiency acquired over time, by the participants. The more that militaries train with one another over time, the more familiar they become with each other's tactical procedures, doctrines, personnel and equipment; sustaining regular exercises is harder without strong commitment and trust.

Utility

How useful are combined-military exercises in addressing participants' security challenges? While all of them would publicly claim that combined exercises help address their security needs, there are often operational mismatches. A large-scale ASW exercise may not be the best response to a participant's need to counter illegal fishing, for example. Such mismatches often arise from participants having different motivating factors in formulating and executing combined-military exercises outside of 'shared threats'.

As noted above, participants may have different strategic-signalling needs. More broadly, combined-military exercises can be used as a 'shaping' tool by participants to create a more favourable environment.[7] Major powers use them to recruit allies, build the capacity of weaker militaries, influence the role of partner forces and even develop trust among adversaries.[8] Non-major powers, especially autocracies unable to attract foreign investment or democratic allies, often use combined-military exercises to strengthen their economic security.[9]

Other major powers may use such exercises as a demonstration of their deployed assets in order to sell them to other participants. Combined-military exercises, after all, have reciprocal relationships with arms-trading networks.[10] Relatedly, combined-military exercises have also been useful in protecting the bureaucratic interests of some armed forces whose budget share declined after the Cold War.[11] In any case, given the plethora of utilities driving the participants' decision-making, whether and how the execution helps them address their security needs remains an important indicator of their value.

Soldiers stand in position in a flag-raising ceremony marking the beginning of *Aman 2023*, a five-day Pakistan-led naval exercise involving forces from 50 countries including China, Indonesia, Turkiye and the US, in Karachi, Pakistan, 10 February 2023

(Muhammed Semih Ugurlu/Anadolu Agency via Getty Images)

Diversity

How many combined-military-exercise partners does each country have and how diverse are they? Minilateral and multilateral exercises should not only build a broader, collective sense of operational habits and inter-operability, but also address misperceptions and alleviate anxieties among a wider set of partners and even potential rivals. For small and middle powers, a broader and diverse set of exercise partners can also act as a strategic hedge against being overly dependent on – and thus vulnerable to – a few partner countries. Some countries are likely to offer better exercise value than others due to their geography, history, expertise, readiness, assets and training area.

Partner diversity is, nevertheless, a luxury item and not essential for policymakers under pressure to get the best value for money. And yet, the politics of exercise inclusion and diversity can accrue significance over time. States with many connections in a combined-military-exercise network attract more partners; they have more institutional knowledge and prestige.[12] Such popular intersections could also encourage its partners to grow defence ties among themselves by facilitating a 'friends-of-friends' cluster over time.[13] These trends, involving the US and its allies and partners in the Asia-Pacific, are described below.

CURRENCY EXCHANGE

Much as trade in goods and services serves as a key indicator of economic exchange, combined-military exercises indicate deeper defence engagement between states. They are more common than foreign-military assistance, for example, and yet harder to develop and sustain. Indeed, combined-military exercises have proliferated to the point that states are now more connected by exercises than by alliances.[14]

Just as economic exchanges are underpinned by social transactions, combined-military exercises are voluntary choices by participants to rehearse for future military

Figure 1.2: **Asia-Pacific: selected multilateral military exercises, 2018–23**

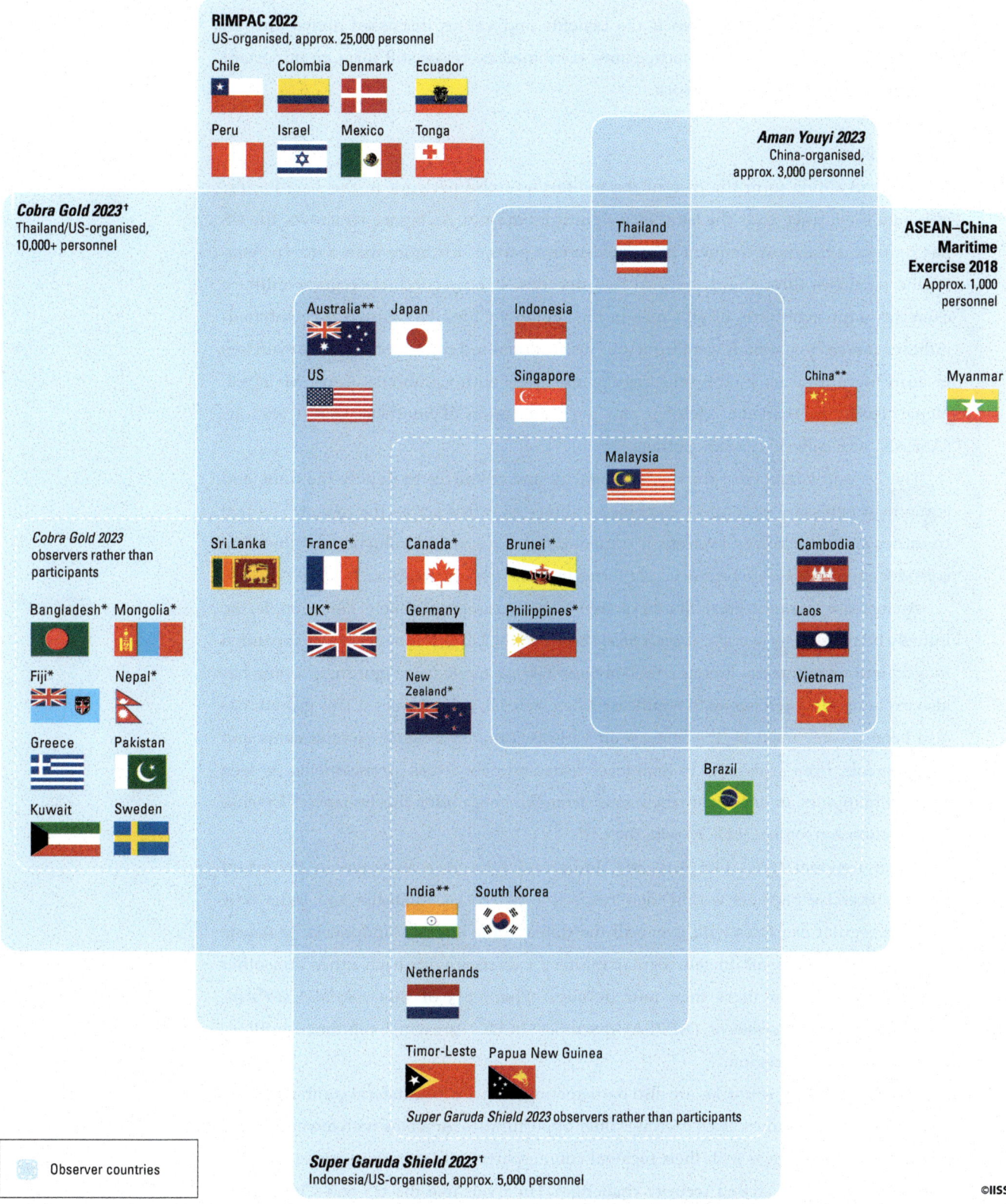

operations and therefore exchange ideas, goods and services. These interactions range from shared threat assessments and defence planning to doctrinal and operational knowledge of each other.[15] Even if the benefits and values discussed above are not often symmetrical between all participants, combined exercises still form an important patterned regional security network.

Frequent flyer

The US and China form the core of the military-exercise network in the Asia-Pacific, although the former leads the latter by a significant margin. As Figure 1.1 shows, the US has remained the most frequent bilateral exercise partner for more than a dozen Asia-Pacific countries throughout the past two decades. It now conducts regular military exercises with two-thirds of all states in the region.[16] China has grown its combined-military exercises as well. It went from four institutionalised combined-military exercises in 2010 to 12 in 2020, establishing regular exercises with Cambodia, Laos, Malaysia, Nepal, Pakistan, Thailand, Vietnam and the Association of Southeast Asian Nations (ASEAN) as a collective, among others.[17]

The US and China have the biggest capacity and resources to deploy the units and equipment necessary to conduct combined-military exercises across the region. The two countries are also involved in strategic competition for access and influence and therefore consider such exercises to be crucial platforms in their strategic toolbox.

An increase in combined-military exercises by both countries is likely. For example, the initially bilateral army exercise *Garuda Shield* between the US and Indonesia was expanded in 2022 into a multilateral exercise dubbed *Super Garuda Shield* (see Figure 1.2). China has also expanded its exercises with Southeast Asian states in recent years.[18] This growth has also been accompanied by the increase in various forms of defence commitments and engagements, from arms sales to high-level visits and new access arrangements, as seen in the Philippines in 2023 with their new arrangements under the Enhanced Defense Cooperation Agreement (EDCA) with the US.

Other regional states like Australia, India and Indonesia also remain important military-exercise partners within their respective networks. Australia and India now conduct regular exercises with over half the states in the region.[19] Indonesia, Malaysia and Singapore have conducted regular military exercises with each other and other regional partners for more than four decades. Chapter 3 of this year's *Asia-Pacific Regional Security Assessment* (APRSA) discusses India's growing combined-military exercises across the region.

More Asia-Pacific countries are also participating in major multilateral combined exercises, as Figure 1.2 shows. Such exercises offer opportunities for states with fewer military resources to still engage with their regional counterparts and learn the various facets of working together on shared security challenges. For rivals like the US and China, such venues could also offer an engagement and communication platform without the need to work closely together on sensitive military capabilities or operational concepts. Most of these major multilateral exercises also tend to focus on broader non-traditional security scenarios such as HADR.

Scripting security

Asia-Pacific countries are part of separate yet overlapping networks of bilateral, minilateral and multilateral military exercises. Some countries like Australia, India, Indonesia and others are strong fulcra within their respective networks, while the US and China are simply the dominant partners across the board. But whether such networks contribute to regional order depends not only on partner selection and frequency, but also on their nature and scale.

As Figure 1.3 shows, the US has conducted more frequent field-training exercises (FTXs) compared to China. FTXs are seen as the more 'realistic' – and therefore the more serious – form of combined exercises that play out operational scenarios on the field with deployed assets and personnel. They require more resources, commitment and trust between the participants, and are therefore better indicators of their operational readiness and the strength of strategic partnership. Compared to China, the US also leads in other forms of exercises, from table-top exercises to command-post exercises and other combinations, across the region.

Further, despite the maritime geostrategic character of the Asia-Pacific, the majority (almost 40%) of China's combined-military exercises with regional partners over the past two decades involved its army, the People's Liberation Army Army (PLAA). Despite the growing combat capabilities of the People's Liberation Army Air Force (PLAAF), discussed in chapter 6 of this year's APRSA, the service has not engaged in as many combined-military exercises as its other People's Liberation Army (PLA) counterparts.

While the amount of service-branch participation alone can only allow for broad inferences around multinational readiness, some scenarios or security themes provide a more nuanced picture. As Figure 1.4 shows, the US also leads in the frequency of exercises across almost half a dozen categories, from HADR to combined-arms warfare, in contrast to China. The issues on which the PLA has most often engaged in combined-military exercises over the past two decades have centred on ground operations, HADR and counter-terrorism. Major naval exercises,

Figure 1.3: **China and the US: selected Asia-Pacific exercises by type, participating services and partners, 2003–22**

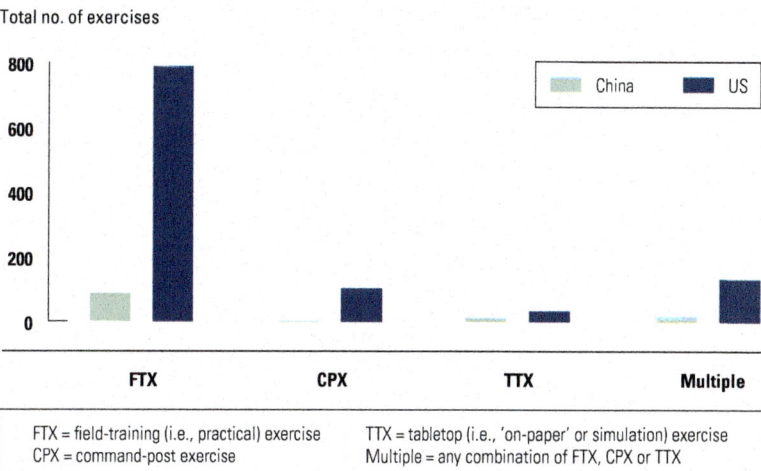

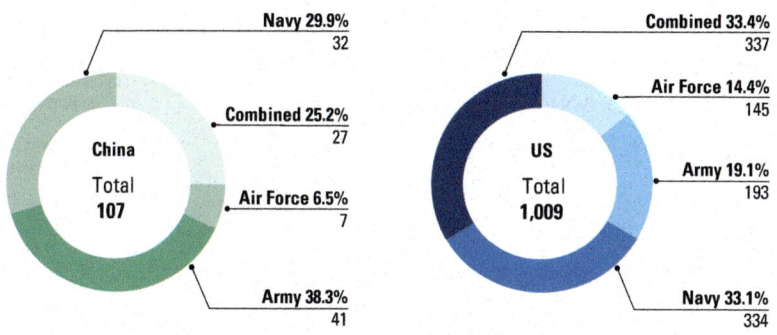

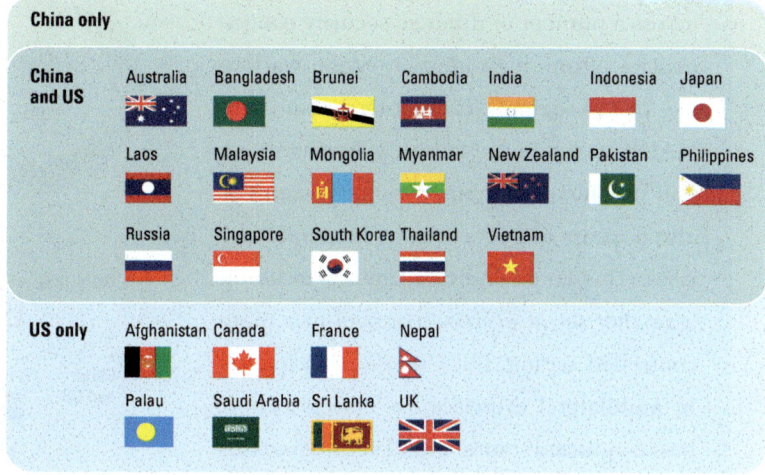

Note: Partner data includes participants in bilateral, minilateral and multilateral exercises.

Pie charts above exclude exercises for which data on participating services is not available.

Source: IISS

such as *Sea Guardian* with Pakistan (discussed below), are a relatively new development and its sustainability remains in question.

Meanwhile, the majority of the United States' combined-military exercises with regional allies and partners have focused on joint warfare, naval and air-combat operations. While the US and China might be gearing for the same conflicts against each other, there is some asymmetry in how they are preparing to fight them. The US relies more on allies and joint or coalition warfare, while China is more focused on self-reliant capabilities and not on fighting alongside allies or partners. This is why, despite the growth in China's naval capabilities, the PLA Navy (PLAN) arguably has less combined-military-exercise experience. But China likely does not define or operationalise war-fighting readiness in the same way as the US does in terms of combined exercises.

The US, on the other hand, is more ready to work with regional allies and partners across a number of different security contingencies, from high-intensity joint warfare to peacekeeping, counter-terrorism and HADR, as noted in Figure 1.4. Furthermore, half of China's combined-military exercises also appears to be focused on bilateral exercises. This could indicate China's focus on a smaller set of exercise partners in a more controlled setting. But China's participation in multilateral exercises has also grown; it has conducted more multilateral exercises as a percentage of its total exercises when compared with the US.

Overall, the US still retains significant leads in exercise complexity, durability, utility and diversity. It simply trains with the most Asia-Pacific states, more frequently, across a wide range of platforms, scales and security challenges. China is certainly catching up, but is held back by limited

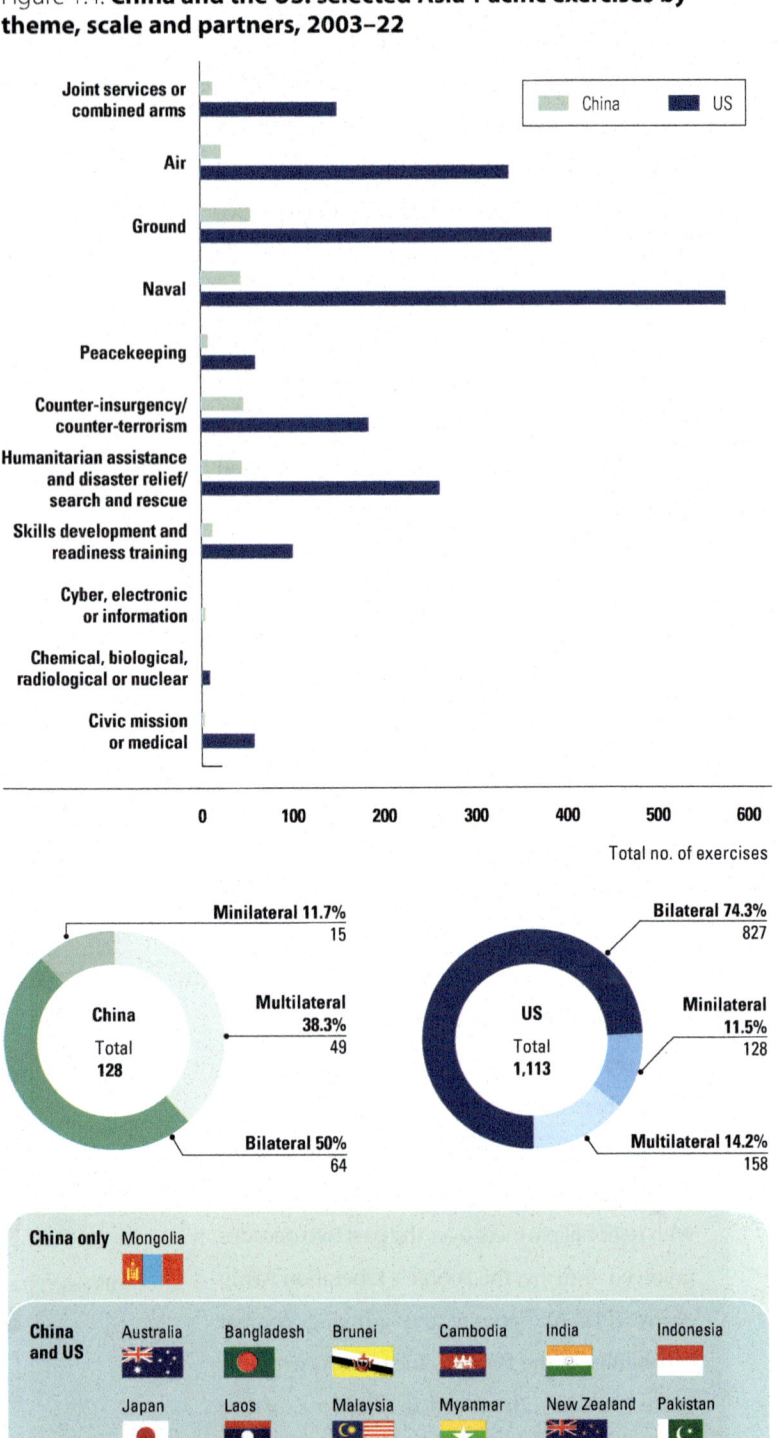

Figure 1.4: **China and the US: selected Asia-Pacific exercises by theme, scale and partners, 2003–22**

Note: Partner data includes participants in bilateral, minilateral and multilateral exercises. For the purposes of this analysis, a 'bilateral' exercise is one involving two countries, 'minilateral' three to five, and 'multilateral' more than five or organised by a regional/global organisation.

Source: IISS

resources and it not seeking to have allies to fight alongside it in the first place. Ousting the US as a defence partner across the Asia-Pacific would be a Herculean task for China.

ANCHORING ALLIANCES

Over the last decade, the US has upgraded its military exercises with its Asian allies and partners. The number of exercises has grown, as has the list of participating countries, the number of personnel and equipment engaged and the scale of ambitions (see Figure 1.1). Tens of thousands of US troops now rotate regularly on assignments west of the International Date Line to plan and staff these exercises. The rationale for this is multi-dimensional, including the desire to build closer working relationships with allies and partners, to give credibility to its regional commitments by assuring friends and deterring adversaries, to practice inter-operability in real-world situations, to respond to the increasing pace of Chinese military exercises and, significantly, to build the regional infrastructure that will sustain any future war effort.

Moving target

Washington's priorities and the contours of its Asia-Pacific exercise strategy have changed over time. Early efforts focused on partner capacity-building as a bulwark against the spread of communism in Southeast Asia.[20] In September 1954, the US, along with Australia, France, New Zealand, Pakistan, the Philippines, Thailand and the UK, formed the Southeast Asia Treaty Organization (SEATO) towards this end. The member states signed a collective-defence treaty and began conducting combined-military exercises annually.[21] Soon afterwards, in September 1956, an American–Thai exercise – *Operation Team-Work* – involved a joint marine force that stormed the beach of Had Chao Samran and attracted 25,000 spectators from across the region.[22]

A surge and retreat of US military engagement in the region occurred during the 1960s and 1970s, alongside the ramping up and ultimate failure of the American war efforts in Vietnam. Washington sought to resurrect its regional military ties by launching the *Cobra Gold* exercise with Thailand in 1982. It has been held every year since. Vietnam called the exercise provocative at the time and accused the US of seeking to reintroduce standing armies in the region; meanwhile, the Soviets began monitoring these exercises from vessels offshore.[23]

But new priorities emerged for Washington after the Cold War. These ranged from responding to Taiwan contingencies and North Korea's weapons programmes, to conducting HADR missions, to engaging in counter-terrorism operations and ensuring freedom of navigation in the South China Sea and other critical maritime theatres. Over the past 30 years, the US has launched a host of new exercises centred around these issues.

All hands on deck

Washington's growing focus on great-power competition with China since the mid- to late-2010s has precipitated a shift in the patterns and practice of US combined exercises. The shift towards more frequent and larger exercises with more partners followed prior trends but along a much steeper trajectory that is set to continue beyond 2024. Washington did not pursue this shift independently; it could not have occurred absent the rising threat perceptions of some Asia-Pacific states that had been clashing for years with an increasingly assertive China.

Many bilateral exercises have become multilateral and expanded further over the past decade.[24] The aforementioned *Cobra Gold* exercise is a prime example, as Map 1.1 shows. Japan has joined the once predominantly bilateral *Malabar* naval exercise between India and the US every year since 2014, with Australia joining in 2020. The once-bilateral *Talisman Sabre* exercise in Australia now involves 15 countries.[25] In 2023, the US completed the largest-ever *Talisman Sabre* with nearly 30,000 personnel and three Pacific Island countries joining for the first time.[26]

As of 2024, the US Army alone is conducting more than 40 combined exercises per year in the Asia-Pacific and seeks to have forces operating in the region for seven or eight months per year.[27] US officials view the fact that more regional countries are interested in participating in US-led military exercises as a clear reaction to China's aggressive posture and as evidence that the US strategy in the region is succeeding.[28]

But the US also conducts exercises to build partner capabilities and increase inter-operability for mission types that are less about deterring China, such as HADR, counter-piracy and counter-terrorism. *Pacific Partnership*, for example, is the largest annual multinational mission focused on HADR missions, with the 2023 version including mission stops in eight countries in Southeast Asia and the Pacific Islands region.[29]

Cobra Gold 2023 also maintained a strong emphasis on HADR operations – though with a stronger multilateral component and involving space operations for the first time – with Indonesia, Japan, Malaysia, Singapore, South Korea and Thailand participating (see Map 1.1). Indonesia, Malaysia and Singapore, which have hedged rather than committed to one side in the US–China rivalry, are more willing to participate in exercises of this type than in those with a war-fighting and clear anti-China salience.

Scripted signalling

The US views combined exercises as credible commitment signals to its allies, partners and potential rivals, as highlighted by public statements issued by the Pentagon since the Cold War. These statements have tended to stress the benefits of the US building closer relationships with regional counterparts, specifically increasing partner capacity through training and the regional US military presence to deter potential rivals. In April 2023, Admiral John C. Aquilino, commander of the US Indo-Pacific Command, stated that 'campaigning normalizes our operations ... delivers interoperable and confident warfighting partners and gives us the ability to rehearse warfighting concepts together'.[30]

In recent years, the US and its allies and partners have made strides in increasing training, integration and inter-operability in emerging domains such as space and cyber. The US focus on inter-operability now creates, implicitly, a contrast with exercises conducted between China and Russia in recent years. As the 2023 Military and Security Developments Involving the People's Republic of China (PRC) report, commonly referred to as the China Military Power Report (CMPR), noted, their manoeuvres 'are scripted and parallel rather than integrated, suggesting that both countries are not capable of operational or tactical interoperability'.[31] This is yet another contrast to the patterns of combined exercises between the US and China noted above.

Yet the Pentagon's evergreen rationale for exercising – integration and capacity-building – does not fully explain their increased number and ambition since the 2010s (see Figure 1.1). Some

SCRIPTED ORDER: COMBINED-MILITARY EXERCISES IN THE ASIA-PACIFIC

Map 1.1: **Thailand et al.: 42nd *Cobra Gold* exercise, 28 February–10 March 2023**

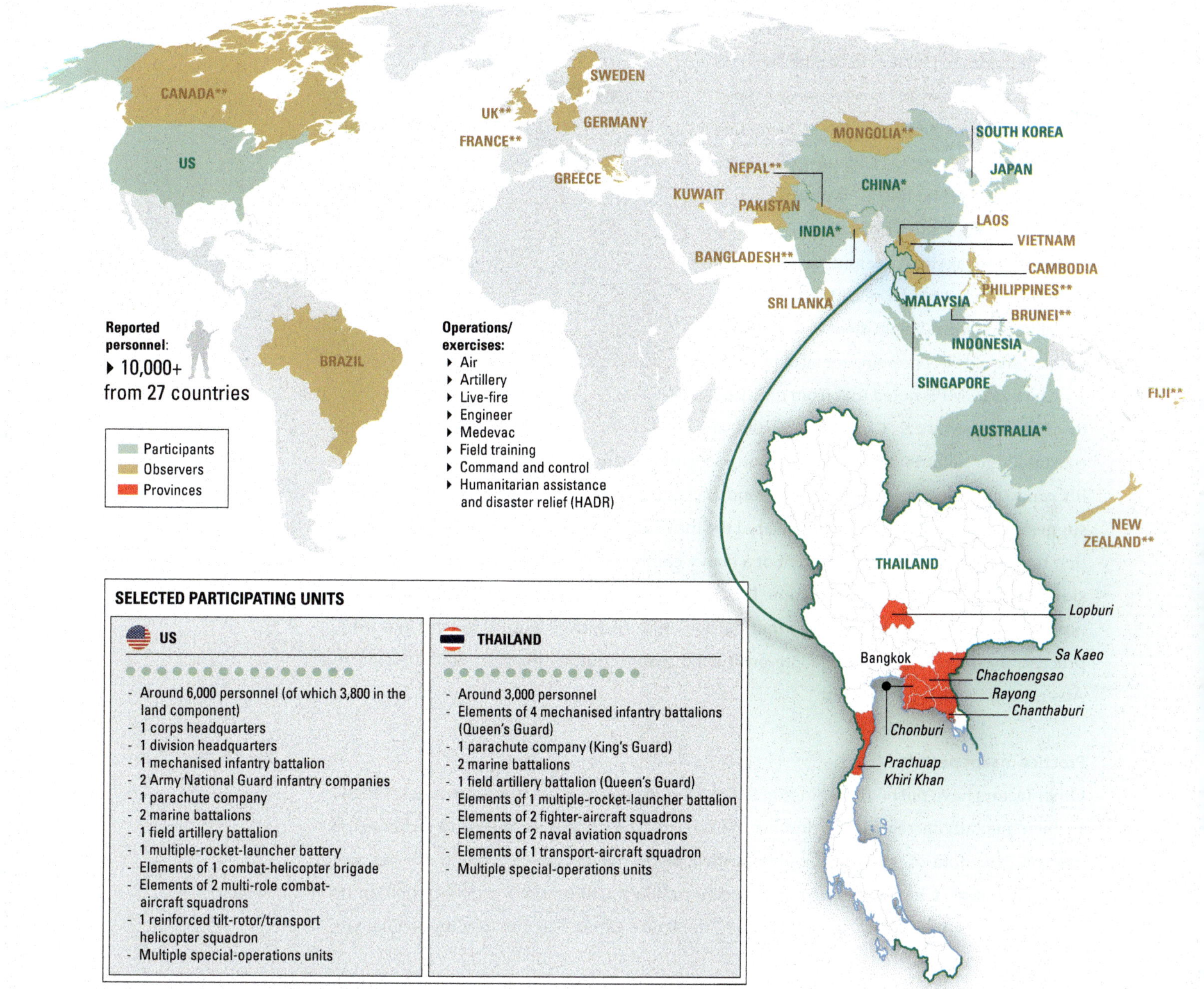

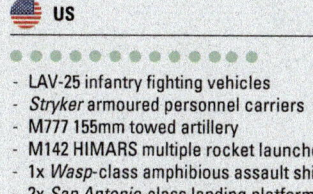

Reported personnel: ▶ 10,000+ from 27 countries

- Participants
- Observers
- Provinces

Operations/exercises:
- Air
- Artillery
- Live-fire
- Engineer
- Medevac
- Field training
- Command and control
- Humanitarian assistance and disaster relief (HADR)

Countries labelled on map: CANADA**, US, SWEDEN, UK**, FRANCE**, GERMANY, GREECE, KUWAIT, MONGOLIA**, SOUTH KOREA, JAPAN, NEPAL**, CHINA*, PAKISTAN, INDIA*, BANGLADESH**, LAOS, VIETNAM, CAMBODIA, PHILIPPINES**, SRI LANKA, MALAYSIA, BRUNEI**, INDONESIA, SINGAPORE, FIJI**, AUSTRALIA*, NEW ZEALAND**, BRAZIL

Thailand provinces: Lopburi, Sa Kaeo, Chachoengsao, Rayong, Chanthaburi, Chonburi, Prachuap Khiri Khan

SELECTED PARTICIPATING UNITS

US
- Around 6,000 personnel (of which 3,800 in the land component)
- 1 corps headquarters
- 1 division headquarters
- 1 mechanised infantry battalion
- 2 Army National Guard infantry companies
- 1 parachute company
- 2 marine battalions
- 1 field artillery battalion
- 1 multiple-rocket-launcher battery
- Elements of 1 combat-helicopter brigade
- Elements of 2 multi-role combat-aircraft squadrons
- 1 reinforced tilt-rotor/transport helicopter squadron
- Multiple special-operations units

THAILAND
- Around 3,000 personnel
- Elements of 4 mechanised infantry battalions (Queen's Guard)
- 1 parachute company (King's Guard)
- 2 marine battalions
- 1 field artillery battalion (Queen's Guard)
- Elements of 1 multiple-rocket-launcher battalion
- Elements of 2 fighter-aircraft squadrons
- Elements of 2 naval aviation squadrons
- Elements of 1 transport-aircraft squadron
- Multiple special-operations units

SELECTED PARTICIPATING EQUIPMENT TYPES

US
- LAV-25 infantry fighting vehicles
- *Stryker* armoured personnel carriers
- M777 155mm towed artillery
- M142 HIMARS multiple rocket launchers
- 1x *Wasp*-class amphibious assault ship
- 2x *San Antonio*-class landing platform docks
- Air-cushioned landing craft
- F-35B multi-role combat aircraft
- F-16C multi-role combat aircraft
- P-8A maritime patrol aircraft
- C-17 heavy transport aircraft
- C-130J-30 & MC-130J medium transport aircraft
- MV-22B tilt-rotor transport aircraft
- AH-64D attack helicopters
- CH-53E heavy transport helicopters
- UH-60 family helicopters

SOUTH KOREA
- KAAV amphibious assault vehicles
- K808 armoured personnel carriers
- K55A1 155mm self-propelled artillery
- 1x *Cheonwangbong*-class landing platform dock

THAILAND
- BTR-3E1 infantry fighting vehicles
- M198 155mm towed artillery
- 1x *Angthong*-class landing platform dock
- 1x *Mataphun*-class utility landing craft
- F-16A fighter aircraft
- F-27-200 maritime patrol aircraft
- S-70B helicopter

OTHER SELECTED PARTICIPATING UNITS

SINGAPORE
- 54 personnel
- 1 special-forces team
- 1 cyber incident response team
- 1 combat engineer team

MALAYSIA
- 1 special-forces team

SOUTH KOREA
- 420 personnel
- 1 marine company

INDONESIA
- 1 special-forces team
- Staff officers

CHINA
- 25 personnel from a support brigade of the 75th Group Army (HADR exercise only)

*Humanitarian-exercise participants. **Multinational Planning Augmentation Team (MPAT).

Source: IISS

senior military officials have begun offering more information publicly about the rationale for growing large-scale regional exercises. General Charles A. Flynn, commander of the US Army Pacific, portrayed US exercises as a direct response and counterweight to the increasing pace and sophistication of Chinese joint-service military exercises and the PLA's construction of military training centres from 2014 to 2021: it is 'a dangerous trajectory', he said; 'what they've done over the last ten years and what they are signalling and intending to do over the next ten years ... should be concerning for all of us'.[32]

The Royal Australian Navy ship HMAS *Adelaide*, US Navy ship USS *America*, Japanese Maritime Self-Defense Force ship JS *Izumo* and South Korean Navy ship ROKS *Marado* sail in formation through the Coral Sea as part of *Talisman Sabre 2023*, 29 July 2023

(US Navy Photo via Alamy Stock Photo)

The 2023 CMPR noted that from mid-July to mid-August 2022, China conducted a coastal 'large-volume lift exercise ... using 12 civilian ships', including eight ferries; 'the lift capacity, number of vessels stops, and the number of participating ground vehicles suggest this training could have simulated the movement of up to a full group army for the first time', replicating the 'movement of a heavy combined arms brigade in a Taiwan invasion'.[33] On the subject of large-volume lift, Secretary of the US Army Christine Wormuth noted ahead of *Talisman Sabre 2023* that participating countries would, for the first time, practise the movement of large pre-positioned army equipment from South Korea to Australia using army watercraft.[34]

Practice makes perfect

Other factors have pushed Washington to raise the ambitions it has for its exercises. Firstly, by incrementally increasing the number of exercises, the US and its allies and partners are asserting freedom-of-navigation rights in their respective exclusive economic zones and in the high seas. China maintains that foreign-military activities are impermissible in its claimed waters, which includes nearly all of the South China Sea, because they violate its domestic laws.

Secondly, major combined exercises force the US service branches to practise integration among themselves in ways they might not otherwise. The army, for instance, gained significant experience in the first two decades of the twenty-first century of fighting land wars in Afghanistan and Iraq, but now must adapt to contingency planning in a maritime theatre dominated by the navy. Exercising alongside allies gives the army real-world opportunities to develop concepts for joint-force sustainment during a conflict.[35] As noted above, bureaucratic interests can occasionally become important drivers of combined exercises.

Thirdly, exercises have enabled the US Indo-Pacific Command to experiment with new war-fighting concepts and technologies in a real-world environment, allowing for faster implementation of concepts that prove successful.[36] This includes executing missions relevant to emerging issues, such as protecting critical minerals and disasters that are due to occur more regularly due to climate change.

Lastly, it is noteworthy that no multilateral military exercises involving the US and its allies Australia, Japan, the Philippines, South Korea and Thailand singularly focus on a Chinese invasion of Taiwan. Instead, participating forces practise discrete operations – some involving kinetic missions targeting a generic adversary and others involving logistics, sustainment and the movement of heavy equipment – that in wartime could be stitched together in unknown ways according to the dictates of strategy. HADR exercises can, therefore, be useful in a future wartime scenario, given that inter-operability, situational awareness and strong supply chains are necessary in all cases.

Philippine and US Air Force troops load medical equipment onto a US Air Force C-130 plane as part of a mass-casualty drill during the *Pacific Airlift Rally* HADR exercise held at Clark Air Base in Mabalacat, the Philippines, 17 August 2023

(Ezra Acayan via Getty Images)

Some Asia-Pacific US partners are not comfortable hosting lethal equipment on their territories in a wartime scenario. Still, they may be willing to act as supply hubs for fuel and other non-lethal supplies, which would significantly contribute to the sustainment of any US regional war effort. The US Army programme *Operation Pathways* sought to make use of the high tempo of exercises to pre-position munitions and other equipment throughout the region, creating theatre distribution centres and improving the related regional infrastructure for use in a potential conflict.[37] Flynn refers to these efforts as the creation of 'joint interior lines', meant to counter China's major structural advantage – short supply lines – in any conflict with the US in the Asia-Pacific.

CREEP BEFORE THE LEAP

China's broad objectives for combined-military exercises roughly follow those of other nations and range from operational self-assessments and building trust to strategic signalling. From 2002 to 2011, the PLA and the People's Armed Police participated in at least 33 ground exercises with 13 foreign armies, while the PLAN conducted 19 international maritime exercises involving 13 foreign navies, and the PLAAF took part in one air-combat exercise.[38] In that decade, those exercises were useful in supporting China's confidence-building strategy and providing opportunities to enhance the PLA's professionalisation efforts.

But since then, China's approach to such exercises has evolved, as can be discerned in its strategic documents, most notably *The Science of Military Strategy* (SMS), outlining strategy and doctrine, published in 2013 and 2020. According to the 2013 edition, military exercises with foreign counterparts are characterised as 'non-warfare military activities'.[39] While these are conducted to 'display the existence of the military, to express security concerns, [and] to decline the strategic bottom line', the document also stresses that China must 'strive to avoid over-drawing the sword and upsetting the opponent, leading to a loss of control in escalation'.[40]

Such 'cooperative non-military activities' revolve around shared security concerns and interests and seek to 'borrow from the understanding of foreign militaries' developmental dynamics to strengthen strategic confidence, increase military transparency, display our nation's excellent image, raise our military's international prestige, and expand our nation's international influence'.[41] For China, then, combined-military exercises help build relationships and capability through learning. Indeed, the 2013 document noted that while China's military capabilities had dramatically improved, its strategic air force and long-range oceanic navy were still at a 'crawling phase'.[42] The army-heavy combined-military-exercises pattern noted above seems to confirm this assessment.

But less than a decade later, the 2020 SMS increasingly emphasised the deterrent effect of signalling strength through military exercises. Indeed, it notes that exercises 'demonstrate the military's combat capabilities to the opponent, cause the opponent to doubt China's intentions, and cause psychological panic to produce a deterrent effect'.[43] While large-scale campaign exercises can 'directly produce a strategic deterrent effect', small and medium-scale tactical exercises also play an important role in signalling and in having a deterrent effect.[44]

The document also notes that combined-military exercises play an important political and diplomatic role through deepening 'mutual understanding with friendly countries' in building political and military trust.[45] But ultimately, the 2020 SMS notes that military exercises are part of a 'strategic game' with opponents, using military power to signal China's combat capabilities as well as to foment panic and doubt over its intentions.[46]

Peripheral centrality

While analysts and policymakers often focus on China's exercises in the East and South China seas, the PLA has also turned its attention to the Indian Ocean region and its strategic and military importance. Both the 2013 and 2020 editions of SMS specifically refer to the northern Indian Ocean (and the wider Indian Ocean) as on China's periphery. This has influenced Chinese defence planning.

The 2013 SMS stressed that the 'core is to rely upon the homeland territory [and] to not be distant from the homeland territory', although it also referenced the creation of overseas 'strategic support points' where necessary, as part of a cooperative approach to Chinese overseas military application.[47] The 2020 SMS subsequently stressed the need for enhanced maritime capabilities, relations and communication with the littoral countries of the Indian Ocean and suggested pursuing overseas supply points and support bases.[48]

China has more broadly made significant political, economic and security investments in the Indian Ocean region. It is the only country to have an embassy in every Indian Ocean island state.[49] China opened its first overseas military base in Djibouti in 2017, with observers speculating that a second base in Africa could be on the horizon.[50] Indeed, the Maritime Silk Road, the maritime leg of China's Belt and Road Initiative (BRI), sought to strengthen Chinese ports and other connectivity across the littoral countries of the Indian Ocean through the creation of a 'China–Indian Ocean–Africa–Mediterranean Sea Blue Economic Passage'.[51]

More recently, China's official Global Security Initiative concept paper (issued in February 2023) proposed to strengthen maritime dialogue, exchange, and practical cooperation 'so as to jointly safeguard maritime peace and tranquility and sea line security'.[52] Concurrently, China seeks to continue to project its power across the Indian Ocean region via submarine and other underwater capabilities.

This is in addition to supporting the submarine-capability development of regional partners and sending research vessels to map the geographical subsea features and characteristics of the Indian Ocean.[53] This has caused concern in India, which views the Indian Ocean as an integral part of its security and sphere of influence. Indeed, as we will see in chapter 4 of this year's APRSA, India's heightened concerns about China after their land-border clashes in recent years have led it to expand its regional defence diplomacy and partnerships.

Chinese research ship *Shi Yan* 6 docks at a port in Colombo, Sri Lanka, 25 October 2023

(Ishara S. Kodikara/AFP via Getty Images)

This follows China's own initial growth in defence diplomacy over the past two decades. From 2004–22, China predominantly conducted bilateral exercises in the Asia-Pacific. Within that period, India, Russia and Thailand were its most frequent bilateral exercise partners (see Figure 1.1), but exercises with Pakistan have also surged in recent years (see below). Geographically, these exercises have generally focused on China's immediate periphery in the South and East China seas, although exercises have also taken place further afield, such as with Russia in the Mediterranean.[54] It is apparent that China has conducted exercises to build partnerships with those whose own security could impact China.

Partnering up

The increasing quality and intensity of China's combined-military exercises is perhaps more visibly shown in the Indian Ocean region, in line with the SMS directives noted above. For one thing, China's military exercises have increasingly focused more on the navy and air force and less on the army, which has remained the broad pattern over the past two decades, as Figure 1.3 outlines.

Furthermore, as China adopts a more maritime-focused strategy to become a blue-water navy and in turn a global maritime power, it is seeking to exercise maritime inter-operability and HADR, as well as search and rescue. More sensitive capabilities, such as ASW, seem to be reserved for China's closest partners, such as Russia.[55] Over time, Pakistan has slowly moved into this partnership category, working on sensitive capabilities.

China's relationship with Pakistan is perhaps its closest among all the Indian Ocean littoral states. President Xi Jinping and Pakistan's then-prime minister Anwaar-ul-Haq Kakar, at the Belt and Road Summit in Beijing in September 2023, highlighted the two countries' all-weather strategic partnership and their status as 'ironclad friends', the importance of the BRI for both countries and their commitment to one another's core interests.[56] In 2013, China and Pakistan launched the BRI's flagship project, the China–Pakistan Economic Corridor, which connects China's Xinjiang Uyghur Autonomous Region with Pakistan's southwest Gwadar Port through rail and infrastructure projects such as energy.[57]

China has also conducted complex combined-military exercises with Pakistan in the Indian Ocean, including the *Sea Guardian* series. The exercise, now in its third iteration, has steadily incorporated more operational-exercise types, assets, participating services and objectives. It first took place in January 2020 in the northern Arabian Sea, in which five PLAN ships, two ship-borne helicopters and naval forces from the Southern Theater Command participated.[58] Dong Jun, China's current minister of national defence and then-general director and deputy commander of the PLA Southern Theater Command, took part in the opening ceremony. The public objective of the exercise was to consolidate the development of the all-weather strategic partnership, to promote joint construction of a safe marine environment and to cope with maritime terrorism and crime.[59]

The second *Sea Guardian* was a four-day exercise off the coast of Shanghai in July 2022, split into two phases.[60] The first phase consisted of on-shore operational planning and cultural exchanges, while the second consisted of maritime exercises. These comprised enhanced joint drills, including attacks on maritime targets, tactical manoeuvres, anti-aircraft and anti-missile operations and ASW operations, amongst others. As noted, China usually reserves ASW exercises for close and strategic partners. The exercises also involved assets from the PLA's Eastern Theater Command, including a submarine, guided-missile frigates, an early-warning aircraft and two fighter jets.

Despite the increased intensity and scale of this second iteration, the stated objectives remained largely similar: deepening bilateral relationships, enhancing the ability of their respective militaries to jointly respond to maritime threats and promoting defence cooperation. The public message seems to be one of non-confrontation and partnership building. Indeed, in both 2020 and 2022, China stressed that the exercises had nothing to do with the regional situation and were not targeted at third countries. This was repeated in the Chinese-language reporting on the exercise.[61]

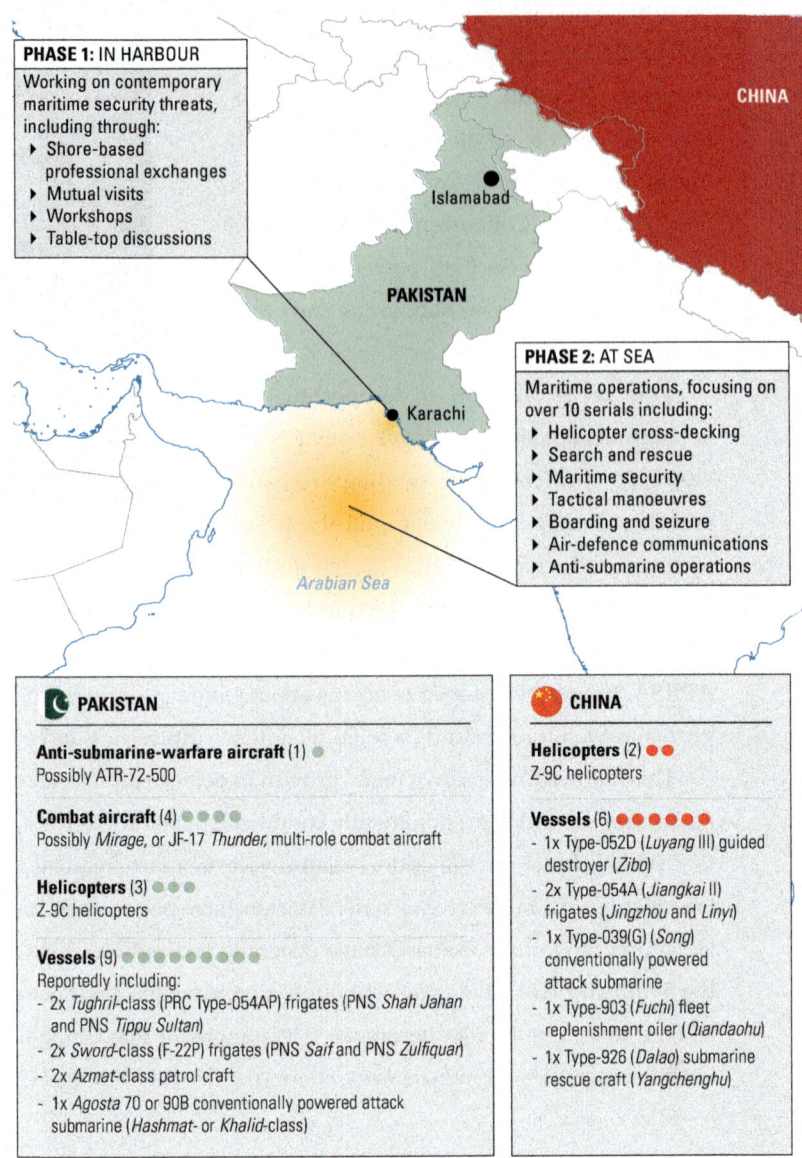

Map 1.2: **China and Pakistan: 3rd *Sea Guardian* exercise, 2023**

Source: IISS

The most recent *Sea Guardian* in November 2023 took place in the north Arabian Sea (see Map 1.2). It was the largest exercise between the PLAN and the Pakistan Navy (PN) at that time, and the first time that Pakistan hosted one of China's most advanced Type-052D destroyers, which reportedly features improved radar detection capabilities.[62] As in 2022, the exercise also involved a Chinese Type-039 (*Song*-class) diesel-electric attack submarine, as well as multiple other support ships and aircraft and a marine-corps unit.[63] Including both a land and a sea phase, the former incorporated scenario consultations. The exercises encompassed training courses on air-defence communication, in addition to visit, board, search and seizure (VBSS) operations and, once again, joint ASW operations.

Signalling greater efforts to build inter-operability and mutual trust, China and Pakistan swapped personnel to observe the organisation and implementation of drills.[64] The joint maritime drills reportedly involved combined arms and focused on joint operational capabilities. In another inter-operability effort, the exercises included the first joint maritime patrol between the two nations, involving the Chinese Type-054A guided-missile frigate *Linyi* and the Pakistani ship PNS *Saif*.[65]

The inclusion of the PNS *Shah Jahan*, one of two recently delivered Type-054AP frigates that Pakistan acquired from China, in the exercise also served to showcase the growing closeness of the two partners.[66] Indeed, as chief PN spokesperson Commodore Syed Rizwan Khalid noted, the exercises 'simulated [a] multi-threat environment' and served to enhance maritime cooperation and inter-operability.[67]

Friends with benefits

For China, military exercises with close partners carry diplomatic, economic and military benefits. These include building political trust, bolstering other areas of China's bilateral relationships, such as BRI investments, as well as offering the PLA valuable overseas operational experience and building inter-operability with foreign militaries.

Indeed, overseas operational experience is perhaps one of the key missing pieces for China and the PLA in terms of overall military readiness in a future regional conflict against an adversary like the US. The comparative combined-military-exercise data with the US noted in Figure 1.4 can attest to this reality. Gradual steps in expanding the scale and complexity of combined-military exercises, such as what China has done with Pakistan, could therefore provide an important contribution to operational proficiency down the line.

These exercises also provide an element of deterrence and political signalling for China. In the case of *Sea Guardian 2022*, observers have noted that the exercises took place in succession following the US–India 2+2 meeting and after India had formally acceded to the Combined Maritime Forces.[68] The exercises were likely timed to send diplomatic signals to the US and India regarding their growing relationship, which China and Pakistan view with a measure of concern considering their own bilateral disputes with the US and India.

ELEVATED EXPECTATIONS

A growing number of European states are deploying their forces to the Asia-Pacific and taking part in combined-military exercises, even as they give renewed focus to European security following Russia's full-scale invasion of Ukraine. The numbers still remain small, and contingents remain limited in relative terms, but there have been recent increases to the capabilities deployed and envisaged for the future and the scenarios exercised, including nascent moves towards greater coordination.[69]

For some European states, strengthening long-standing defence relationships is an important driver for the deployment of these capabilities. So too are the imperatives deriving from territorial possessions in the region (e.g., France). In this case, in-place forces provide greater flexibility to host incoming forces and for more persistent engagements. Defence sales and defence-related technology cooperation are other drivers. Indeed, deployments and exercise participation can improve partner inter-operability and signal the strategic relevance of a particular region whilst also demonstrating the technological prowess of some assets offered by their manufactures, as noted above. For all European states with regional defence ambitions, perhaps the most important drivers are the economic interests and related concerns about regional security dynamics, particularly China's growing assertiveness.

Growing engagement

Germany will reportedly send eight *Typhoon*s and 12 *Tornado*s, as well as four A400Ms and four A330 multi-role tanker transports (MRTTs), to the Asia-Pacific in 2024.[70] Dubbed *Pacific Skies 24*, this air deployment is a significant increase not only in comparison to Berlin's 2022 commitment, but also in comparison to contingents dispatched by other European states. The air force is planning to deploy quickly, travelling east to west, continuing to demonstrate power-projection capability but enabling a different range of engagement options than in 2021 while en route to the Pacific. The German contingent will also be part of a broader deployment with its partner nations in the Future Combat Air System programme; France and Spain will send *Rafale*s, A400Ms, MRTTs and *Typhoon*s respectively.

Germany's maritime contingent will also expand in 2024, with the addition of a support ship to accompany *Baden-Wurttemberg*, one of Germany's latest F125-class frigates. In 2021, the German Navy sent the frigate *Bayern* on a six-month deployment that included port calls and exercises with regional states; it was the navy's first deployment to the region for some 20 years. A year later, the German Air Force's first Asia Pacific deployment, dubbed *Rapid Pacific 2022*, saw it send six *Typhoon* combat aircraft, four A400M transport aircraft and three A330 MRTT tankers to the region, where they took part in Australia's *Pitch Black* and *Kakadu* exercises, among other activities.[71] This engagement was followed in 2023 by the participation of a German contingent in Australia's *Talisman Sabre* exercise.[72]

It is also noteworthy that Germany's planned 2024 military deployments are already being associated with greater exercise participation than the previous deployments: the United States' *Rim of the Pacific* (RIMPAC)

Crew members pose for photos aboard the German Navy frigate *Bayern* at Changi Naval Base, Singapore, 21 December 2021

(Ore Huiying/Bloomberg via Getty Images)

2024 naval exercise, *Pitch Black* and India's *Tarang Shakti* have been reported as potential activities. In its 2021 voyage, most of the *Bayern*'s exercises were passage exercises, and Berlin avoided overt military drills and transiting the Taiwan Strait (though it did take part in Japan's ANNUALEX 2021).[73] Its partners in the *Pacific Skies 24* deployment – France and Spain – are also slated to take part in *Pitch Black* and *Tarang Shakti*.

These increased military deployments and activities are a result of Germany's development of a greater policy focus on the Asia-Pacific in recent years. German Minister of Defence Boris Pistorius said at the 2023 IISS Shangri-La Dialogue that Germany 'cannot afford to neglect this region'.[74] In 2020, Berlin issued its Policy Guidelines for the Indo-Pacific, reflecting the economic and political importance of the region, as well as regional security challenges and the importance of the rules-based order.[75] This document stated that Germany would expand its regional security and defence cooperation, including participation in exercises.[76]

Broadening base

The UK has been seeking to further develop its foundational defence ties in the region with a greater presence and more exercise engagement. The Integrated Review 2021, a comprehensive articulation of the UK's national-security and international policy, announced that the UK would 'tilt' towards the Indo-Pacific, assessing the region to be critical to the UK's economy and security. The subsequent Defence Command Paper (DCP) stated that the UK would increase its presence and engagement and enhance exercise participation in the region, particularly with Australia, India, Japan and South Korea.

The Carrier Strike Group 21 deployment of the aircraft carrier *Queen Elizabeth* and escorts, including the Dutch frigate *Evertsen*, saw a series of exercises take place with forces from Australia and Japan, with one UK frigate conducting a passage of the Taiwan Strait during the deployment.[77]

The UK's presence and participation have increased modestly since then. The region was still prominent in the Integrated Review Refresh 2023, but not to the same extent as before, given the renewed focus on the Euro-Atlantic. There was also criticism of the UK's Indo-Pacific policy development from the Defence Committee last year. The UK's regional military presence in the Indo-Pacific, the committee said, 'remains limited and the strategy to which it contributes is unclear'.[78]

Two offshore-patrol vessels (OPVs) have been present in the region since 2021, but the Littoral Response Group (LRG) deployment – which the 2021 DCP had said would take place in 2023 and which would have provided more exercise opportunities – has not yet occurred. The two support ships forming the LRG were on their way when the Hamas–Israel conflict erupted, and they were held up on standby in the eastern Mediterranean. But London reaffirmed the intention for the LRG to deploy into the Indian Ocean in 2024, and perhaps still further afield.[79]

Deeper, larger and more complex UK combined exercises with Japan are under way in the wake of defence tie-ups such as the Reciprocal Access Agreement, the Hiroshima Accord and the Global Combat Air Programme (also including Italy).[80] For instance, the exercise *Vigilant Isles 2023* was the 'first time British troops have

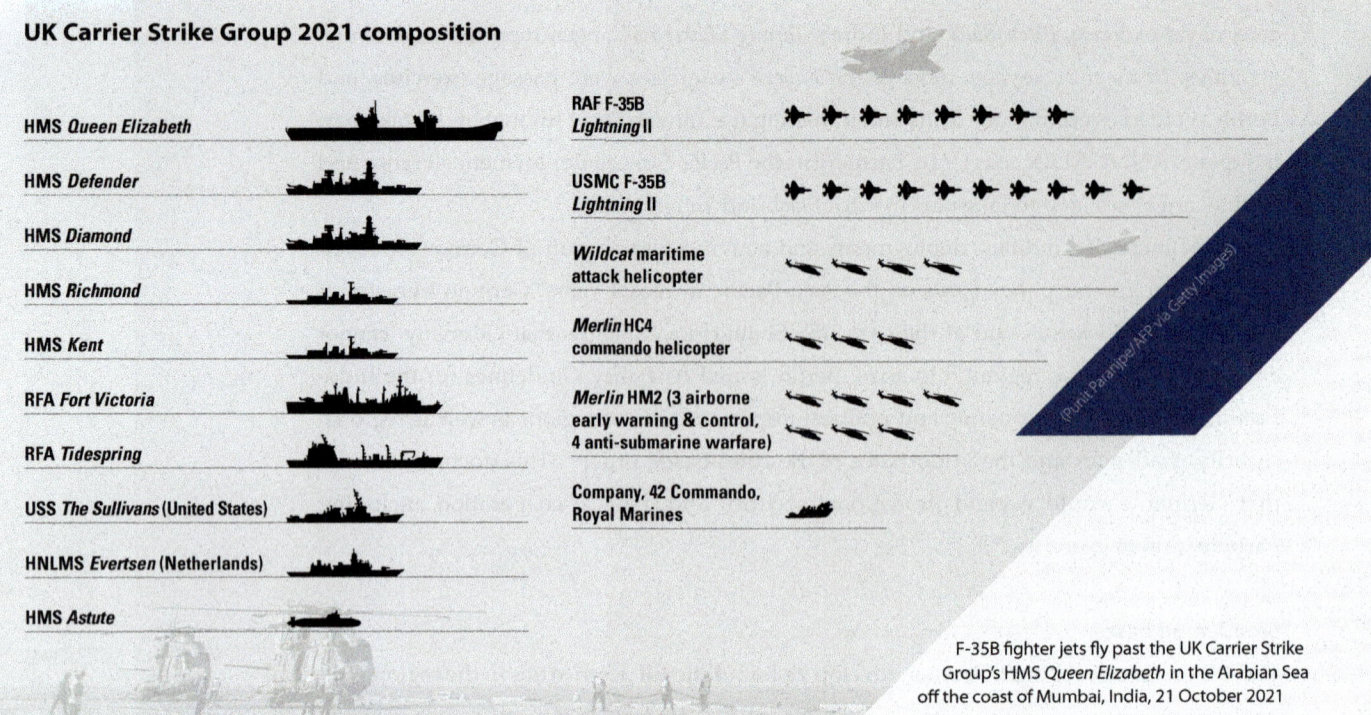

F-35B fighter jets fly past the UK Carrier Strike Group's HMS *Queen Elizabeth* in the Arabian Sea off the coast of Mumbai, India, 21 October 2021

been embedded with their Japanese counterparts'. The personnel component was still limited, though this was double the number sent for the 2022 exercise. *Vigilant Isles* has progressed since its first 2018 iteration to now include live-fire components and scenarios focused on surveillance and reconnaissance, including the use of uninhabited aerial vehicles (UAVs).[81]

Similarly, combined exercises with Australia will deepen once the Australia–UK–US partnership (AUKUS) sees the forward-deployment of a UK *Astute*-class submarine and, eventually, when the new submarine design for the Australian and UK navies (dubbed SSN-AUKUS) is built. Currently, UK forces regularly deploy to routine Australian exercises such as *Pitch Black* and *Talisman Sabre*; furthermore, in mid-2023 they deployed an A400M to the US-led *Mobility Guardian* exercise in Guam and in late 2023 took part, along with the Australian and US air forces, in the *Global Dexterity* exercise, which brought together elements of the three nations' C-17 fleets for inter-operability training.[82]

Other UK regional exercises are based on long-standing defence relationships, such as with Brunei or with Australia, Malaysia, New Zealand and Singapore through the Five Power Defence Arrangements (FPDA) framework. Set up in 1971, FPDA exercises have evolved to reflect changing security concerns and developments in military capabilities. UK contributions routinely involve modest numbers of *Typhoon* combat aircraft. The UK also maintains a military base in Brunei, including a Gurkha infantry garrison and a jungle-warfare training facility. UK forces conduct exercises with the Royal Brunei Armed Forces, and the Gurkha contingent engages on other exercises and training activities with partners across the region that, while small in scope, contribute to a relatively high tempo of engagement.[83]

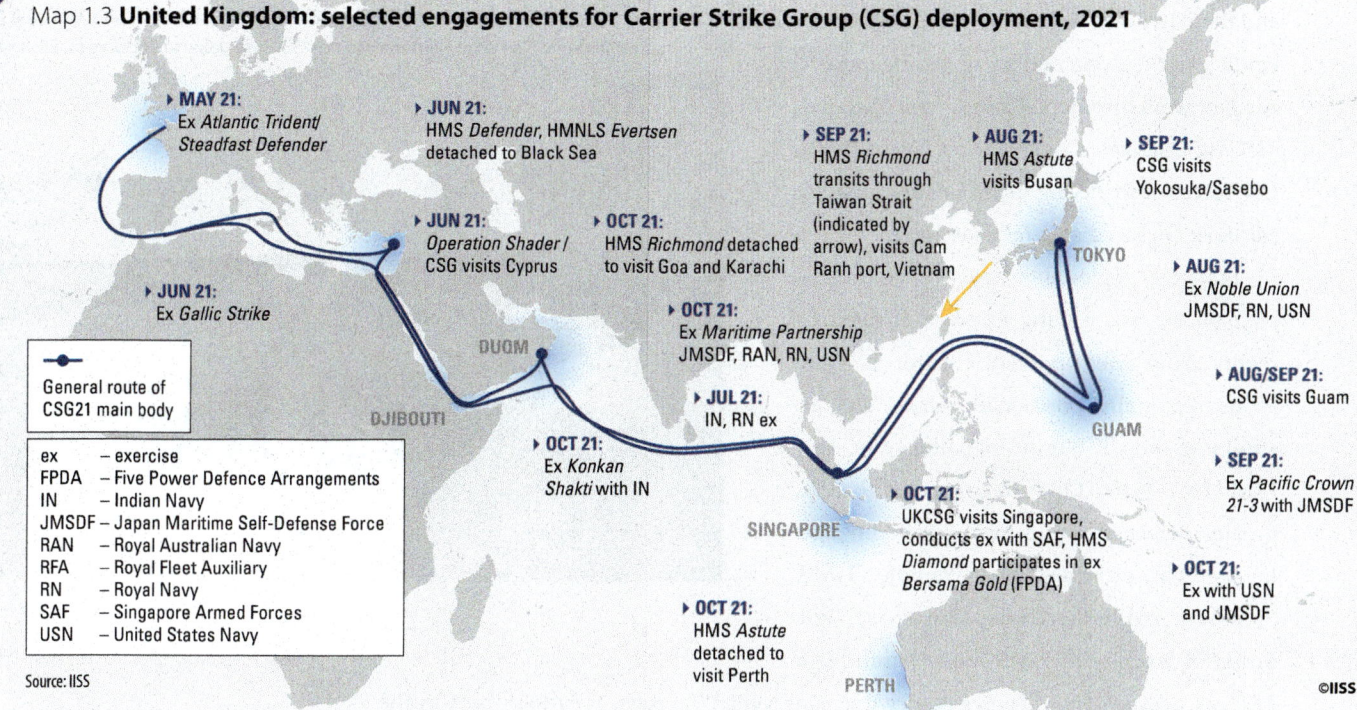

Map 1.3 **United Kingdom: selected engagements for Carrier Strike Group (CSG) deployment, 2021**

Forward presence

France considers itself a Pacific nation due to its regional territories and standing military presence. It also considers itself as 'contributing to regional security through military and security cooperation', including through regular exercises, such as *La Pérouse* in the Indian Ocean and *Croix du Sud* in the Pacific Ocean, as well as other 'bilateral and multilateral exercises'.[84] France's regionally based forces are also larger than the UK's and are used for defence engagement and exercise.

Its military assets include a small number of *Floréal*-class frigates and *d'Entrecasteaux*-class patrol ships and ground and air components in French Polynesia and New Caledonia. Its amphibious assault vehicles are regular visitors on France's *Jeanne d'Arc* training deployments: *Tonnerre* transited the region with an escort in 2021, *Mistral* in 2022 and *Dixmude* in 2023, all taking part in a range of exercises. In 2019 the aircraft carrier *Charles de Gaulle* visited the region, docking in Singapore at the time of the 2019 IISS Shangri-La Dialogue and conducting exercises during its voyage with Indian, Japanese and US naval forces.[85] In 2023, meanwhile, *Rafale*s deployed from the *Charles de Gaulle* conducted a power-projection exercise by flying over 4,000 kilometres from the Indian Ocean to Singapore as part of the *Rastaban* exercise.[86]

Air components form a key aspect of France's regional exercises. Air transits enable the air force to demonstrate power projection and practise the logistics tail required to operate at such distances and, similar to Germany, Spain and the UK, deliver the capacity to engage in exercises with regional partners. The *Pegase* missions are notable in this regard. The 2023 mission was larger than previous deployments. Nineteen aircraft took part, including ten *Rafale*s, five A330 MRTT tankers and four A400M heavy air transports. France utilised several bases for the deployment, routing via the Al-Dhafra Air Base in the United Arab Emirates and then dividing the deployment, with some landing in Malaysia and some in Singapore.[87] Aircraft were dispatched in July to the US-led *Mobility Guardian 23* exercise in Guam (with UK forces also taking part), in addition to *Northern Edge 23-2* and *Talisman Sabre*.[88]

France's regional exercise posture is enabled by its growing number of deployments from Metropolitan France, as well as its regionally positioned forces. This is similar to the UK but on a smaller scale. The Royal Navy's two OPVs have granted the UK greater persistence and flexibility to engage in regional exercises. For example, HMS *Spey* took part in the US–Japan exercise *Keen Sword* in 2022, with HMS *Tamar* joining the FPDA's *Bersama Shield* exercise later the same year.[89] In 2023, *Spey* took part in the exercise *Konkan* with the Indian Navy and the exercise *Sama Sama* with US and Philippines naval forces.[90] But while these platforms have enabled greater maritime participation, they remain limited in terms of their military capability.

During an annual *Pegase* mission, French Air Force personnel work on a Dassault *Rafale* combat aircraft at Halim Perdanakusuma Air Base, Jakarta, Indonesia, 26 July 2023

(Aditya Irawan/NurPhoto via Getty Images)

There are also gaps in Europe's ability to field a regular carrier presence in the region. Italy may fill that in 2024 and the UK in 2025, but importantly, the UK and French governments have identified this as a potential area of cooperation, saying in 2023 that they will 'explore opportunities for the UK and France to demonstrate the sequencing of more persistent European carrier strike group (CSG) presence in the Indo-Pacific'.[91]

Dipping toes in the water

Aside from France, Germany and the UK, other European states are also looking to deploy their military assets in various engagements and exercises, albeit on a smaller scale. The Dutch frigate *Tromp*, for example, may take part in the RIMPAC exercise as part of its regional deployment in 2024.[92]

If approved, Italy's planned Asia-Pacific deployment could consist of the *Cavour* carrier and escorts, a significant increase to the six-month deployment of one of its new *Paolo Thaon di Revel*-class frigates in 2023. Elements of the *Cavour* group could participate in *Pitch Black* as well as RIMPAC.[93] The Italian Air Force also sent four F-35As, three KC-767A tanker/transports, one G-550 airborne early warning aircraft and two C-130J *Hercules* to Komatsu Air Base for a joint exercise in 2023; Japan is the third country in the Global Combat Air Programme, alongside Italy and the UK, providing another motivation for Rome to engage the region.[94]

In recent years, Italy has developed a greater policy focus on the Asia-Pacific. A range of trade and defence-cooperation agreements have been reached with regional states, and while Italy's concept of 'the enlarged Mediterranean' outlines priorities up to and including the western Indian Ocean, the government has also developed bureaucratic structures – such as a standing committee for Asia-Pacific foreign policy – that could support broader regionally focused policy development.[95] Italy's most recent defence-programming document, meanwhile, explicitly connected Italian national interests with the Asia-Pacific.[96]

With the likely deployment of various European military assets and contingents, several Asia-Pacific countries privately question their coordination given the occasional confusion over whether such activities fall under an EU or a national flag. Indeed, coordination is an ambition of the EU. In its Indo-Pacific paper of 2021, the EU said it would assess the opportunity of establishing 'maritime areas of interest in the Indo-Pacific', also exploring 'ways to ensure enhanced naval deployments by its Member States in the region'.[97] Thus far, EU-level regional exercises have been focused on interactions between Asia-Pacific and EU members' navies, operating as part of EU NAVFOR *Operation Atalanta* taking place in the Indian Ocean. While the EU said that it would seek to conduct 'more exercises and port calls with Indo-Pacific partners', for those EU member states currently deploying forces, their national deployments seem to reflect their national interests rather than an EU-level framework.[98]

BACK TO THE FUTURE?

The first edition of APRSA, published in 2014 and then called *Regional Security Assessment*, focused on the proliferation of security challenges, from the nuclear crisis in the Korean Peninsula, to the flashpoints in the South and East China seas, to the armed conflicts across Southeast Asia, along with the growing challenge of water and energy security and military modernisation. The responses to these challenges then were shaped by a focus on strategic partnerships and multilateralism – especially ASEAN – across the Asia-Pacific.

Combined-military exercises as one of the pillars of the regional security architecture were largely missing from the debate. And yet, as we have seen above, combined-military exercises have multiplied over the past two decades, perhaps indicating a worsening security environment with increasingly strained multilateral arrangements. While it is perhaps unsurprising that the US continues to lead ahead of China in combined-military exercises across the region, unpacking the network of military exercises remains useful in better understanding the deeper structure and nature of the regional security order.

Moving ahead, the trajectory of US military exercises in the region will be to continue to adapt to China's operational strategy, including its training patterns and posture towards Taiwan. The Pentagon expects the PLA to broaden its international military footprint; to participate increasingly in bilateral and multilateral military drills; to increase its capacity to deliver humanitarian aid; to participate in naval escort missions; and to make port visits in the region.[99] This is incentive for the US to expand its regional-exercise footprint.

RIMPAC – typically the world's largest maritime-warfare exercise – will occur in June and July 2024 in Victoria, Canada. The last iteration in 2022 included 26 participant countries. Vietnam joined as a full participant for the first time in 2018, although it skipped 2022.[100] Its decision about whether to participate or not will be noteworthy; in September 2023, Hanoi and Washington upgraded their relationship to a 'comprehensive strategic partnership', and the US may be hoping that it can attract Vietnam's participation in a fuller array of multilateral exercises in the region.[101]

The defence ambitions of Japan, a key US ally, will also make a mark on multilateral exercises in the years ahead. At the *Yama Sakura 85* exercise in December 2023, for example,

Tokyo invited Australia to participate for the first time, allowing trilateral coordination with the US on 'workflow, systems, equipment, and command and control'.[102] Likewise, the Philippines will play an important role in multilateral exercises and support the United States' attempt to build new training and operations infrastructure under their EDCA. This agreement facilitates joint training efforts, enables the strategic pre-positioning of military equipment and supports infrastructure construction, including that of airstrips, fuel depots and personnel accommodation.[103]

The US faces significant challenges and threats in Europe and the Middle East. Seeking operational and deterrence benefits from multinational exercises in multiple theatres simultaneously will, even for Washington, strain budgets and cause personnel and equipment gaps. These constraints became clear in 2023 when the US relied on major naval assets to play a regional deterrence role after the 7 October Hamas attack against Israel. One counterpoint, however, is that the US establishment in 2022 of the Joint Pacific Multinational Readiness Center in Hawaii will allow Washington to continuously train foreign-military personnel without having to deploy American assets and soldiers in the region.[104]

Meanwhile, China's immediate strategic priorities will continue to lie in the South and East China seas. It has, nonetheless, been increasing its own military and civilian deployments in the Indian Ocean and to the region. This should not be a surprise. Since 2015, China has stressed that wherever Chinese citizens, companies and investments go, it will need to be able to protect its assets in times of crisis.[105] China's need to evacuate citizens from Libya and Yemen in 2011, in particular, highlighted to senior leadership the need for an overseas military presence.[106] As the recent attacks in the Red Sea have indicated, threats to maritime security, communication and trade in the periphery of the Indian Ocean remain.

As a result of this changing security environment, and China's own desire to deepen and diversify partnerships in the region, China will likely engage in joint military exercises in the Indian Ocean region through new formations of partnerships or with new intensity. In October 2023, China and Saudi Arabia conducted the second iteration of the *Blue Sword* exercise, in which both countries' navies conducted activities such as UAV operations and ship-to-ship firing, as well as a comprehensive drill on rescuing a hijacked merchant ship by force at sea.[107] Once again, the value of relationship building and inter-operability was stressed.

However, China has also engaged in trilateral military exercises in the region, including with Iran and Russia. In February 2024, joint naval drills were announced against a backdrop of renewed US strikes against the Iran-backed and Yemen-based Houthi rebels.[108] Though the exact timeline and location have not been made public yet, previous trilateral exercises between these partners in March 2023 took place in the Gulf of Oman.[109] Similar trilateral exercises took place in 2019 and 2022. Although not a formal trilateral exercise, in June 2023 China held the first meeting of the China–Pakistan–Iran consultation on counter-terrorism and other security matters.[110] It is not inconceivable that in time, such political groupings may potentially evolve into incremental military engagement.

Finally, Europe's increasing defence engagement will continue to raise expectations in the near future. There is an understandable focus, for example, on the prospects for the next UK carrier deployment to the region. In December 2023, UK Defence Secretary

Grant Shapps announced that the UK's carrier strike group would visit Japan as part of the Carrier Strike Group 2025 (CSG25) deployment to the region. Should this transpire, it would likely lead to exercises with the Japanese Maritime Self-Defense Force, but also with others in the region.[111] The CSG itself may take on a more multinational appearance, with increased participation by regional navies.

However, given the gradual increase in European defence engagement, there are important questions over whether regional states might consider that it will translate ultimately into a defence commitment if a

Iranian Navy sailors pilot a speedboat near a Chinese PLA Navy replenishment ship during the *Maritime Security Belt 2024* combined naval exercise between China, Iran and Russia in the Gulf of Oman, 12 March 2024

(ZUMA Press, Inc. via Alamy Stock Photo)

crisis arises. Gauging intentions and managing expectations on that front will be important, as the practical effect of any greater European military interest will inevitably be limited in scale, constrained by scarce resources and the distances involved, and perhaps also by political will and the growing imperative of worries closer to home.

Moreover, all of the European regionally focused strategy documents, whether explicitly or otherwise, refer to maintaining freedom of navigation or safe maritime passage in the Asia-Pacific.[112] There is a particular focus on the South China Sea and the Taiwan Strait, where the US (among select others) has routinely exercised its right of free passage by sending naval vessels through waters claimed by China. Of European navies, it is noteworthy that only France and the UK have conducted passages of the Taiwan Strait in recent years.[113] And even if EU foreign-policy chief Josep Borrell reportedly urged European navies to patrol the Taiwan Strait, it is uncertain which other European nations would currently be willing to do this, even if they had the capability.[114]

Even so, events elsewhere may already be affecting all of these military-exercise plans. An increased European naval presence in the waters of the southern Red Sea to counter Houthi attacks on shipping could affect those plans. In the debate that has taken place in the UK over whether to deploy a UK carrier to the Middle East, one of the factors weighing on the minds of UK officials will have been the potential effect on the CSG25 deployment. In that sense, much like the US, while there may be plans for greater presence and participation in the region, crises elsewhere may be introducing more uncertainty about the plans of European defence ambitions for the Asia-Pacific.

Taken together, a growth in combined-military exercises across the Asia-Pacific should be expected. The US will seek to maintain its lead via its plethora of military exercises with almost all regional countries. China will try and narrow the gap by deepening its exercise ties with a small number of regional partners, while some European countries seek a niche, although not necessarily limited, role in the Asia-Pacific domain. The military 'currency exchanges' underpinning the regional security order will grow as the market for military-exercise and defence partnerships more broadly continues to expand.

NOTES

1 Defence analysts and policymakers use different terms to describe a military exercise involving two nations or more. These terms include 'joint military exercises', 'multi-national exercises' and 'combined-military exercises'. We use 'combined-military exercises' to distinguish them from 'joint' exercises within a single armed forces involving three different branches or services (army, navy, air force) or more.

2 See Beatrice Heuser, 'Reflections on the Purposes, Benefits and Pitfalls of Military Exercises', in 'Military Exercises: Political Messaging and Strategic Impact', *NATO Defence College Forum Paper*, no. 26, April 2018, pp. 11–16.

3 Jordan Bernhardt and Lauren Sukin, 'Joint Military Exercises and Crisis Dynamics on the Korean Peninsula', *Journal of Conflict Resolution*, vol. 65, no. 5, 1 May 2021, pp. 855–88, https://journals.sagepub.com/doi/abs/10.1177/0022002720972180; and Marcel De Haas, 'War Games of the Shanghai Cooperation Organization and the Collective Security Treaty Organization: Drills on the Move!', *The Journal of Slavic Military Studies*, vol. 29, no. 3, 1 August 2016, pp. 378–406, https://www.tandfonline.com/doi/full/10.1080/13518046.2016.1200383.

4 Erik Lin-Greenberg, 'Non-traditional Security Dilemmas: Can Military Operations Other Than War Intensify Security Competition in Asia?', *Asian Security*, vol. 14, no. 3, 2018, pp. 282–302, https://www.tandfonline.com/doi/full/10.1080/14799855.2017.1414044; and Pauline Therese Collins and Rosalie Arcala Hall (eds), *Military Operation and Engagement in the Domestic Jurisdiction: Comparative Call-out Laws* (Leiden: Martinus Nijhoff Publishers, 2022).

5 Beatrice Heuser and Diego Ruiz Palmer, 'Military Exercises: Political Messaging and Strategic Impact', *NATO Defence College Forum Paper*, no. 26, April 2018, p. 1.

6 Wilson Chun Hei Chau, 'Explaining China's Participation in Bilateral and Multilateral Military Exercises', *Security Challenges*, vol. 7, no. 3, 2011, p. 52, https://www.jstor.org/stable/26467108.

7 Kyle J. Wolfley, 'Military Power Reimagined: The Rise and Future of Shaping', *Joint Force Quarterly*, vol. 102, no. 3, 2021, p. 20, https://ndupress.ndu.edu/Media/News/News-Article-View/Article/2679810/military-power-reimagined-the-rise-and-future-of-shaping/.

8 Kyle J. Wolfley, 'Military Statecraft and the Use of Multinational Exercises in World Politics', *Foreign Policy Analysis*, vol. 17, no. 2, 2021, p. 3, https://academic.oup.com/fpa/article-abstract/17/2/oraa022/6123995?redirectedFrom=fulltext.

9 Brian G. Forester, *Globalization, Hierarchy, and Bureaucracy: Exploring the Politics of Joint Military Exercises*, PhD dissertation, University of North Carolina at Chapel Hill, 2023.

10 *Ibid.*

11 Jordan Bernhardt, *The Causes and Consequences of Joint Military Exercises*, PhD dissertation, Stanford University, 2020.

12 Kevin Galambos, 'Military Exercises and Network Effects', *International Studies Quarterly*, vol. 68, no. 1, 2024, p. 2, https://academic.oup.com/isq/article-abstract/68/1/sqae004/7571530?redirectedFrom=fulltext.

13 *Ibid.*

14 *Ibid.*, p. 3

15 *Ibid.*; Derrick V. Frazier and J. Wesley Hutto, 'The Socialization of Military Power: Security Cooperation and Doctrine Development Through Multinational Military Exercises', *Defence Studies*, vol. 17, no. 4, 2017, pp. 379–97, https://www.tandfonline.com/doi/full/10.1080/14702436.2017.1377050; and Matías Ferreyra and Joseph Soeters, 'Multinational Military Cooperation in the Global South', *Armed Forces & Society*, vol. 50, no. 1, 2024, pp. 25–54, https://journals.sagepub.com/doi/abs/10.1177/0095327X221114928.

16 Brian L. Willis, *Diversification: Middle States, Security Institutions, and the Shadow of Great Power Rivalry*, PhD dissertation, University of California San Diego, 2022, p. 110.

17 *Ibid.*

18 Ian Storey, 'China's Military Exercises in Southeast Asia Belie Lack of Trust', *Fulcrum*, 27 December 2023, https://fulcrum.sg/2023-top-10-chinas-military-exercises-in-southeast-asia-belie-lack-of-trust/.

19 Willis, *Diversification: Middle States, Security Institutions, and the Shadow of Great Power Rivalry*, p. 110.

20 Dean Acheson, 'Foreign Relations of the United States, 1950, East Asia and the Pacific', US Department of State Office of the Historian, vol. 6, 9 March 1950, https://history.state.gov/historicaldocuments/frus1950v06.

21 US Department of State Office of the Historian, 'Milestones in the History of US Foreign Relations: Southeast Asia Treaty Organization (SEATO), 1954', https://history.state.gov/milestones/1953-1960/seato.

22 Valerie Jackson, 'Old Friends in Southeast Asia: U.S. Marines in Thailand', *Fortitudine: Bulletin of the Marine Corps Historical Progam*, vol. 33, no. 1, 2008, pp. 16–17, https://www.marines.mil/Portals/1/Publications/Fortitudine%20Vol%20 33%20No%201.pdf; and Elbridge Durbrow, 'Vietnam Embassy Memorandum to the US Department of State', *Foreign Relations of the United States, 1955–1957, East Asian Security; Cambodia; Laos*, vol. 11, 12 August 1957, https://history.state.gov/historicaldocuments/frus1955-57v21/d163.

23 Jackson, 'Old Friends in Southeast Asia: U.S. Marines in Thailand', pp. 16–17.

24 Brendan Taylor, 'Conceptualizing the Bilateral–Multilateral Security Nexus', in William T. Tow and Brendan Taylor (eds), *Bilateralism, Multilateralism and Asia-Pacific Security: Contending Cooperation* (London: Routledge, 2013).

25 'Strategic Landpower Dialogue: A Conversation with General Charles Flynn', Center for Strategic and International Studies, Washington DC, 12 October 2023, https://www.csis.org/analysis/strategic-landpower-dialogue-conversation-general-charles-flynn.

26 Joseph Clark, 'Growth in Partnerships Signals US Success in Indo-Pacific', DOD News, 7 September 2023, https://www.defense.gov/News/News-Stories/Article/Article/3519047/growth-in-partnerships-signals-us-success-in-indo-pacific.

27 Christopher Hurd, 'USARPAC: Landpower Essential in Defending Indo-Pacific', Army News Service, 20 October 2023, https://www.army.mil/article/270956/usarpac_landpower_essential_in_defending_indo_pacific; see also 'Not Just an Air and Maritime Theater: The Army's Role in the Indo-Pacific', discussion at the American Enterprise Institute, 27 February 2023, https://www.aei.org/wp-content/uploads/2023/02/230227-The-Armys-Role-in-the-Indo-Pacific.pdf.

28 Clark, 'Growth in Partnerships Signals US Success in Indo-Pacific'.

29 US Indo-Pacific Command, 'Pacific Partnership Concludes Final 2023 Mission in the Kingdom of Tonga', 20 November 2023, https://www.pacom.mil/Media/News/News-Article-View/Article/3595119/pacific-partnership-concludes-final-2023-mission-in-the-kingdom-of-tonga/.

30 Admiral John C. Aquilino, 'US Indo-Pacific Command Posture', statement to the Armed Services Committee, US House of Representatives, 18 April 2023, https://www.congress.gov/118/meeting/house/115680/witnesses/HHRG-118-AS00-Wstate-AquilinoJ-20230418.pdf.

31 US Department of Defense, 'Military and Security Developments Involving the People's Republic of China 2023', p. 179, https://media.defense.gov/2023/Oct/19/2003323409/-1/-1/1/2023-MILITARY-AND-SECURITY-DEVELOPMENTS-INVOLVING-THE-PEOPLES-REPUBLIC-OF-CHINA.PDF.

32 'Strategic Landpower Dialogue: A Conversation with General Charles Flynn', Center for Strategic and International Studies.

33 US Department of Defense, 'Military and Security Developments Involving the People's Republic of China 2023', p. 143.

34 'Not Just an Air and Maritime Theater: The Army's Role in the Indo-Pacific', American Enterprise Institute.

35 *Ibid.*

36 For example, the US has developed the Pacific Multi-Domain Test and Experimentation Capability, which allows allied military forces across the theatre to link their training operations, simulation centres and mobile training-support systems, creating the world's largest military-training network. See Admiral John C. Aquilino, 'US Indo-Pacific Command Posture', statement to the Armed Services Committee.

37 'Not Just an Air and Maritime Theater: The Army's Role in the Indo-Pacific', American Enterprise Institute.

38 Chau, 'Explaining China's Participation in Bilateral and Multilateral Military Exercises', p. 51.

39 Academy of Military Science Military Strategy Department, *The Science of Military Strategy* (Beijing, Haidian District, Qinglong Bridge: China Aerospace Studies Institute Military Science Press, December 2013), p. 148, https://www.airuniversity.af.edu/Portals/10/CASI/documents/Translations/2021-02-08%20 Chinese%20Military%20Thoughts-%20In%20 their%20own%20words%20Science%20of%20 Military%20Strategy%202013.pdf?ver=Nx-AWg4BPw_NylEjxaha8Aw%3d%3d.

40 *Ibid.*

41 *Ibid.*
42 *Ibid.*, p. 133.
43 China Aerospace Studies Institute, 'In Their Own Words: Science of Military Strategy', December 2020, p. 136, https://www.airuniversity.af.edu/Portals/10/CASI/documents/Translations/2022-01-26%202020%20Science%20of%20Military%20Strategy.pdf.
44 *Ibid.*
45 *Ibid.*, p. 314.
46 *Ibid.*, pp. 313–14.
47 *Ibid.*, p. 148.
48 *Ibid.*, p. 325.
49 Darshana Baruah, 'Surrounding the Ocean: PRC Influence in the Indian Ocean', Testimony before the House of Representatives Foreign Affairs Committee Subcommittee on the Indo-Pacific, 18 April 2023, https://carnegieendowment.org/files/HHRG-118-FA05-Wstate-BaruahD-20230418.pdf.
50 Alex Vines, Henry Tugendhat and Armida van Rij, 'Is China Eyeing a Second Military Base in Africa?', United States Institute of Peace, 30 January 2024, https://www.usip.org/publications/2024/01/china-eyeing-second-military-base-africa.
51 Zhao Lei, '3 Sea Routes Planned for Belt & Road Initiative', *China Daily*, 21 June 2017, https://english.www.gov.cn/state_council/ministries/2017/06/21/content_281475692760102.htm.
52 See Ministry of Foreign Affairs of the People's Republic of China, 'The Global Security Initiative Concept Paper', 21 February 2023, https://www.mfa.gov.cn/eng/wjbxw/202302/t20230221_11028348.html.
53 See Cate Cadell, 'Chinese PLA-linked Vessels Map the Indian Ocean for Submarine Warfare', *Washington Post*, 10 January 2024, https://www.washingtonpost.com/national-security/2024/01/10/china-submarine-military-indian-ocean/; and Ken Moriyasu and Kiran Sharma, 'Indian Ocean Rivalry: China's Naval Maneuvers Irk New Delhi', Nikkei Asia, 27 September 2022, https://asia.nikkei.com/Spotlight/Asia-Insight/Indian-Ocean-rivalry-China-s-naval-maneuvers-irk-New-Delhi.
54 Magnus Nordenmann, 'Why the Chinese Navy Is In the Mediterranean', US Naval Institute, 14 May 2015, https://news.usni.org/2015/05/14/why-the-chinese-navy-is-in-the-mediterranean.
55 'Russia and China Hold Naval Drills, Practise Submarine Capture', Reuters, 28 December 2022, https://www.reuters.com/world/russia-china-hold-naval-drills-practise-submarine-capture-2022-12-28/; and Yukio Tajima, 'China and Russia Kick Off Military Exercises in Sea of Japan', Nikkei Asia, 21 July 2023, https://asia.nikkei.com/Politics/International-relations/Indo-Pacific/China-and-Russia-kick-off-military-exercises-in-Sea-of-Japan.
56 Chinese Embassy to Indonesia, 'Xi Jinping Meets with Prime Minister of Pakistan Anwaar-ul-Haq Kakar', 19 October 2023, http://id.china-embassy.gov.cn/indo/wjyw/202310/t20231020_11165084.htm; and Sun Zhiying, 'Zhōnghuá rénmín gònghéguó hé bājīsītǎn yīsīlán gònghéguó liánhé xīnwén shēngming' 中华人民共和国和巴基斯坦伊斯兰共和国联合新闻声明 [Joint press statement of the People's Republic of China and the Islamic Republic of Pakistan], Xinhua News Agency, 20 October 2023, http://www.81.cn/zt/2023nzt/dsjydylg-jhzgflt/yw_246474/16260824.html.
57 'PM: Pakistan Progresses with CPEC Projects Under BRI', Xinhua News Agency, 1 November 2023, http://english.scio.gov.cn/beltandroad/2023-11/01/content_116787907.htm.
58 Huang Panyue, 'China, Pakistan Kick Off "Sea Guardians–2020" Naval Drill in Karachi', China Military Online, 6 January 2020, http://eng.mod.gov.cn/xb/News_213114/TopStories/4858081.html.
59 *Ibid.*
60 Chen Zhuo, 'China, Pakistan Kick Off Joint Naval Exercise "Sea Guardians – 2" in Shanghai', Ministry of National Defense of the People's Republic of China, 10 July 2020, http://eng.mod.gov.cn/xb/News_213114/TopStories/4915287.html.
61 'Zhōng bā "hǎiyáng wèishì-3" hǎishàng liánhé yǎnxí kāimù' 中巴"海洋卫士-3"海上联合演习开幕 [China–Pakistan 'ocean guard-3' joint maritime exercise opens], Xinhua News, 12 November 2023, http://www.news.cn/world/2023-11/12/c_1129971543.htm.
62 Li Weichao, 'China–Pakistan Sea Guardian 2023 Joint Exercise Enters Maritime Drills Phase', China Military Online, 16 November 2023, http://eng.chinamil.com.cn/CHINA_209163/TopStories_209189/16267195.html; and Usman Ansari, 'China, Pakistan Wrap Up Naval Drill Featuring Sub, High-tech Destroyer', DefenseNews, 18 November 2023, https://www.defensenews.com/training-sim/2023/11/17/

china-pakistan-wrap-up-naval-drill-featuring-sub-high-tech-destroyer/.
63 Ansari, 'China, Pakistan Wrap Up Naval Drill Featuring Sub, High-tech Destroyer'; and Ayaz Gul, 'China Holds Naval Drills with Pakistan in Arabian Sea', *VOA News*, 13 November 2023, https://www.voanews.com/a/china-holds-naval-drills-with-pakistan-in-arabian-sea/7353002.html.
64 'China–Pakistan "Ocean Guard–3" Joint Maritime Exercise Opens', Xinhua News.
65 Huang Panyue, 'China, Pakistan Kick Off "Sea Guardians-2020" Naval Drill in Karachi'; Li Weichao, 'China–Pakistan Sea Guardian 2023 Joint Exercise Enters Maritime Drills Phase'.
66 Tayfun Ozberk, 'Chinese Shipyard Delivers Final Two Type 054 A/P Frigates to Pakistan Navy', Naval News, 11 May 2023, https://www.navalnews.com/naval-news/2023/05/chinese-shipyard-delivers-final-two-type-054-a-p-frigates-to-pakistan-navy/.
67 Ansari, 'China, Pakistan Wrap Up Naval Drill Featuring Sub, High-tech Destroyer'.
68 Abhijit Singh, 'Deciphering China–Pakistan Naval Exercises in the Indian Ocean', Observer Research Foundation, https://www.orfonline.org/expert-speak/deciphering-china-pakistan-naval-exercises-in-the-indian-ocean.
69 Takahashi Kosuke, 'Japan, France to Conduct First Joint Fighter Jet Drill', *Diplomat*, https://thediplomat.com/2023/07/japan-france-to-conduct-first-joint-fighter-jet-drill; and Gabriel Dominguez, 'France and Japan Expand Defense Ties with First Joint Fighter Jet Drills', *Japan Times*, 26 July 2023, https://www.japantimes.co.jp/news/2023/07/26/japan/japan-france-first-fighter-jet-exercises/.
70 Sebastian Sprenger, 'German Air Force Plans Major Asia-Pacific Tour in 2024', DefenseNews, 27 November 2023, https://www.defensenews.com/global/europe/2023/11/27/german-air-force-plans-major-asia-pacific-tour-in-2024/.
71 Airbus, 'Pitch Black 2022: Behind the Scenes of Operation Rapid Pacific 2022', 31 August 2022, https://www.airbus.com/en/newsroom/stories/2022-08-pitch-black-2022-behind-the-scenes-of-operation-rapid-pacific-2022; and Australian Government Department of Defence, 'Navy's Largest Exercise Comes to a Close', 28 September 2022, https://www.defence.gov.au/news-events/news/2022-09-28/navys-largest-exercise-comes-close.
72 German Bundeswehr, 'Talisman Sabre 23', https://www.bundeswehr.de/de/organisation/heer/aktuelles/schwerpunkte/talisman-sabre.
73 Sprenger, 'German Air Force Plans Major Asia-Pacific Tour in 2024'; German Bundeswehr, 'Indo-Pacific Deployment: "Bayern" Back Home', 18 February 2022, https://www.bundeswehr.de/en/organization/navy/news/indo-pacific-deployment-bayern-back-home-5357646; and German Bundeswehr, 'Naval Exercises: The "Bayern" at ANNUALEX 2021', 9 December 2021, https://www.bundeswehr.de/en/organization/navy/news/naval-exercises-frigate-bayern-at-annualex-2021-5320470.
74 Germany Ministry of Defence, 'Verteidigungsminister Pistorius besucht die Indo-Pazifik-Region' [Defence minister Pistorius visits the Indo-Pacific region], June 2023, https://www.bmvg.de/de/themen/dossiers/engagement-im-indopazifik/minister-besucht-strategisch-bedeutsame-indo-pazifik-region.
75 Federal Government of Germany, 'Policy Guidelines for the Indo-Pacific', 1 September 2020, https://www.auswaertiges-amt.de/blob/2380514/f9784f7e3b3fa1bd7c5446d274a4169e/200901-indo-pazifik-leitlinien--1--data.pdf.
76 Federal Government of Germany, 'Policy Guidelines for the Indo-Pacific', p. 35.
77 Question by Andrew Rosindell MP in UK Parliament Discussions of UIN 1063718, 8 December 2022, https://questions-statements.parliament.uk/written-questions/detail/2022-12-08/106371/.
78 UK House of Commons Defence Committee, 'UK Defence and the Indo-Pacific – Report Summary', 24 October 2023, https://publications.parliament.uk/pa/cm5803/cmselect/cmdfence/183/summary.html.
79 UK Government, 'UK Plans to Deploy Spearhead Carrier Strike Group to Indian Ocean Region in 2025', 10 January 2024, https://www.gov.uk/government/news/uk-plans-to-deploy-spearhead-carrier-strike-group-to-indian-ocean-region-in-2025#:~:text=Plans%20to%20send%20UK's%20high,bolstering%20UK%2DIndia%-20security%20ties.
80 UK Government, 'The Hiroshima Accord: An Enhanced UK–Japan Global Strategic Partnership', 18 May 2023, https://assets.publishing.service.gov.uk/media/64662b0b0b72d30013344777/The_Hiroshima_Accord.pdf; and Government

of Japan, 'Agreement Between Japan and the United Kingdom of Great Britain and Northern Ireland Concerning the Facilitation of Reciprocal Access and Cooperation Between the Self-Defense Forces of Japan and the Armed Forces of the United Kingdom of Great Britain and Northern Ireland', 11 January 2023, https://www.mofa.go.jp/files/100445053.pdf.

81 UK Army, 'British Troops Embed with Japanese Armed Forces for First Time', 27 November 2023, https://www.army.mod.uk/news-and-events/news/2023/11/british-troops-embed-with-japanese-armed-forces-for-first-time/; and UK Army, 'British Troops Exercise in Japan for the First Time', 4 October 2018, https://www.army.mod.uk/news-and-events/news/2018/10/british-troops-exercise-in-japan-for-the-first-time/.

82 Air Mobility Public Affairs, 'AMCs Largest Global Exercise Process Success in Indo-Pacific Theatre', 24 July 2023, https://www.af.mil/News/Article-Display/Article/3468805/amcs-largest-global-exercise-proves-success-in-indo-pacific-theater/; and UK Royal Airforce, 'RAF Lands in Australia to Participate in Exercise Global Dexterity for the First Time', 2 December 2023, https://www.raf.mod.uk/news/articles/raf-lands-in-australia-to-participate-in-exercise-global-dexterity-for-the-first-time/.

83 UK Royal Navy, 'HMS Albion's Royal Marines Exercise with Brunei Forces', 13 September 2019, https://www.royalnavy.mod.uk/news-and-latest-activity/news/2018/september/13/180913-hms-albion-royal-marines-exercise-with-brunei-forces; Defence Australia, 'Exercise Croix du Sud 2023 Force Integration Training New Caledonia', YouTube, 5 May 2023, https://www.youtube.com/watch?v=qmzEpNqY2sY; and UK Army, 'Gurkhas Go Down Under for Urban and Amphibious Warfare Training', 14 August 2023, https://www.army.mod.uk/news-and-events/news/2023/08/gurkhas-down-under-for-urban-and-amphibious-warfare-training/.

84 French Ministry for Europe and Foreign Affairs, 'France's Indo-Pacific Strategy', 16 September 2021, p. 54, https://www.diplomatie.gouv.fr/IMG/pdf/en_dcp_a4_indopacifique_022022_v1-4_web_cle878143.pdf.

85 Japanese Ministry of Defense, 'Indo-Pacific Deployment 2019', https://www.mod.go.jp/msdf/en/exercises/IPD19.html; and French Carrier Strike Group (@FRENCH_CSG), tweet, 17 January 2023, https://twitter.com/French_CSG/status/1615394087879704626?ref_src=twsrc%5Etfw%7Ctwcamp%5Etweetembed%7Ctwterm%5E1615394087879704626%7Ctwgr%5E110f5d186e88b555007c60478b65141c-383c260a%7Ctwcon%5Es1_&ref_url=https%3A%2F%2Fnews.usni.org%2F2023%2F01%2F18%2Fcharles-de-gaulle-carrier-strike-group-operating-in-indian-ocean-deploys-fighters-to-singapore.

86 Ibid.

87 French Ministry of Defence, 'Mission Pegase', https://www.defense.gouv.fr/operations/operations/mission-pegase; and Paco Milhiet, 'Pegase 2023: The French Air Force Flies Across the Indo-Pacific', *Diplomat*, 4 August 2023, https://thediplomat.com/2023/08/pegase-2023-the-french-air-force-flies-across-the-indo-pacific/.

88 French Air Force, 'Pegase 23: From Exercise to Reality, a Research Mission in the Pacific', 12 July 2023, https://air.defense.gouv.fr/armee-de-lair-et-de-lespace/actualite/pegase-23-exercise-reality-research-mission-pacific; 'Pegase 23 Bolsters French Indo-Pacific Presence', *Indo Pacific Defense Forum*, 6 August 2023, https://ipdefenseforum.com/2023/08/pegase-23-bolsters-french-indo-pacific-presence/; and Michelle Chang and Hannah Strobel, 'US and Allies Benefit from Exercise Northern Eagle 23-2', US Pacific Air Forces, 4 August 2023, https://www.pacaf.af.mil/News/Article-Display/Article/3484084/us-and-allies-benefit-from-exercise-northern-edge-23-2/.

89 UK Royal Navy, 'Royal Navy Joins One of the Largest Military Exercises in Pacific for First Time', 21 November 2022, 'https://www.royalnavy.mod.uk/news-and-latest-activity/news/2022/november/21/20221121-royal-navy-joins-one-of-the-largest-military-exercises-in-pacific-for-first-time; and UK Royal Navy, 'UK Military Complete First of Two Major Exercises in East Asia', 1 April 2022, https://www.royalnavy.mod.uk/news-and-latest-activity/news/2022/april/01/220401-uk-military-complete-first-of-two-major-exercises-in-east-asia.

90 UK Royal Navy, 'Sama Lovin' – Spey Enjoys Taking Part in Major Philippines Naval Exercise', 19 October 2023, https://www.royalnavy.mod.uk/news-and-latest-activity/news/2023/october/19/20231019-spey-enjoys-

taking-part-in-major-philippines-naval-exercise; British High Commission in New Delhi, 'Royal Navy Warship HMS Spey Makes Inaugural Visit to India', 24 November 2023, https://www.gov.uk/government/news/royal-navy-warship-hms-spey-makes-inaugural-visit-to-india.

91 UK Ministry of Defence, 'UK and France Commit to Greater Defence Cooperation at Paris Summit', 10 March 2023, https://www.gov.uk/government/news/uk-france-commit-to-greater-defence-cooperation-at-paris-summit.

92 Minister of Defence of the Netherlands Kajsa Ollongren (@DefensieMin), tweet, 31 January 2024, https://twitter.com/DefensieMin/status/1752617907949875656.

93 Aaron-Mathew Lariosa, 'Italian Navy to Ramp Up Indo-Pacific Engagement in 2024', Naval News, 10 January 2024, https://www.navalnews.com/event-news/sna-2024/2024/01/italian-navy-to-ramp-up-indo-pacific-engagement-in-2024/. Note that one Italian source reports that the *Cavour* deployment could be accompanied by up to four escort and support units (Gabriele Carrer and Emanuele Rossi, 'Italia e India giocano in Difesa: L'accordo Crosetto-Singh' [Italy and India play defence: the Crosetto–Singh agreement], *Formiche*, October 2023, https://formiche.net/2023/10/italia-india-difesa-rinnovata-intesa/). It is reported that Italy will declare initial operational capability for the *Cavour* with its F-35B capability, which raises the potential for experience-sharing discussions with the Japan Self Defense Force, looking to establish this capability on its *Izumo*-class vessels.

94 Tom Kington, 'Italy Air Force Hauls an F-35 Contingent to Japan for First-ever Drill', DefenseNews, 8 August 2023, https://www.defensenews.com/global/europe/2023/08/08/italy-air-force-hauls-an-f-35-contingent-to-japan-for-first-ever-drill/; and European Air Traffic Command, 'WATC Supports Italian Air Force Deployment to Japan', 9 August 2023, https://eatc-mil.com/post/eatc-supports-italian-air-force-deployment-to-japan.

95 'Hearing on Italy's Role in the Indo-Pacific', Istituto Affari Internazionali, 27 September 2023, https://documenti.camera.it/leg19/resoconti/commissioni/bollettini/pdf/2023/09/27/leg.19.bol0171.data20230927.com03.pdf.

96 Italian Ministry of Defence, 'Documento Programmatico Pluriennale Della Difesa per il Triennio 2023–2025' [Multi-Annual Defence Programme 2023–2025], 2023, https://www.difesa.it/assets/allegati/2569/4acffd61-84fa-4df3-bdab-806066fa5d56.pdf.

97 'The EU Strategy for Cooperation in the Indo-Pacific', European Commission, https://eur-lex.europa.eu/legal-content/EN/TXT/HTML/?uri=CELEX:52021JC0024&from=EN.

98 European Union, 'Joint Communication to the European Parliament and the Council: The EU Strategy for Cooperation in the Indo-Pacific', 16 September 2021, p. 13, https://www.eeas.europa.eu/sites/default/files/jointcommunication_2021_24_1_en.pdf; and Council of the EU, 'Press Release: Coordinated Maritime Presences: Council Extends Implementation in the Gulf of Guinea for Two Years and Establishes a New Maritime Area of Interest in the North-western Indian Ocean', 21 February 2022, https://www.consilium.europa.eu/en/press/press-releases/2022/02/21/coordinated-maritime-presences-council-extends-implementation-in-the-gulf-of-guinea-for-2-years-and-establishes-a-new-concept-in-the-north-west-indian-ocean/.

99 US Department of Defense, 'Military and Security Developments Involving the People's Republic of China 2023', p. 149.

100 US Department of State Bureau of Political-Military Affairs, 'Fact Sheet: U.S. Security Cooperation with Vietnam', 11 September 2023, https://www.state.gov/u-s-security-cooperation-with-vietnam.

101 White House, 'Joint Leaders' Statement: Elevating United States–Vietnam Relations to a Comprehensive Strategic Partnership', 11 September 2023, https://www.whitehouse.gov/briefing-room/statements-releases/2023/09/11/joint-leaders-statement-elevating-united-states-vietnam-relations-to-a-comprehensive-strategic-partnership.

102 Marc Jacob Prosser, 'Yama Sakura Expands to Multilateral Exercise, Sees Largest Participation', *Indo-Pacific Defense Forum*, 25 December 2023, https://ipdefenseforum.com/2023/12/yama-sakura-expands-to-multilateral-exercise-sees-largest-participation.

103 AP News, 'Philippines Names 4 New Camps for U.S. Forces', *Indo-Pacific Defense Forum*, 18 December 2023, https://ipdefenseforum.com/2023/12/philippines-names-4-new-camps-for-u-s-forces.

104 US Army, 'Joint Pacific Multinational Readiness Center Rotation Begins in Hawaii', 2 November 2022, https://www.army.mil/article/261685/joint_pacific_multinational_readiness_center_rotation_begins_in_hawaii.

105 'China's Military Strategy', Xinhua News, 27 May 2015, https://english.www.gov.cn/archive/white_paper/2015/05/27/content_281475115610833.htm.

106 Jonathan Marcus, 'Business Interests Propel Change in China's Global Role', BBC News, 30 May 2015, https://www.bbc.com/news/world-asia-32933447.

107 Li Jiayao, 'China–Saudi Arabia "Blue Sword–2023" Launches Maritime Training', China Military Online, 25 October 2023, http://eng.mod.gov.cn/xb/News_213114/OverseasOperations/JointTrainingandExercises/16261863.html; and Lin Congyi, 'China–Saudi Arabia "Blue Sword–2023" Naval Special Operations Joint Training Concluded', China Military Online, 27 October 2023, http://eng.mod.gov.cn/xb/News_213114/OverseasOperations/JointTrainingandExercises/16262628.html.

108 Dewey Sim, 'China, Russia and Iran to Hold Navy Drills Aimed at "Regional Security", Admiral Says as Middle East Tensions Flare', *South China Morning Post*, 6 February 2024, https://www.scmp.com/news/china/military/article/3251127/china-russia-and-iran-hold-navy-drills-aimed-regional-security-admiral-says-middle-east-tensions.

109 Liu Zhen, 'China, Russia, Iran Launch Five Days of Navy Drills in Gulf of Oman, Close to US-led Middle East Sea Exercise', *South China Morning Post*, 15 March 2023, https://www.scmp.com/news/china/military/article/3213657/chinese-russian-and-iranian-navies-launch-five-days-drills-gulf-oman-close-us-led-middle-east-sea?module=inline&pgtype=article.

110 Ministry of Foreign Affairs of the People's Republic of China, 'The First Meeting of the China–Pakistan–Iran Trilateral Consultation on Counter-terrorism and Security Held in Beijing', 7 June 2023, https://www.mfa.gov.cn/eng/wjbxw/202306/t20230614_11096165.html.

111 UK Ministry of Defence, 'UK Carrier Strike Group to Visit Japan in 2025', 14 December 2023, https://www.gov.uk/government/news/uk-carrier-strike-group-to-visit-japan-in-2025.

112 Both France and Germany's Asia-Pacific strategies refer to freedom of navigation, while the UK's Integrated Review Refresh of 2023 also noted the term, but without specifying a region. The UK currently lacks a cross-government Indo-Pacific strategy (see House of Commons Defence Committee, 'UK Defence and the Indo-Pacific – Report Summary'). The Dutch government's 2020 'Guidelines for Strengthening Dutch and EU Cooperation with Partners in Asia' refers to maritime safe passage (see Government of the Netherlands, 'Indo-Pacific: Guidelines for Strengthening Dutch and EU Cooperation with Partners in Asia', 13 November 2020, https://www.government.nl/binaries/government/documenten/publications/2020/11/13/indo-pacific-guidelines/Indo-Pacific+Guidelines+EN.pdf); Spain's 2021 National Security Strategy reflected the region's importance for Madrid (see Government of Spain, 'Estrategia de Seguridad Nacional 2021' [National Security Strategy 2021], https://www.dsn.gob.es/es/estrategias-publicaciones/estrategias/estrategia-seguridad-nacional-2017), as did the 2018 Strategic Vision for Asia (see Government of Spain, 'A Strategic Vision for Spain in Asia, 2018–2022', February 2018, https://www.exteriores.gob.es/es/ServiciosAlCiudadano/PublicacionesOficiales/2018_02_ESTRATEGIA%20ASIA%20ENG.pdf).

113 In remarks in 2021 at the 42nd IISS Fullerton Lecture, then-German naval chief Vice Admiral Kay-Achim Schönbach said that the 2021 *Bayern* deployment was reflective of a step-by-step approach given the time since the previous naval deployment, indicating that a future transit of the Taiwan Strait was a possibility (The International Institute of Strategic Studies, '42nd IISS Fullerton Lecture – Germany's Chief of Navy, Vice Admiral Kay-Achim Schönbach', YouTube, 21 December 2021, https://www.youtube.com/watch?v=PG26J-GD3DQ.

114 Stuart Lau, 'Send Warships to Taiwan Strait, Borrel Urges EU Governments', Politico, 23 April 2023, https://www.politico.eu/article/china-joseb-taiwan-borrell-eu-warships-to-patrol-strait/.

CHAPTER 2

MIDDLING AND MUDDLING THROUGH? MANAGING ASIA-PACIFIC CRISES

MEIA NOUWENS

Senior Fellow for Chinese Security and Defence Policy, IISS

Illustration of 'spy' balloons over Chinese and US flags (Jakub Porzycki/NurPhoto via Getty Images)

OBJECTIVE:

This chapter analyses the existing crisis-prevention and -management mechanisms between the United States and China and within the broader Asia-Pacific, as well as evaluating their development and effectiveness. It also seeks to better understand and map regional incidents at air and sea.

ARGUMENTS AND FINDINGS:

Asia-Pacific countries are concerned about the lack of communication between the United States and China, two nuclear-armed powers, in an era of great-power competition. Simultaneously, the heightened activity and increased interaction between their militaries has increased the need for crisis prevention and management. Numerous mechanisms between China and regional countries already exist, as they also do between regional countries excluding it. Mechanisms which include China are reportedly used infrequently and are therefore of questionable effectiveness. This infrequent use stems from Beijing's staunch opposition to any activity that it deems to be a provocation, including activity deemed as legal under the United Nations Convention on the Law of the Sea (UNCLOS). Regional mechanisms that exclude China have been more effective and are regularly used. While multilateralism is unlikely to provide effective solutions to regional crisis management soon, there is growing momentum behind regional minilateral initiatives.

REGIONAL SECURITY IMPLICATIONS:

Regional crisis-management mechanisms that include China are numerous but so far have not brought stability to the Asia-Pacific. To remedy this, regional states could build a localised security framework by employing a greater web of bilateral and minilateral crisis-management mechanisms and codes of conduct.

Crisis-management mechanisms between the US and the People's Republic of China (PRC) became a central topic in discussions about Asia-Pacific stability for much of 2023, as regional and extra-regional countries became increasingly concerned about the escalating potential for conflict. US–China relations had reached their lowest point since 1979 following the visit of then-speaker of the house Nancy Pelosi to Taiwan in 2022 and the US shooting down of the suspected PRC spy balloon.

Simultaneously, the US and China increasingly operate in closer proximity across the maritime, air, cyber, electromagnetic and space domains. The Pentagon reported in 2023 that between the autumn of 2021 and autumn of 2023, 'the US has documented over 180 instances of PLA [People's Liberation Army] coercive and risky air intercepts against US aircraft in the region – more in the past two years than in the previous decade'.[1] Add to this equation other regional countries' growing activity across each of these domains, and the need for enhanced crisis-management mechanisms becomes only more urgent.

And yet various management mechanisms already exist in the Asia-Pacific, from bilateral and minilateral to multilateral forms. Some have been in place since the late 1990s and remain relevant, such as the Japan–China Maritime and Air Communication Mechanism, while others, like the Six-Party Talks involving China, Japan, North Korea, Russia, South Korea and the US, over the North Korean nuclear challenge, had a relatively short shelf life. These mechanisms generally focus on trust- and confidence-building measures, have taken the form of hotlines, and include regular meetings and dialogues to promote ongoing communication and problem solving. Seen more broadly, such mechanisms seek to prevent crises or, failing this, to manage them.

However, the effectiveness of these existing mechanisms remains questionable. They are usually non-obligatory, open to interpretation and apply only to national militaries. Multilateral efforts have failed or are predominantly preoccupied with institutional processes, rather than with actively preventing conflict. The codes of conduct that have been established have not prevented incidents from escalating into crises.

Lastly, most conflict-management mechanisms are limited to the maritime and air domains across Southeast Asia and around Taiwan. Few are directly applicable to the South Pacific and Northeast Asia. Furthermore, the perception gap between the PRC and regional countries as to what constitutes 'risky behaviour' complicates the effectiveness of existing mechanisms. To fill the existing gaps in current regional efforts to enhance stability and security, it has become increasingly necessary to improve PRC-inclusive bilateral mechanisms. Where that fails, there must be efforts to further broaden the matrix of minilateral efforts between regional countries.

TALKING PAST EACH OTHER

At the 20th IISS Shangri-La Dialogue in 2023, US Secretary of Defense Lloyd Austin reiterated that the US believes that open lines of communication between it and the PRC are essential to bolster peace, security and stability in the Asia-Pacific region. 'The more we talk, the more we can avoid misunderstandings and miscalculations that could lead to crisis or conflict.'[2] Austin also voiced concerns about the PRC's unwillingness to engage seriously on crisis-management mechanisms between the two countries' militaries. This highlighted the importance of dialogue between Washington and Beijing, along with their armed forces, to mitigate and, if needed, manage crises.

As US–China bilateral relations become more tense in the context of great-power competition and systemic rivalry, the need for crisis-management mechanisms is increasing. Since 1997, the US and China have already agreed to a series of such mechanisms. These include crisis- and conflict-prevention regimes through dialogue channels and agreements on rules of behaviour in domains in which the US and Chinese armed forces have expe-

US Secretary of Defense Lloyd Austin addresses attendees during the 2023 IISS Shangri-La Dialogue in Singapore, 3 June 2023

(IISS)

rienced increasingly dangerous encounters. Further mechanisms have been established to serve as hotlines (direct communication links, both audio and video) between heads of state, heads of militaries or combatant commands, or specific branches of each countries' armed forces that are responsible for particular war-fighting domains.

In 1998, the defence ministers of the US and China signed the Military Maritime Consultative Agreement (MMCA).[3] This established an operator-level exchange to discuss maritime safety. During the first working-group meeting in July that year, the two sides discussed communication at sea between aircraft and ships from a technical and procedural perspective. The goal of these discussions was to establish a common understanding of operational procedures between the PLA Navy (PLAN) and US Navy. The second working-group meeting included tours to the PLAN's North Sea Fleet headquarters in Qingdao, the naval museum and the PLAN's newest guided-missile destroyer at the time. This allowed both sides to improve their understanding of the other's capabilities.

As US Navy Lieutenant Commander George Capen stated in 1999, 'As the PLAN expands its fleet and operating areas, encounters at sea will become more frequent. It is necessary to meet periodically to ensure misunderstandings are minimized and prevented whenever possible.'[4] Despite this, in 2001 a PLAN J-8IIM fighter collided with a US EP-3 surveillance plane on a signals-intelligence mission that included overflights of the South China Sea.[5]

In June 2013, president Barack Obama and President Xi Jinping both reaffirmed the importance of military-to-military communications during a press conference following their bilateral meeting.[6] This was put to the test in December that year, when the USS *Cowpens* was forced to take evasive action to avoid a collision with a Chinese warship manoeuvring near the Chinese aircraft carrier *Liaoning*. In that case, bridge-to-bridge communication between the two crews was effective in managing the incident.

Both vessels ultimately manoeuvred to ensure safe passage, and while a US official initially stated that the Chinese warship was trying to 'impede and harass' the USS *Cowpens*, the Pentagon played down the issue. Pentagon spokesperson Colonel Steve Warren stated that he did not think the incident 'was a crisis level incident by any stretch.

Figure 2.1: **Selected unsafe or unprofessional maritime and air incidents involving China, 2001–24**

Incident no.	Date	Incident	Other party	Incident no.	Date	Incident	Other party
		The US has documented over 180 instances of PLA coercive and risky air intercepts against US aircraft in the region between the fall of 2021 and fall of 2023, more in that two-year period than in the decade before that. Over the same period, the PLA has conducted around 100 instances of coercive and risky operational behaviour against US allies and partners.					
1	Apr 2001	A US EP-3 collided with a PLAN J-8IIM fighter, killing the Chinese pilot and forcing the EP-3 to land on Hainan.	US	11	Feb 2017	Unsafe interaction between a Chinese KJ-200 aircraft and a US Navy P-3C aircraft. Aircraft came within 300 m of each other.	US
2	Mar 2009	USNS *Impeccable* (unarmed, civilian-operated ocean surveillance ship belonging to Military Sealift Command) surrounded by 5x Chinese vessels: PLAN intelligence ship, FLEC patrol vessel, China Marine Surveillance cutter and 2x Chinese-flagged fishing trawlers.	US	12	May 2017	2x PLAAF Su-30 fighters intercepted a US Air Force Boeing WC-135 *Constant Phoenix* aircraft, coming within 45 m of each other and one of the Su-30 fighters flying inverted over the WC-135.	US
				13	Jul 2017	2x PLAAF Chengdu J-10 fighters conducted an intercept within 90 m of a US Navy EP-3 *Aries* surveillance aircraft.	US
3	Jan 2013	Chinese navy frigates locked their weapon-targeting radars on a Japanese navy ship (30 January) and a Japanese military helicopter (19 January).	Japan	14	Oct 2018	*Luyang* destroyer approached USS *Decatur* in an unsafe and unprofessional manoeuvre.	US
4	Nov 2013	PLA Air Force (PLAAF) scrambled fighter jets to identify US and Japanese military aircraft.	US / Japan	15	Jun 2019	2x Chinese Su-30s flew within 300 m of the bow of Canadian frigate HMCS *Regina* at 90 m above the water.	Canada
5	Dec 2013	USS *Cowpens* had to take evasive action to avoid a collision with the *Liaoning* manoeuvring nearby.	US	16	Feb 2022	A Chinese naval ship directed a laser at an Australian P-8A *Poseidon* aircraft operating in Australia's exclusive economic zone (EEZ).	Australia
6	Aug 2014	Shenyang J-11BH came within 10 metres of a patrolling Boeing P-8 *Poseidon* aircraft and performed aerobatic manoeuvres including a barrel roll.	US	17	Apr–May 2022	PLAAF fighter jets conducted close approaches to the Canadian CP-140 patrol aircraft, forcing it to alter its flight path to avoid collision.	Canada
7	Sep 2015	2x Chinese JH-7 fighters performed an 'unsafe' manoeuvre in front of a US RC-135 surveillance aircraft, coming within 150 m.	US	18	May 2022	A Chinese J-16 conducted a dangerous intercept manoeuvre of an Australian P-8A on a maritime surveillance flight.	Australia
8	May 2016	A US Navy EP-3 was intercepted by 2x PLAAF Shenyang J-11 fighters, with one Chinese fighter coming within 15 m.	US	19	Jun 2022	A Chinese J-16 cut across the nose of and released a round of chaff into another Australian P-8A *Poseidon*.	Australia
9	Jun 2016	Unsafe intercept by 2x Chinese J-10 fighter planes of a US Air Force RC-135 reconnaissance plane, coming within 30 m of each other.	US	20	Dec 2022	A PLA J-11 fighter came within 6 m of the nose of a US military aircraft.	US
10	Dec 2016	*Dalang* III-class submarine rescue vessel seized a US UUV glider and brought it aboard as USNS *Bowditch* was attempting to retrieve it.	US	21	Feb 2023	A Chinese Coast Guard (CCG) vessel engaged in dangerous manoeuvres against a Philippine Coast Guard vessel operating within Manila's EEZ, including deploying a military-grade laser that temporarily blinded Philippine crew members.	Philippines

● Air ● Maritime ● Air + Maritime ○ No specific location details found

MIDDLING AND MUDDLING THROUGH? MANAGING ASIA-PACIFIC CRISES

Incident no.	Date	Incident	Other party
22	Apr 2023	Chinese navy ship 'crossed paths' with Philippine coastguard ships.	Philippines
23	Apr 2023	Philippines coastguard ships were intercepted by 2x CCG ships that 'exhibited aggressive tactics' two days after previous April encounter.	Philippines
24	May 2023	A PLA J-16 intercepted and 'thumped' a US RC-135 aircraft by flying 200–300 m in front of it and forcing the US aircraft to fly directly behind it in its wake turbulence.	US
25	Jun 2023	PLA vessels cut across USS *Chung-Hoon*'s bow on their power side at 140 m distance.	US
26	Aug 2023	A CCG vessel blocked and water-cannoned a chartered Philippine boat on a rotation and resupply mission.	Philippines
27	Oct 2023	CCG vessel 5203 conducted blocking manoeuvres and caused a collision with a Philippine-contracted resupply boat.	Philippines
28	Oct 2023	Chinese J-11 pilot executed a night-time intercept of a US Air Force B-52 aircraft, coming within 3 m.	US
29	Nov 2023	Australian naval divers injured after being subjected to Chinese warship's sonar pulses.	Australia
30	Dec 2023	CCG fired water cannons at BRP *Cabra*, *Unaizah Mae* 1 and civilian-operated Philippine-government fishing vessel M/L *Kalayaan*, ramming its resupply vessels and a coastguard ship.	Philippines

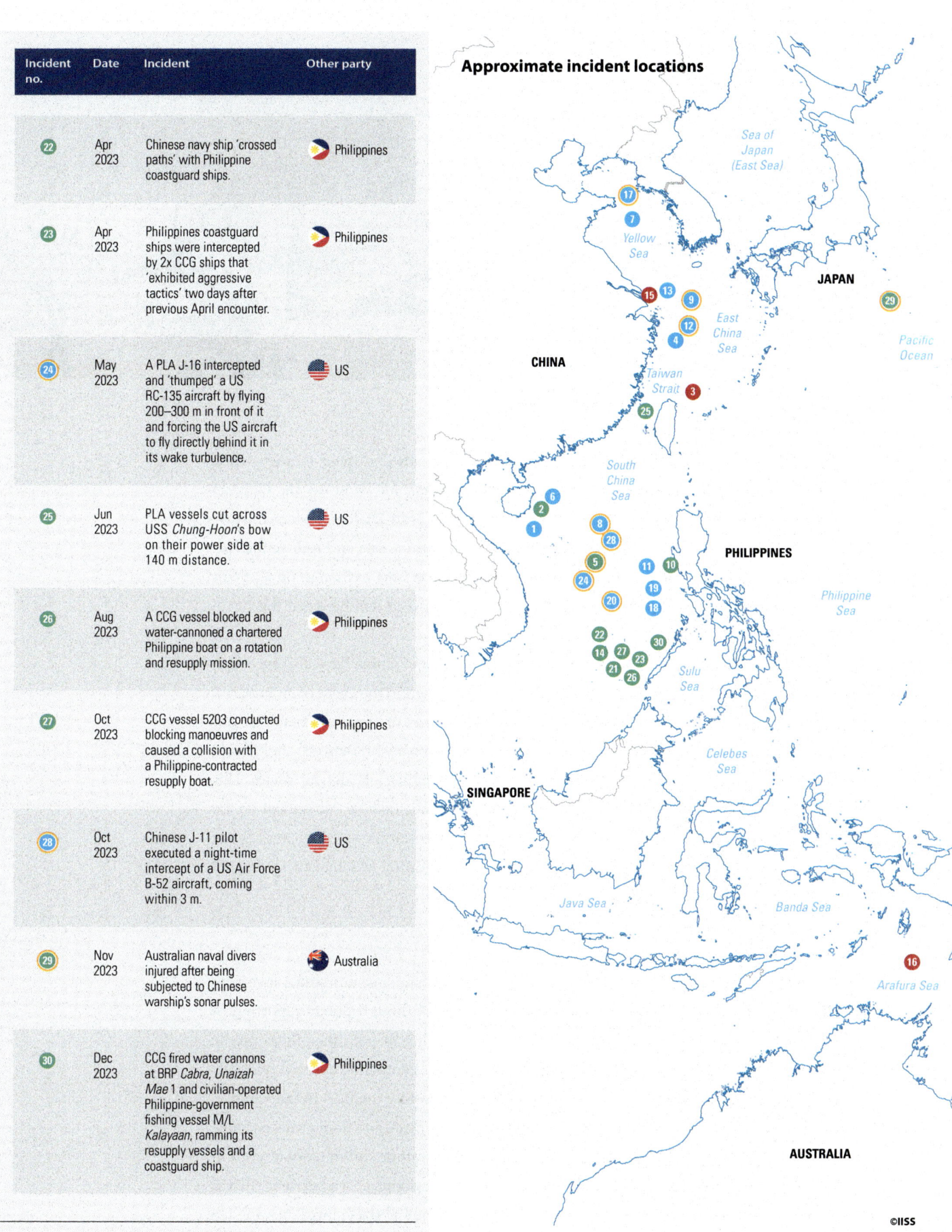

Approximate incident locations

Source: IISS; US Department of Defense, www.defense.gov; Asia-Pacific Leadership Network, www.apln.network

I don't believe tensions have heightened.'[7] The PRC's Ministry of National Defense similarly stated that the 'Chinese naval vessel strictly followed protocol and handled the incident' and that 'the two defence departments used normal working channels to stay informed about the situation and communicated effectively'.[8]

In 2014, the US and China signed two memorandums of understanding (MoUs) to further improve their bilateral communication channels and crisis-prevention mechanisms. These include the MoU of Notification of Major Military Activities Confidence-Building Measures Mechanism and the MoU on the Rules of Behavior for the Safety of Air and Maritime Encounters.[9] A framework was also adopted in 2017 when Marine Corps general and chairman of the Joint Chiefs of Staff Joe Dunford and General Fang Fenghui, chief of China's Joint Staff, signed the Joint Staff Dialogue Mechanism.[10] These agreements seek to further 'enable [both sides] to communicate and reduce the risk of miscalculation' by establishing platforms for conversation and exchange on difficult issues and establish rules of behaviour for safety during encounters between the naval vessels and aircrafts of the US and China.

A team of Lockheed Martin employees disassemble a US Navy EP-3 surveillance plane after it collided with a PLAN J-8IIM fighter over Hainan Island, 18 June 2001

(Lockheed Martin Aeronautics Co./US Navy via Getty Images)

In addition to these crisis-prevention mechanisms, the US and China have also agreed to a number of crisis-management mechanisms, the latter to be used in the event of an incident. In theory, these hotlines would be confidential, high-level lines of communication for top leaders to prevent an incident turning into a crisis or a crisis into a war. Between the US and China, several hotlines have been created at heads of state or military-leadership levels. This includes the 1997 Heads of State Direct Communications hotline, the 2008 Agreement on the Establishment of a Secure Defense Telephone Link at defence-minister level, the 2015 Space Direct Communication hotline and the 2015 Direct Communication Mechanism for Urgent Cybercrime and Significant Cybersecurity.[11]

WALKING THE TALK

Despite the existing crisis-prevention and -management mechanisms, numerous incidents between the US and China have been reported since 2014. Although public reporting of such instances is limited, with the US and China likely opting to not make them public and manage them through diplomatic channels instead, the Pentagon reported over 180 instances of coercive and risky air intercepts against US aircraft by the PLA in the region.[12]

Incidents for which details are publicly available include unsafe and dangerous encounters between US surveillance aircraft and PLAAF fighter aircraft or surveillance aircraft in 2015, 2016, three times in 2017, 2022, twice in 2023 and interceptions at sea between the US and Chinese navies in 2016, 2018 and 2023. In the most serious of these incidents, the US accused the PLAAF and PLAN of unsafe and unprofessional conduct.

Military-to-military encounters have not been limited to near collisions. They have also included incidents of Chinese coercive acts intended to send signals, such as seizing property belonging to the US Navy. In December 2016, a PLAN vessel seized one of the United States' uncrewed underwater vehicle (UUV) gliders and brought it aboard as the USNS *Bowditch* was attempting to retrieve it. One US expert described this as a 'brazen, calculated act of coercive diplomacy' that was intended to send a message to president-elect Donald Trump ahead of his inauguration in January 2017.[13]

This called into question the above mechanisms' utility and effectiveness. Indeed, in addition to failing to stem the risky operational behaviour in the South and East China seas and around Taiwan, existing channels of crisis communication have also reportedly not been used during crises. For example, the hotlines were reportedly not used during the 2001 Hainan Island incident, even though president Bill Clinton had previously said that the crisis hotline would 'make it easier to confer at a moment's notice'.[14]

Furthermore, the defence telephone link that was established in 2008 has also reportedly rarely been used and was not used during the PLA's seizure of a US UUV in 2016.[15] In 2001, then-deputy secretary of state Richard Armitage stated that the US had tried to resolve the incident behind the scenes through high-level phone calls, but that this was unsuccessful. 'It seems to be the case that when very, very difficult issues arise, it is sometimes hard to get the Chinese to answer the phone.'[16]

The difficulty in agreeing to and using these crisis-management mechanisms stems from fundamental differences in how the US and China view each other's actions, as well as their different crisis-management philosophies. For example, the Pentagon noted in a 2023 report that coercive and risky air and maritime behaviour by China seeks 'to impinge on the ability of the United States and other nations to safely conduct operations where international law allows'. The PRC's goal, according to the same report, is to 'pressure the United States and other nations to reduce or cease lawful operations near areas Beijing claims territorial sovereignty'.[17]

The US, meanwhile, has tended to describe Chinese behaviour during incidents as unsafe, unprofessional, dangerous, aggressive and coercive (see Figure 2.2). The PRC has described US behaviour in turn as deliberately provocative, intentional, threatening to China's national security and the root cause of US–China tensions. From Beijing's

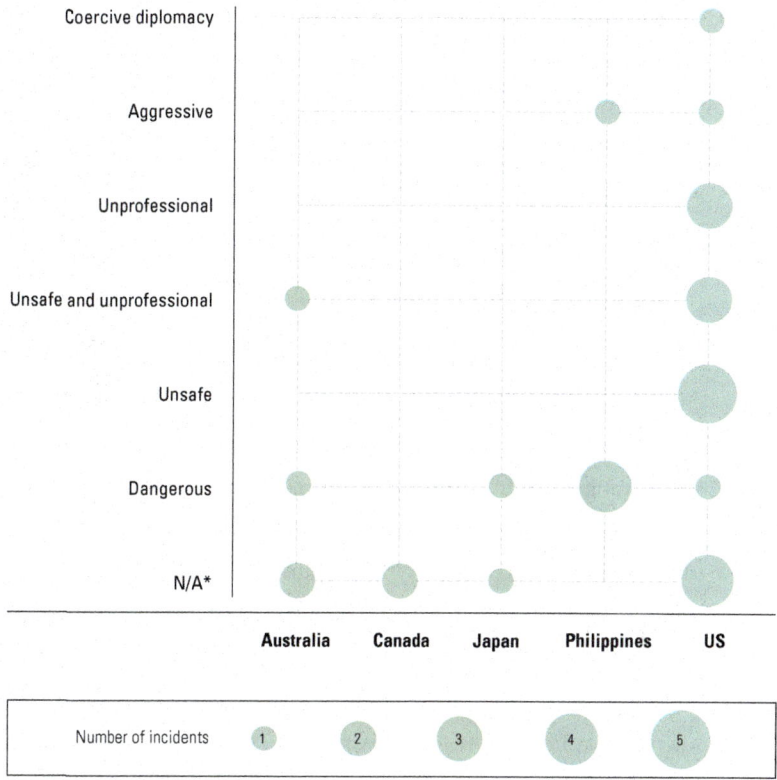

Figure 2.2: **Other parties' characterisation of China's behaviour in maritime and air incidents, 2001–24**

*No public response to incident.

Source: IISS; US Department of Defense, www.defense.gov; Asia-Pacific Leadership Network, www.apln.network

perspective, the United States' activity in what it views as its own backyard is aimed at provocation. When a US spy plane was alleged by China to have entered a no-fly zone over live-fire military drills, the PRC's defence ministry stated that 'it was an act of naked provocation, and China is resolutely opposed to it, and have already lodged stern representations with the US side'.[18]

The US views the current mechanisms as a way to establish crisis 'guardrails'. Such guardrails would allow both countries to compete in a 'healthy manner' while preventing crises from escalating into conflict.

A US Air Force pilot observes a suspected Chinese surveillance balloon during its passage over the continental US, 3 February 2023

(US Department of Defense/Handout/Anadolu Agency via Getty Images)

However, China views US calls for such guardrails and other additional mechanisms as disingenuous. Then-minister of foreign affairs Qin Gang stated in 2023 that 'the US claims that it seeks to "out-compete" China but does not seek conflict. Yet in reality, its so-called "competition" means to contain and supress China in all respects and get the two countries locked in a zero-sum game.' Beijing interprets US calls for the establishment of guardrails then as a call for China to 'not respond in words or action when slandered or attacked'.[19]

Beijing thus believes that the US uses such mechanisms not to prevent crises or resolve them, but as cover for actions that Beijing disagrees with and finds provocative. In its official responses to incidents at sea and in the air with the US, the PRC's spokespersons often push back on US claims of dangerous and unlawful behaviour. In particular, they variously label 'the PLA's behaviour during incidents as professional, safe, responsible, justified, legal and having followed protocol. In addition, the PRC often claims that the United States' behaviour and activity in its backyard is the 'root cause' of incidents.

In his speech at the 20th IISS Shangri-La Dialogue in 2023, then-PRC minister of national defence and state councillor Li Shangfu stated that while the PRC observes UNCLOS, 'what is key now is that we must prevent attempts that want to use those freedom of navigation and innocent passage as a pretext to exercise hegemony of navigation'.[20] China's leadership instead puts greater emphasis on crisis prevention. Indeed, Li stated 'to truly prevent such incidents in the future, we not only need the codes [of conduct]. The best way is for other countries, especially the naval vessels and fighter jets of all countries, not to do close-in actions around other countries' territories.' Essentially, Li's suggestion to the US to avoid further problems was 'mind your own business'.[21] For this reason, mechanisms like the Code for Unplanned Encounters at Sea (CUES) are also unlikely to be effective, as the PRC does not believe that such encounters are unplanned.[22]

If this lack of trust continues to characterise this bilateral relationship, crisis-prevention and -management mechanisms will likely continue to fail to have an impact. When Austin attempted to communicate with then-Chinese defence minister Wei Fenghe following the 2023 balloon incident, Wei refused to take the call because the US had 'not created the proper atmosphere for dialogue'.[23] During a 2021 MMCA, China implied that crisis prevention would only come from the US ceasing operations within the first island chain and instead focusing on building trust, stating that 'with no mutual political or military trust, China finds it impossible to use the so-called military hotline to avoid possible conflicts'.[24]

Other issues undermine crisis-management mechanisms. Prior to joining the Biden administration as deputy director for China and Taiwan at the National Security Council, Rush Doshi argued that the mechanisms in place to manage US–China tensions are inadequate, particularly when compared to past mechanisms between the US and Soviet Union. He argues that the mechanisms in place today 'lack a conscious effort at the command level to reduce the risk of inadvertent war' and are not 'binding, detailed, or effective' as their US–Soviet predecessors.[25] Furthermore, the current mechanisms rely on the subjective perspectives of each party and are suggestive in their language, rather than decisive or obligatory.

New mechanisms are also needed to cover new domains in which the US and China are increasingly active and where the potential for crises is heightened, such as subsea, cyber and outer space. Though the US and China agreed to a space hotline in 2015, there were several reports in 2023 that the US is exploring a potential space-force hotline with China.[26] This suggests that the previous channel of communication is not yet sufficient to address Washington's concerns for a potential crisis in the space and electromagnetic domains.

Current mechanisms are also limited to the PLA and the US military. Yet paramilitary forces have also been involved in US–China incidents, as well as other incidents in the Asia-Pacific involving the PRC. Mechanisms should, therefore, be expanded to also include regional coastguard forces and maritime militias, though the latter will be more difficult to incorporate and enforce as they provide states with plausible deniability in the event of a crisis.

Lastly, existing crisis-prevention and -management mechanisms are also at risk of being suspended to send political signals. Following Pelosi's visit to Taiwan, Beijing suspended bilateral Theater Commander talks, Defense Policy Coordination talks and the MMCA meetings.[27] Talks only resumed in late 2023 and 2024, following a limited rapprochement between US President Joe Biden and Xi.[28]

CROWDED SPACE

Tensions in the Asia-Pacific have increased not just between the US and China, but also between China and other regional countries. Furthermore, as maritime claims overlap between claimant states in the South China Sea, countries have also sought to establish crisis-management mechanisms with each other that do not include the PRC. Indonesia, Malaysia, Thailand and Vietnam have all established such mechanisms. While many of these mechanisms predominantly cover the maritime domain, they also include references to the air and land domains as well.

However, in addition to its crisis-management mechanisms with the US, China has also established bilateral mechanisms with other regional countries. These include countries that China has both close and challenging relations with. Bilateral agreements have been signed with Brunei, Cambodia, India, Indonesia, Japan, the Philippines, Singapore, Taiwan, Thailand and Vietnam.

Chinese bilateral crisis communications with these countries include direct communication mechanisms, such as navy hotlines, defence hotlines, general military hotlines, coastguard hotline protocols, cross-border hotlines for terrorism and security, hotlines for

Figure 2.3: **Asia-Pacific: selected bilateral crisis-management mechanisms**

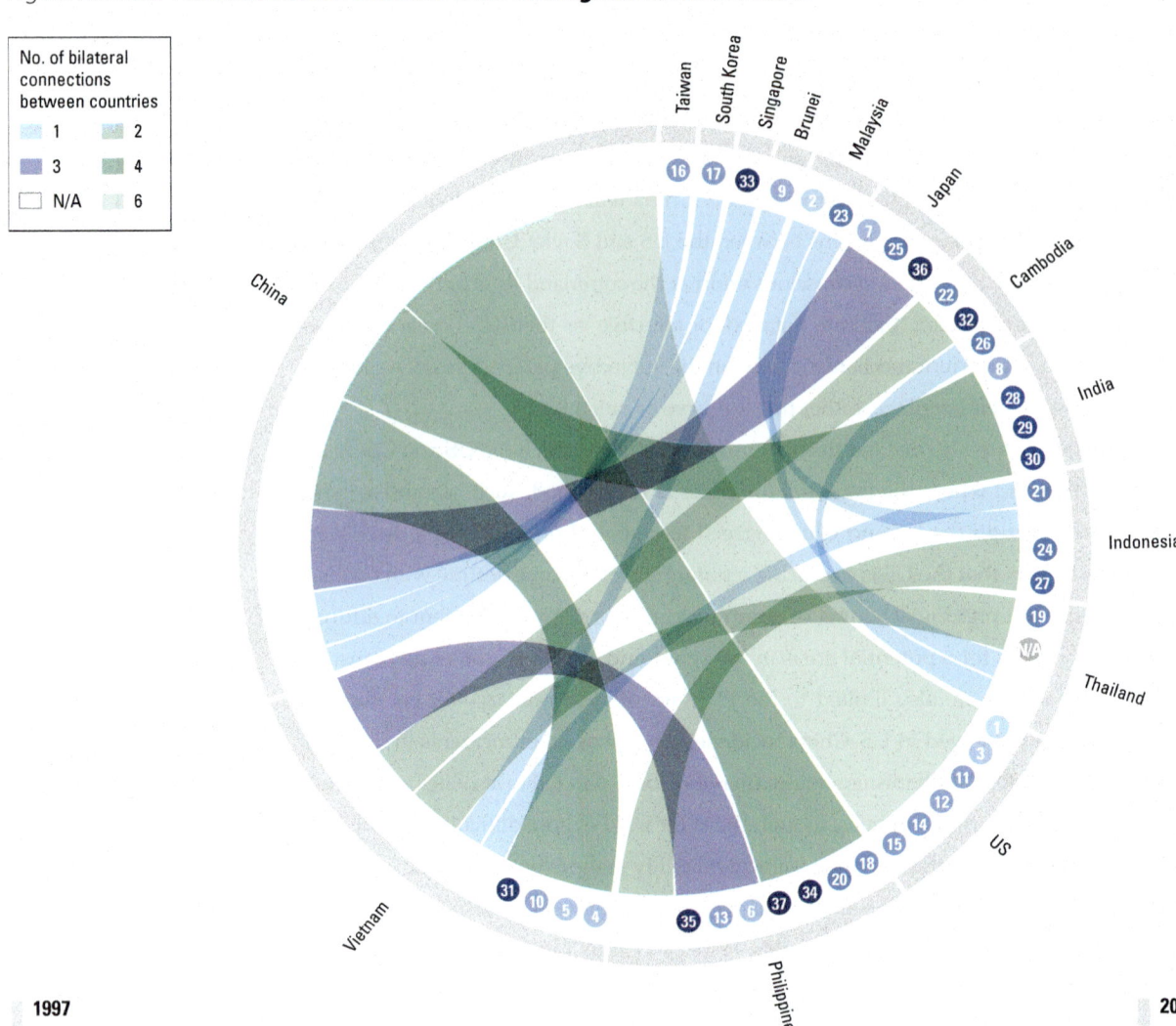

1997
1. Heads of State direct communication (hotline).

2001
2. MALINDO Prevention of Sea Incidents Cooperative Guidelines.

2008
3. Agreement on the establishment of a secure defence telephone link (updated in 2015).

2011
4. Agreement on basic principles guiding settlement of sea-related issues.
5. Agreement to guide settlement of maritime issues (including hotline).
6. Coast Guard direct communication hotline.

2012
7. High-level Consultation on Maritime Affairs.*

2013
8. Border Personnel Meetings.
9. Navy direct communication hotline.

2014
10. Direct high-level communications between defense leaders (hotline).
11. Memorandum of Understanding (MoU) on Notification of Major Military Activities Confidence-Building Measures Mechanism.
12. MoU on the Rules of Behavior for the Safety of Air and Maritime Encounters.
13. Navy direct communication hotline.

2015
14. Space direct communication (hotline).
15. Direct communication mechanism for urgent cyber crime and significant cyber security incidents.
16. Direct communication between China's Taiwan Affairs Office and Taiwan's Mainland Affairs Council.**
17. Defence authorities' hotline.

2016
18. Bilateral Consultative Mechanism on the South China Sea.

2017
19. MoU on hotline communication on fisheries at sea.
20. Direct communication under Joint Coast Guard Committee on Maritime Cooperation.
21. Coast Guard direct-communication-hotline letter of intent.
22. Coast Guard direct-communication-hotline protocol.

2018
23. Cross-border hotline (terrorism and security).
24. Cross-border hotline (terrorism and security).
25. Maritime and Air Communication Mechanism (military only).
26. Defence hotline on border management.

2019
27. MoU on Maritime Security Cooperation.

2020
28. Corps Commander Level Meetings.

2021
29. Commander-level military hotlines.
30. Foreign-minister hotline.

2022
31. Direct high-level communication to deal with marine fisheries incidents (hotline).
32. General military direct communication hotline.

2023
33. Direct high-level communications between defence leaders (hotline).
34. Direct-communication mechanism between foreign ministries.
35. Coast Guard direct-communication hotline.
36. Direct high-level communications between defence leaders (hotline).

2024
37. Direct communications between foreign ministries and coastguards over maritime issues.

N/A. Navy direct communication hotline – exact year unclear.

*Included both China's and Japan's armed forces and coastguards. Frozen in 2013. **Frozen in 2017.

Source: IISS

fisheries at sea, commander-level military hotlines, foreign-minister hotlines and maritime and air-communication mechanisms.

In contrast to the US–PRC bilateral mechanisms, the PRC has coastguard communication-hotline protocols with three countries: Cambodia, Indonesia and the Philippines.

Where the PRC shares disputed land borders, for example with India, it has established cross-border mechanisms. These include the Border Personnel Meetings (agreed in 2013), corps commander-level meetings (signed in 2020) and commander-level military hotlines (agreed in 2021).[29] However, these mechanisms have done little to impact the situation following the 2020 Galwan Valley clash between Indian and Chinese forces in 2020, as chapter 3 of this year's *Asia-Pacific Regional Security Assessment* (APRSA) notes.

The Philippine military boat ML *Kalayaan* travels to resupply the BRP *Sierra Madre*, a ship currently operating as a Philippine military outpost in the Second Thomas Shoal in the disputed South China Sea, 11 November 2023

(Lisa Marie David/Bloomberg via Getty Images)

One possible factor in Beijing's willingness to sign such agreements is the increase in incidents involving China with regional countries. Over half of the non-US bilateral mechanisms established by the PRC were agreed to after 2016, following the UNCLOS tribunal ruling in favour of Manila and effectively deeming China's 'nine-dash line' claims in the South China Sea illegal. The Sino-Indian agreements were signed between 2020 and 2021 following deadly clashes in the disputed border area of Galwan Valley. In recent years, the PRC has had bilateral incidents at sea with Japan, the Philippines and Vietnam as well. In remedy to this, in 2022 and 2023 the PRC established direct high-level communication lines with these countries.

However, the US alliance system may have also played a role in Beijing's considerations. Following Pelosi's visit to Taiwan in 2022, the PRC severed communication channels with the US, and the US under Biden continues to consolidate its Asia-Pacific alliances. The PRC has since established communication mechanisms with three defence- and foreign-ministry leaders of key US allies in the region: Japan, the Philippines and Singapore. In doing so, the PRC is signalling to regional countries that it is not opposed to crisis-management mechanisms in general, and instead indirectly placed blame on the US for the deterioration of the bilateral relationship.

Aside from the PRC, Indonesia signed two crisis-management mechanisms with the Philippines in 2018 and 2019 on cross-border hotlines focused on counter-terrorism and maritime-security cooperation. The Philippines and Vietnam signed a navy hotline in 2014 and a coastguard hotline in 2024. These hotlines are a regional effort to prevent crises in the South China Sea. For example, the recent Philippines–Vietnam MoU on maritime cooperation is intended to strengthen 'the understanding, mutual trust, and confidence between the two parties through development of a Joint Coast Guard Committee'.[30]

This mechanism is meant to work within the Association of Southeast Asian Nations (ASEAN) and with other dialogue partners as well. One analyst stated that the Philippines has recently deepened its cooperation in the maritime domain with Vietnam in order to 'form a united front [against China] but Hanoi does not want to publicly show that', while another called it 'a clever move in breaking China's dominance by peaceful means'.[31] The latter is in reference to the lack of progress on negotiations on the China–ASEAN Code of Conduct in the South China Sea. By signing bilateral agreements between claimant states without the PRC, the Philippines seeks to cooperate with other claimant states and regional countries to establish a code of conduct without the PRC.

MORE THAN TWO-WAY CHANNELS

The Asia-Pacific is also equipped with minilateral and multilateral institutions that often include crisis mechanisms as well. The Malacca Straits Patrol (MSP), first established in 2004, includes a hotline involving Indonesia, Malaysia, Singapore and Thailand and consists of the Sea Patrols, the Eyes-in-the-Sky Combined Maritime Air Patrols and the Intelligence Exchange Group. The navies from these countries regularly meet to coordinate and review operations and engage in intelligence and information sharing.[32] The inclusion of intelligence sharing and active cooperation in the trust-building exercises differentiates such a minilateral mechanism from the US–PRC or PRC-led bilateral arrangements. They simultaneously improve sub-regional security.

Building off the successful MSP model, Indonesia, Malaysia and the Philippines agreed in 2016 to a Trilateral Cooperative Arrangement (TCA), which also includes a hotline as well as regular patrols, joint exercises, coordination and intelligence sharing. The patrols have reportedly been effective at countering piracy and terrorism. In 2017, 99 cases of piracy and armed robbery were reported in the patrol area; in the first half of 2023 there were no reported events.[33]

Widening the scope of membership further, multilateral arrangements in the Asia-Pacific which cover crisis management include the Western Pacific Naval Symposium and ASEAN-led arrangements. The former resulted in the establishment of CUES, which was signed in 2014 between 21 countries and which one non-signatory party reportedly adheres to. The arrangement includes China, Russia and the US, alongside more than a dozen other Asia-Pacific countries. However, CUES is not legally binding and is limited to naval forces.

HOW JAPAN MANAGES CRISES

Japan currently participates in crisis-management mechanisms with the PRC. While Japan previously participated in the Six-Party Talks, it currently does not participate in any Northeast Asian crisis-management mechanisms.

Japan and China agreed to the Maritime and Air Communication Mechanism (MACM) in 2007, and a general framework in 2012. However, progress stalled three months later when the Japanese government at the time nationalised the Senkaku/Diaoyu islands. The MACM finally became operational in 2015 after several rounds of talks between then-prime minister Abe Shinzo and then-Chinese premier Li Keqiang. The MACM entails regular meetings and a hotline between defence authorities, and communication mechanisms between Japanese Self-Defense Forces and PLA vessels and aircraft. Its purpose is to enhance cooperation, avoid incidents in air and at sea, and prevent crises from escalating. It was not until 2023 that Japan and China actually installed a hotline and held the first call between defence ministers. The two countries are also signatories of CUES.

However, the MACM also has its weaknesses. Since 2019, the two countries' militaries no longer conduct exchanges, and it currently lacks military communication channels at the operational or commander level. As CUES has already proved ineffective, the two militaries have had little opportunity to build mutual trust and confidence. In the minilateral domain, Japan, the US and South Korea have agreed to deepen their military cooperation following the Camp David summit in 2023. Finally, Japan also participates in the ASEAN Defence Ministers' Meetings Plus (ADMM-Plus) and joined the ASEAN Direct Communications Infrastructure (ADI) in 2023. Japan was the first of the 'Plus' countries to operationalise the ADI that same year, and expressed at ADMM-Plus in Jakarta its 'expectations for the ADI to become available for daily communication in the future'.

*Sources: Komeito, 'Japan and China agree on regime to prevent air-sea mishaps', 14 May 2018, https://www.komei.or.jp/en/; Japan Ministry of Defense, 'First telephone call of the Hotline Between Japan-China Defense Authorities by Japanese and Chinese Defense Ministers', 16 May 2023, https://www.mod.go.jp/en/; White House, 'FACT SHEET: The Trilateral Leaders' Summit at Camp David', 18 August 2023, https://www.whitehouse.gov; and Japan Ministry of Defense, 'State Minister of Defense Miyazawa's Participation in the 10th ASEAN Defence Ministers' Meeting-Plus', 16 November 2023, https://www.mod.go.jp/en/.

This has limited the utility of CUES in the Asia-Pacific, where maritime incidents often involve coastguard or maritime militia (i.e., civilian) vessels. It is noteworthy that ASEAN and China issued a joint statement in 2016 declaring the applicability of CUES in the South China Sea. However, incidents involving unsafe manoeuvres by Chinese coastguard vessels against Indonesia, Malaysia, the Philippines and Vietnam since then cast doubt on the effectiveness of the statement. A few 'track two' efforts involving experts from think tanks and universities, as well as officials in a private capacity, to promote a CUES-like mechanism for maritime-law enforcement involving South China Sea claimants have not been successful thus far.

Delegates greet each other during the 14th Western Pacific Naval Symposium in Qingdao, Shandong province, eastern China, 22 April 2014

(Imago via Alamy Stock Photo)

More broadly at the regional level, the ASEAN Defence Ministers' Meeting (ADMM) has agreed to the guidelines for maritime interaction in 2019. However, this mechanism appears limited to the signatories' navies (the maritime interaction guidelines were agreed to at an ASEAN Navy Chiefs Meeting in 2023) and has been criticised for being ineffective when dealing with challenges that occur in the 'grey zone'.

The ADMM also launched a Direct Communications Infrastructure mechanism in 2017, expanding it into the ADMM-Plus in 2019 and inviting the dialogue-partner states to join. Experts claim, however, that 'there are simply too many bureaucratic procedures and contextual requirements built into the ASEAN Direct Communications Infrastructure to make it an effective hotline for rapid response in times of emergency and crisis'.[34] The ADMM-Plus, nonetheless, remains the 'highest ministerial-defence and security-consultative and cooperation mechanism for regional security issues' and 'de facto multilateral security mechanism' in the region.[35] Working groups include maritime security, counter-terrorism, humanitarian assistance and disaster relief, peacekeeping operations, military medicine, humanitarian mine action and cyber security. The ADMM-Plus also includes operational confidence building, with 20 large-scale exercises carried out across the grouping's priority areas between 2010 and 2020.[36] Although these mechanisms are aimed at preventing incidents and crisis management, they are more focused on establishing institutional processes and are yet to be tested in a crisis.[37]

In Northeast Asia, the picture is even less promising. Following the disintegration of the Six-Party Talks, there is no replacement multilateral crisis-management mechanism in place.[38] It should be noted that the ASEAN Regional Forum (ARF) counts China, Japan, North Korea, Russia, South Korea and the US as members; the original Six-Party Talks initially came out of its sidelines. And the ARF itself has worked since 1994 to move the region from confidence building to preventive diplomacy and conflict resolution, but no concrete and operational mechanisms have been agreed to thus far.

Indonesian Navy sailors in a ship wheelhouse conducting routine operations during *ASEAN Solidarity Exercise in Natuna 2023* in Batam, Riau Islands province, 20 September 2023

In 2023, Japan, South Korea and the US agreed to deepen their trilateral military relationship by holding military exercises annually and sharing real-time information on North Korean missile launches and illicit cyber activities by the end of the year.[39] However, there is currently no dedicated and focused mechanism in place that includes China, North Korea and Russia, a requirement for any improvement to Korean Peninsula stability. As North Korea deepens its ties with Russia, crisis-management mechanisms will need to include both Beijing and Moscow.[40] This may prove difficult as Russia's second invasion of Ukraine continues.

TAILORED TALKING POINTS

Despite the number of regional incidents involving China and rising tensions between it and its neighbours, China is the most prolific actor in regional crisis-management mechanisms in the Asia-Pacific. China has signed crisis-management mechanisms with 13 countries and entities in the Asia-Pacific which are publicly known of.

However, these mechanisms do not always serve their intended purpose. China has reportedly failed to answer hotline calls during crises, or the mechanisms have reportedly not been used at all. This is particularly the case for the US–China mechanisms. But the Philippines, which last year signed a defence-leader hotline with the PRC, has also had calls go unanswered during crises at sea in 2023 involving PRC and Philippines vessels.

China individualises its narrative of each crisis according to which other country is involved (see Figure 2.4). In encounters with the US, the PRC often argues that crises evolve because the US failed to address the root cause of incidents: US air and maritime activity within the 'first island chain'. As a result, China justifies its responses as a legitimate, responsible and professional reaction to provocation.

Figure 2.4: **China's characterisations of other parties' and its own behaviour in maritime and air incidents, 2001–24**

US	PHILIPPINES	AUSTRALIA	CANADA	JAPAN
• Root causes are US actions (close-in surveillance). • Deliberate disinformation. • Deliberate, malicious, provocative actions. • National security threat. • Intentionally causing trouble in China's backyard.	• Invaded. • Illegal entry. • Ignored China's warnings. • Conducted dangerous approach. • Intentionally unprofessional and dangerous conduct. • Provocative acts.	• Information is untrue; spreading malicious disinformation; spreading false information. • Disregarded warnings. • Threatened China's security. • Instigated hostility and confrontation. • Making trouble on China's doorstep.	• Provocative behaviour. • Risky acts. • Threatened China's national security and frontline personnel.	• Stirring up tensions.
CHINA	**CHINA**	**CHINA**	**CHINA**	**CHINA**
• Followed protocol. • Legal, professional, responsible reaction. • Legal, professional, responsible, safe and justified response.	• Acted in accordance with domestic, law enforcement and international law, including UNCLOS. • Professional and restrained response. • Necessary response.	• China's response in line with international law and practice. • Legal and legitimate response. • Professional, safe, reasonable and legitimate response.	• Monitored the Taiwan Strait.	• Kept normal observation.

Sources: IISS; US Department of Defense, www.defense.gov; Asia-Pacific Leadership Network, www.apln.network

The PRC meanwhile characterises the Philippines' actions as unprofessional, dangerous, failing to heed warnings, illegal and an invasion of Chinese territory. The PRC characterises its own response as legal and in accordance with domestic and international law and practice, as well as professional and restrained. Against Australia, the PRC often claims that Canberra's facts are incorrect or, at worst, that Australia is purposefully spreading disinformation about the PRC. The element consistent to each of these responses is the claim of defending its national security.

The PRC, however, appears to have been relatively less harsh in responding to incidents involving Canada and Japan (compared to those involving the Philippines and Australia). The PRC has remained relatively quiet regarding incidents with Japanese forces and acknowledged that it monitored these situations. Similarly, the PRC only noted that the Canadian transit of the Taiwan Strait was observed and noted. With both Canada and Japan, nonetheless, Beijing laid the blame on them for provocations and threatening China's national security.

Beijing attempts to deflect blame onto other parties involved in incidents where PLA vessels or aircraft have operated unprofessionally or without due regard to safety. It employs various arguments and tones to justify its behaviour. It is a predominantly legalistic framing of incidents which is not ameliorated by existing crisis-management mechanisms, especially when considering Beijing's unwillingness to use them to prevent incidents.

The only solution that Beijing proposes is for regional states to refrain from conducting any activity that it disagrees with, even if it is within their legal right under UNCLOS. Additionally, Beijing has openly stated that it is suspicious of crisis-management mechanisms and codes of conduct, as it believes participation in these mechanisms to be disingenuous and provide second parties with the immunity to continue behaviour that it finds provocative.

Figure 2.5: **Asia-Pacific: selected minilateral and multilateral crisis-management mechanisms**

ASEAN Defence Ministers' Meeting Plus, 2019
ASEAN Direct Communications Infrastructure expanded to Dialogue Partners

ASEAN and Japan, 2023
Japan joining ASEAN Direct Communications Infrastructure

Western Pacific Naval Symposium (WPNS), 2014
Code for Unplanned Encounters at Sea

ASEAN and Australia, 2021
Australia announcing intent to join ASEAN Direct Communications Infrastructure

Russia, Japan, New Zealand, Brunei, Cambodia, Myanmar, Vietnam, Singapore, Laos, South Korea, Philippines, Indonesia, US, Australia, China, Canada, Papua New Guinea, Chile, Peru, France, Tonga, Pakistan, Mexico, Bangladesh, India, Malaysia, Thailand

Trilateral Cooperative Arrangement, 2016*

Malacca Straits Patrol, 2004*

ASEAN Defence Ministers' Meeting:
2017 ASEAN Direct Communications Infrastructure
2019 Guidelines for Maritime Interaction

WPNS observer countries

ASEAN and China:
2016 Joint Statement on The Application of The Code for Unplanned Encounters at Sea in The South China Sea
2017 Guidelines for Hotline Communications among Senior Officials of the Ministries of Foreign Affairs in Response to Maritime Emergencies in the Implementation of the Declaration on the Conduct of Parties in the South China Sea

*Including hotline
Source: IISS

©IISS

In the multilateral domain, meanwhile, codes of conduct are either pending (such as between ASEAN and China in the South China Sea) or have failed, such as the Six-Party Talks over North Korea's nuclear programme. Beyond China, Southeast Asian countries have enacted bilateral mechanisms to address common threats such as cross-border crime and terrorism and maritime safety, reportedly with success.

Bilateral and trilateral mechanisms that exclude the PRC could become an important way of creating a matrix of codes of conduct and crisis-management mechanisms between like-minded countries in the Asia-Pacific, though few if any regional official would publicly make the case. If coordinated, such a tailored matrix could eventually result in standards of operation and conduct in the region's most contested spaces. This could also serve to highlight Beijing's transgressions. Furthermore, countries could potentially and more easily improve their cooperation in new domains, such as space and cyber.

Equally urgent is the need to address the absence of crisis-management mechanisms in Northeast Asia given the lack of operational progress within the ARF. Following the failure of the Six-Party Talks, North Korea is currently excluded from all operational crisis-management mechanisms. Any inclusive crisis-management mechanism will require the involvement of North Korea and Russia, though this is unlikely while Russia wages war against Ukraine.

An alternative solution could be the formation of crisis-management mechanisms between regional countries that exclude China, North Korea or Russia, though these would instead focus on building ties to increase information sharing, coordinate regional responses to crises and prepare for conflict as a means of deterrence, rather than managing crises. It is likely that ASEAN or the majority of Southeast Asian countries would refuse to participate, limiting it to like-minded states, and thus diluting its possible effectiveness.

THE MORE THINGS CHANGE

The overall strategic picture in 2024 may not look fundamentally different to when the first *Asia-Pacific Regional Security Assessment* (APRSA), then titled *Regional Security Assessment 2014* (hereafter RSA 2014), was published in the same year. Regional concerns focused on potential flashpoints and ongoing territorial disputes in the South China Sea, East China Sea and on the Korean Peninsula. By 2024, Korean Peninsula security and stability has perhaps taken a backseat to issues that have commanded immediate policy attention: maritime and air incidents in Southeast and Northeast Asia.

However, RSA 2014 noted that the factors leading to instability and preventing crisis management were predominantly domestic in nature. Chapters on Southeast Asian and Northeast Asian security developments noted the importance of developments in national political scenes and in government as inhibitors to conflict resolution and diplomatic resolution of disputes.

For example, one chapter pointed to the changes in prime minister Abe Shinzo's second government, and the series of corruption scandals within Japan's Ministry of Foreign Affairs in the early 2000s which led to the decline of the influence of China-focused diplomats.[41] Generational changes in political-elite circles also had an impact. For example, in Japan, the generation of politicians who were instrumental in the normalisation of relations in the 1970s had passed away by 2014.[42]

In China, growing nationalism rising from economic and political confidence, and government encouragement through propaganda campaigns, has led to greater domestic activism on foreign-policy issues. For example, in 2012 a group of seven Chinese activists travelled to the Senkaku/Diaoyu islands as part of an organised tour.[43] Furthermore, 'fervent nationalism' also rose in the 1990s, and though it closely resembled the Chinese Communist Party's line at times, it was also independent of it. Despite Xi's dominant control of the state in 2013, Chinese commentators voiced hardline views about Chinese claims in the Spratly Islands.[44] Domestic public opinion has, at times, created a dilemma for Chinese leaders by restricting their policy options.[45]

Though various chapters in RSA 2014 discussed the lack of trust between China and the US, this was not the central lens through which regional stability and security was perceived. This outlook, at the time, led to very different views of potential areas for cooperation and confidence building. One chapter even promoted deepening Chinese economic integration across Southeast Asia as a positive development.[46] In 2024, Chinese investment and trade dependencies are instead viewed more cautiously through the lens of economic security, de-risking and supply-chain resilience. Previously considered a positive inhibitor of conflict, economic ties could now be viewed suspiciously as precursors to economic coercion and influence.

Members of the Chinese 'Action Committee for Defending the Diaoyu Islands' activist group hold a press conference on their planned second expedition to the disputed Senkaku/Diaoyu islands at Shau Kei Wan Typhoon Shelter, Hong Kong, 8 August 2013

(Dickson Lee/South China Morning Post via Getty Images)

However, multilateral efforts have not changed much by 2024. Indeed, though the RSA 2014 chapters discussed the push to resume the Six-Party Talks and the potential for a China–ASEAN Code of Conduct for the South China Sea, they were generally pessimistic about the mechanisms' progress back then. Instead, they focused on developments within individual bilateral relationships as potential sources of regional stability. Solutions to crisis prevention and management were therefore also predominately bilateral in nature. The exception centred around a discussion of Japan–South Korea relations, and the potential for the US to facilitate confidence building between Seoul and Tokyo.[47] It was hoped that this would also contribute to greater alignment on the countries' policies on North Korea in the absence of Six-Party Talks.

Perhaps the greatest change, then, in regional crisis-prevention and -management mechanisms is the growing network of bilateral and trilateral relationships across the Asia-Pacific, including those centred on the PRC as well as those that exclude it. The US approached the region through similar bilateral means. In 2014, countries that should have been natural allies seemingly mistrusted one another. Today, however, integrated deterrence and sub-regional initiatives to build inter-state trust and confidence point to a more optimistic tone for regional stability, despite a lack of functioning mechanisms that include the PRC or North Korea.

NOTES

1. US Department of Defense, 'Military and Security Developments Involving the People's Republic of China: A Report to Congress', 19 October 2023, https://media.defense.gov/2023/Oct/19/2003323409/-1/-1/1/2023-MILITARY-AND-SECURITY-DEVELOPMENTS-INVOLVING-THE-PEOPLES-REPUBLIC-OF-CHINA.PDF.
2. See '"A Shared Vision for the Indo-Pacific": Remarks by Secretary of Defense Lloyd J. Austin III at the Shangri-La Dialogue', US Embassy in Singapore, 5 June 2023, https://sg.usembassy.gov/a-shared-vision-for-the-indo-pacific-remarks-by-secretary-of-defense-lloyd-j-austin-iii-at-the-shangri-la-dialogue-as-delivered/.
3. US Department of State, 'Maritime Matters: Military Safety: Agreement Between the United States of America and the People's Republic of China', 19 January 1998, https://www.state.gov/wp-content/uploads/2019/02/12924-China-Maritime-Matters-Misc-Agreement-1.19.1998.pdf.
4. George S. Capen, 'The Military Maritime Consultative Agreement', *US Naval Institute Proceedings*, vol. 125, no. 8, August 1999, https://www.usni.org/magazines/proceedings/1999/august/military-maritime-consultative-agreement.
5. 'EP-3 Collision, Crew Detainment and Homecoming', Naval History and Heritage Command, 18 August 2021, https://www.history.navy.mil/content/history/nhhc/research/archives/Collections/ncdu-det-206/2001/ep-3-collision--crew-detainment-and-homecoming.html; and Jim Garamone, 'Chinese Trawlers Harass USNS Impeccable', Military News, 11 March 2009, https://www.militarynews.com/norfolk-navy-flagship/news/top_stories/chinese-trawlers-harass-usns-impeccable/article_217a5b7c-6e43-51df-84f8-7569d1769eee.html.
6. See 'Remarks by President Obama and President Xi Jinping of the People's Republic of China After Bilateral Meeting', speech by Barack Obama and Xi Jinping, The White House, 8 June 2013, https://obamawhitehouse.archives.gov/the-press-office/2013/06/08/remarks-president-obama-and-president-xi-jinping-peoples-republic-china-.
7. Scott Neuman, 'Beijing: Near Miss as U.S. Warship "Harassed" Chinese Vessel', NPR, 18 December 2013, https://www.npr.org/sections/thetwo-way/2013/12/18/255249605/beijing-near-miss-as-u-s-warship-harassed-chinese-vessel.
8. *Ibid.*
9. US Department of Defense, 'Memorandum of Understanding Between the United States of America Department of Defense and the People's Republic of China Ministry of National Defense on Notification of Major Military Activities Confidence-Building Measures Mechanism', https://dod.defense.gov/Portals/1/Documents/pubs/141112_MemorandumOfUnderstandingOnNotification.pdf; and US Department of Defense, 'Memorandum of Understanding Between the Department of Defense of the United States of America and the Ministry of National Defense of the People's Republic of China Regarding the Rules of Behavior for Safety of Air and Maritime Encounters', https://dod.defense.gov/Portals/1/Documents/pubs/141112_MemorandumOfUnderstandingRegardingRules.pdf.
10. Jim Garamone, 'U.S., Chinese Military Leaders Sign Agreement to Increase Communication', US Department of Defense, 15 August 2017, https://www.defense.gov/News/News-Stories/Article/Article/1278684/us-chinese-military-leaders-sign-agreement-to-increase-communication/.
11. The White House, 'Joint U.S.–China Statement', 29 October 1997, https://1997-2001.state.gov/regions/eap/971029_usc_jtstmt.html; US Department of State, 'Agreement on the Establishment of a Secure Defense Telephone Link between the Department of Defense, the United States of America and the Ministry of National Defense, the People's Republic of China', 29 February 2008, https://2009-2017.state.gov/documents/organization/108917.pdf; Sam Jones, 'US and China Set Up "Space Hotline"', *Financial Times*, 20 November 2015, https://www.ft.com/content/900870f4-8f9f-11e5-a549-b89a1dfede9b; and John W. Rollins, 'U.S.–China Cyber Agreement', Congressional Research Service, 16 October 2015, https://www.everycrsreport.com/reports/IN10376.html.
12. US Department of Defense, 'Military and Security Developments Involving the People's Republic of China: A Report to Congress'.
13. Missy Ryan and Dan Lamothe, 'Pentagon: Chinese Naval Ship Seized an Unmanned U.S. Underwater Vehicle in South China Sea', *Washington Post*, 16 December 2016, https://www.washingtonpost.com/news/checkpoint/wp/2016/12/16/defense-official-chinese-naval-ship-seized-an-unmanned-u-s-ocean-glider/.

14 See 'Press Conference by President Clinton and President Jiang Zemin', speech delivered by Bill Clinton and Jian Zemin, US Department of State Archive, 29 October 1997, https://1997-2001.state.gov/regions/eap/971029_clinton_china2.html.

15 Ellen Knickmeyer, '"It Just Rang": In Crises, US–China Hotline Goes Unanswered', AP News, 10 February 2023, https://apnews.com/article/politics-united-states-government-lloyd-austin-china-9d1b7c9aa40b22d0bda497ba29be8d9b; and Sam Lagrone, 'Chinese Seize U.S. Navy Unmanned Vehicle', USNI News, 16 December 2016, https://news.usni.org/2016/12/16/breaking-chinese-seize-u-s-navy-unmanned-vehicle.

16 Shirley A. Kan et al., 'CRS Report for Congress: China–U.S. Aircraft Collision Incident of April 2001: Assessments and Policy Implications', 10 October 2001, https://sgp.fas.org/crs/row/RL30946.pdf.

17 US Department of Defense, 'Military and Security Developments Involving the People's Republic of China: A Report to Congress'.

18 'China Protests U.S. Spy Plane Watching Drills', Reuters, 26 August 2020, https://www.reuters.com/article/us-china-usa-security/china-protests-u-s-spy-plane-watching-drills-idUSKBN25L1Q2/.

19 'Foreign Minister Qin Gang Meets the Press', Ministry of Foreign Affairs of the People's Republic of China, 7 March 2023, https://www.mfa.gov.cn/eng/zxxx_662805/202303/t20230307_11037190.html.

20 'Fifth Plenary Session – Q&A with Dr John Chipman and General Li Shangfu', IISS, 4 June 2023, https://www.iiss.org/globalassets/media-library---content--migration/files/shangri-la-dialogue/2023/final-transcripts/p-5/fifth-plenary-session---qa---as-delivered.pdf.

21 *Ibid.*

22 Sam Lagrone, 'Code for Unplanned Encounters at Sea', USNI News, 17 June 2014, https://news.usni.org/2014/06/17/document-conduct-unplanned-encounters-sea.

23 Jennifer Jett and Isaac Lee, 'China Says It Rejected U.S. Call Over Balloon Because "Atmosphere" Wasn't Right', NBC News, 10 February 2023, https://www.nbcnews.com/news/world/china-balloon-rejected-us-defense-ministry-call-rcna70046.

24 Song Zhongping, 'Bottom Line Must Be Respected Despite of Hotlines', *Global Times*, 11 May 2021, https://www.globaltimes.cn/page/202105/1223187.shtml.

25 Rush Doshi, 'Improving Risk Reduction and Crisis Management in US–China Relations', in 'The Future of US Policy Toward China: Recommendations for the Biden Administration', November 2020, https://www.brookings.edu/wp-content/uploads/2020/11/Future-U.S.-policy-toward-China-v8.pdf.

26 Sakura Murakami and Nobuhiro Kubo, 'US Exploring Potential Space Force Hotline with China', Reuters, 25 September 2023, https://www.reuters.com/technology/space/us-exploring-potential-space-force-hotline-with-china-us-commander-says-2023-09-25/.

27 Phelim Kane, 'Beijing Cuts U.S. Cooperation to Protest Pelosi's Taiwan Visit', Politico, 5 August 2022, https://www.politico.com/news/2022/08/05/beijing-protest-pelosi-taiwan-00050155.

28 Noah Robertson, 'US–China Defense Talks Resume as Two Sides Meet in Washington', DefenseNews, 9 January 2024, https://www.defensenews.com/pentagon/2024/01/09/us-china-defense-talks-resume-as-two-sides-meet-in-washington/.

29 See 'China–India Crisis Communications Mechanisms', United States Institute of Peace, 'Crisis Communications with China in the Indo-Pacific', https://www.usip.org/programs/crisis-communications-china-indo-pacific.

30 'Philippines, Vietnam Set to Boost Cooperation in South China Sea', Benar News, 30 January 2024, https://www.benarnews.org/english/news/philippine/philippines-vietnam-boost-south-china-sea-cooperation-01302024043808.html.

31 *Ibid.*

32 MINDEF Singapore, 'Fact Sheet: The Malacca Straits Patrol', 21 April 2015, https://www.mindef.gov.sg/web/portal/mindef/news-and-events/latest-releases/article-detail/2016/april/2016apr21-news-releases-00134/.

33 Gusty Da Costa, 'Indonesia, Malaysia, Philippines Renew Commitment to Cooperation', IP Defense Forum, 25 July 2023, https://ipdefenseforum.com/2023/07/

indonesia-malaysia-philippines-renew-commitment-to-cooperation/.

34 Hoang Thi Ha, 'Repositioning the ADMM-Plus in a Contested Region', *ISEAS Perspective*, vol. 13, 10 February 2021, https://www.iseas.edu.sg/articles-commentaries/iseas-perspective/iseas-2021-13-repositioning-the-admm-plus-in-a-contested-region-hoang-by-thi-ha/; and Siti Rahil, 'Major Powers to Welcome Expansion of ASEAN Security Hotline', Kyodo News, 15 June 2021, https://english.kyodonews.net/news/2021/06/b691e1c32b14-major-powers-to-welcome-expansion-of-asean-security-hotline.html?phrase=shinkansen&words=.

35 Association of Southeast Asian Nations, 'Joint Declaration of the ASEAN Defence Ministers on Partnering for Change, Engaging the World', 24 October 2017, https://asean.org/joint-declaration-of-the-asean-defence-ministers-on-partnering-for-change-engaging-the-world/; and Association of Southeast Asian Nations, 'Chairman Statement of the 5th ADMM-Plus', 20 October 2018, https://asean.org/storage/2018/10/Final-5th-ADMM-Plus-Chairmans-Statement.pdf.

36 'Dedication to Ensure Regional Peace and Stability Stronger Than Ever Amid Ongoing Security Challenges', MINDEF Singapore, 10 December 2020, https://www.mindef.gov.sg/web/portal/mindef/news-and-events/latest-releases/article-detail/2020/December/10dec20_nr.

37 Association of Southeast Asian Nations, 'Joint Declaration of the ASEAN Defence Ministers on Partnering for Change, Engaging the World'; Association of Southeast Asian Nations, 'Ha noi Joint Declaration on the First ASEAN Defence Ministers' Meeting-Plus', 12 October 2010, https://www.asean.org/wp-content/uploads/images/archive/defence/JointDeclaration101012.pdf; and Association of Southeast Asian Nations, 'Chairman Statement of the 5th ADMM-Plus'.

38 'Factbox: History of Failure: Efforts to Negotiate on North Korean Disarmament', Reuters, 7 March 2018, https://www.reuters.com/article/idUSKCN1GI2PQ/.

39 Trevor Hunnicutt, David Brunnstrom and Hyonhee Shin, 'US, South Korea and Japan Condemn China, Agree to Deepen Military Ties', Reuters, 19 August 2023, https://www.reuters.com/world/us-south-korea-japan-agree-crisis consultations-camp-david-summit-2023-08-18/; and Hyunsu Yim and Ju-Min Park, 'U.S., South Korea, Japan to Step Up Actions on North Korea Cyber Threats', Reuters, 9 December 2023, https://www.reuters.com/world/us-skorea-japan-security-advisors-seoul-trilateral-meeting-2023-12-09.

40 'Russia Says It Will Build Close Ties with North Korea "In All Areas"', Reuters, 26 October 2023, https://www.reuters.com/world/russia-says-it-will-build-close-ties-with-north-korea-in-all-areas-2023-10-26/.

41 'Sino-Japanese Tensions in the East China Sea and the Senkaku/Diaoyu Dispute', in *Asia-Pacific Regional Security Assessment* (London: International Institute for Strategic Studies, 2014), p. 63.

42 *Ibid.*

43 Sheila A. Smith, 'Why Japan, South Korea, and China Are So Riled Up Over a Few Tiny Islands', *Atlantic*, 16 August 2012, https://www.theatlantic.com/international/archive/2012/08/why-japan-south-korea-and-china-are-so-riled-up-over-a-few-tiny-islands/261224/.

44 'The South China Sea Disputes in 2013', in *Asia-Pacific Regional Security Assessment* (London: International Institute for Strategic Studies, 2014), pp. 75–6.

45 'Sino-Japanese Tensions in the East China Sea and the Senkaku/Diaoyu Dispute', p. 63.

46 'The South China Sea Disputes in 2013', p. 81.

47 'The Korean Peninsula: North–South Relations in 2013', in *Asia-Pacific Regional Security Assessment* (London: International Institute for Strategic Studies, 2014), p. 93.

CHAPTER 3

PREFERRED SECURITY PARTNER: ANCHORING INDIA IN THE ASIA-PACIFIC

ANTOINE LEVESQUES

Research Fellow for South and Central Asian Defence, Strategy and Diplomacy, IISS

VIRAJ SOLANKI

Research Fellow for South and Central Asian Defence, Strategy and Diplomacy, IISS

An Indian soldier peers upwards at an Indian fighter plane from a vantage point on a convoy of trucks in Gagangir, India, 19 June 2020; the trucks are in transit to Leh in the aftermath of a violent conflict with Chinese troops in Galwan Valley in the Himalayas (Yawar Nazir via Getty Images)

OBJECTIVE:

This chapter examines India's growing defence diplomacy and engagement as a means of enhancing its regional posture in the Asia-Pacific while countering China's concurrent presence and influence following the rise in India–China tensions since 2020.

ARGUMENTS AND FINDINGS:

India has increased its focus on regional defence diplomacy, engagement and issue-based partnerships. The frequency and scope of India's defence diplomacy ranges from military exercises and port calls to ministerial visits, arms sales and defence lines of credit (LoC). For India, being a 'preferred security partner' through defence partnerships increases its regional presence, which in turn enhances its influence and trust with Asia-Pacific countries while simultaneously countering Beijing's regional influence. India's defence engagement is and will continue to be focused on the Indian Ocean region, although it is working to increase its presence in Southeast Asia and the Pacific Ocean. Over the next decade, China will continue to be India's primary defence and security challenge.

REGIONAL SECURITY IMPLICATIONS:

India's expanding defence role and partnerships will likely further contribute to the increasingly competitive nature of India–China relations. It is already the case that should India–China relations deteriorate further, the region could find itself increasingly polarised between the two regional powers, with defence relationships growing even more exclusionary. The status of preferred security partner, therefore, carries risks and challenges alongside defence-specific benefits for regional recipients. India will, nevertheless, choose to become increasingly anchored in the Asia-Pacific.

Following the election of Narendra Modi as India's prime minister in 2014, India's 'middle power' trajectory has risen substantially. Several Asia-Pacific and European countries now increasingly engage India over their shared strategic priority of countering China's growing assertiveness. The *Regional Security Assessment 2014* states that 'even if its military clout, diplomatic influence and economic weight remain well below China's, India will still be a major power, capable of defending its interests in an asymmetric way, affecting its strategic environment and complicating China's strategic calculations'.[1] It added that 'India's security establishment is increasingly becoming fixated on China as its long-term strategic challenge'.

Quad leaders – Australian Prime Minister Anthony Albanese, US President Joe Biden, Japanese Prime Minister Kishida Fumio and Indian Prime Minister Narendra Modi – meet on the sidelines of the G7 summit in Hiroshima, 20 May 2023

(Kenny Holston/POOL/AFP via Getty Images)

This has taken place as India's primary and long-term strategic challenge has changed from Pakistan and Afghanistan to China, especially following the India–China border skirmish in the Galwan Valley in June 2020. Subsequently, India has focused on its engagement, including defence partnerships, with key partners across the Asia-Pacific to counter China's rising regional diplomatic, economic and defence influence. The rupture in New Delhi's relations with Beijing occurred just as tensions between China and the United States and the latter's regional allies were escalating. As such, India opted to increasingly engage with the US and the two other members of the Quad – Australia and Japan – as well as other European, Middle Eastern and other Asia-Pacific partners, including some in Southeast Asia, to bolster its regional strategy.

However, India's 'military clout' clearly remains below China's, with China's 2023 defence budget of USD219 billion nearly three times higher than India's USD74bn budget. Due to this budget and capacity constraint, India has changed its ambition since Modi's first term (2014–19) from becoming a 'net security provider' – primarily to the island and littoral states of the Indian Ocean – to a 'preferred security partner' for Asia-Pacific nations.[2]

Being a preferred security partner, through defence partnerships in particular, increases India's regional presence and enhances its influence and trust. This enables New Delhi to cooperate with partners more fully on sensitive issues and encourages them to engage with India more regularly. The defence-diplomatic efforts have included ministerial and service-chief visits, minilateral and multilateral engagements, arms exports, military exercises and port calls. India also increasingly prefers trilateral and minilateral engagements as they allow it to engage with numerous partners simultaneously, without straining its limited diplomatic and military resources.

India's middle-power trajectory has continued to rise alongside its perceived counterbalancing role to China's growing influence and presence in the Asia-Pacific. India's growing defence partnerships across the region should strengthen that rise as more countries support its aspirations to become a global power. However, there is a discrepancy between India's rhetoric of becoming a global power and its economic, diplomatic and defence capabilities to do so. India's primary diplomatic and defence focus will continue, for the foreseeable future, to be in the Indian Ocean region and only secondary to the wider Asia-Pacific region, despite this region's growing significance for New Delhi.

CHANGING CURRENTS

China's increasing presence and influence in the Asia-Pacific has affected India's regional posture and engagement partners. China ultimately has more military, diplomatic and economic capabilities to engage the region than India does, which continues to face budgetary and capacity constraints. While New Delhi cannot match Beijing's spending level on infrastructure and economic projects, it could and has increased its defence and security cooperation with various partners from the Quad, the Indian Ocean region, Southeast Asia, the Gulf and Europe.

These defence partnerships have grown more significant as India–China relations have become more acrimonious. India needed to become a more attractive defence partner and provide an alternative to Beijing for Indian Ocean and Southeast Asian countries in particular. Indeed, defence engagement now forms a key part of India's 'issue-based alignment' or 'multi-alignment' policy. This is an attempt to build meaningful ties on specific issues, like defence, with different partners while remaining short of an alliance relationship.

Changing Chinese threat

India has far greater security concerns about China in 2024 than it did in 2014. A step change came in June 2020, when four Chinese and over 20 Indian soldiers died during violent clashes in the Galwan Valley on their undemarcated, unresolved Himalayan border.[3] This resulted in relations between Asia's two largest nuclear-armed countries deteriorating to their lowest point since the 1962 Sino-Indian war. Indian officials and experts have claimed to be at a loss to explain why China mobilised troops in Ladakh that summer and pushed to occupy new land in such a way that led to conflict and increased tension on the border.

Instead, it demonstrated that India was now subjected to the same assertive and revisionist Chinese statecraft as other regional countries. India's assessment and driver of its Asia-Pacific strategy now sees the fusion of the two challenges – China as a bilateral problem and a regional one. India can therefore no longer assume that engagement with China can be based mainly on the bilateralism they had developed in the early 1990s, which had allowed them to set aside their differences and focus on border, political and economic cooperation.

Since Galwan, India has decided to place greater emphasis on deterrence, defence and containment of, rather than solely engagement with, China. In 2022–23, Modi and President Xi Jinping re-engaged minimally

Indian soldiers stand guard at Zoji La, a key pass along the highway to the Ladakh region bordering China, 19 March 2022

(Yawar Nazir via Getty Images)

and with little trust. On the border, de-escalation meetings take place with little impact. In the border regions, India has begun increasing the size and sophistication of its military forces and defence-related infrastructure.[4]

India's strategic deterrence of China, meanwhile, continues to rely on its unaltered nuclear doctrine and capabilities. On the economic front, minor punitive trade measures against China – its largest trade partner – after the Galwan Valley clash have not been increased. India is also building up its capacity to deny China political, diplomatic and economic inroads within South Asia and the Indian Ocean.[5] Yet, being the smaller power, India is wary of the limitations of an unrestrained or a single-tool – defence or otherwise – approach to Beijing, which may attract adverse Chinese counter-reactions. China, for example, could respond forcefully against India if Beijing concluded that India is strategically and resolutely siding with the West and against it.[6]

Different defence partner

India and the US are increasingly converging on the strategic need to counter China's role in the Asia-Pacific. Although the mix of deterrence, defence, containment and engagement vis-à-vis China in their respective strategies is not identical, they have become far more analogous since 2008. Relations between India and the US have improved substantially over the last 16 years, having been defined by mistrust and tension during the Cold War.

The bilateral relationship underwent a significant transformation due to the landmark India–US civil nuclear-cooperation agreement signed in 2008. Since then, the US has become India's all-round defence partner in providing arms and technology. Indeed, as the security threat from Beijing and Islamabad worsened, India's arms procurements from the US increased from USD200 million in 2000 to over USD20bn worth, per contracts signed, by 2020.[7]

Along with US diplomatic support for New Delhi, defence cooperation has been a major factor in increased Indian engagement with the US.[8] Key elements of the partnership include the United States' recognition of India as a 'major defence partner' in 2016, and the signing of three defence-cooperation agreements between 2016 and 2019. This has recently been expanded via the US–India Initiative on Critical and Emerging Technology (iCET), signed in January 2023 as part of a wider effort to strengthen long-term security and technology ties.[9] During Modi's first state visit to the US in June 2023, Washington announced its decision to share GE Aerospace's F414 jet-engine technology with India.[10]

These developments show that the US–India defence ties were already growing before the 2020 Galwan clash. While the conflict was not the main catalyst in the US–India defence ties, it gave further impetus and

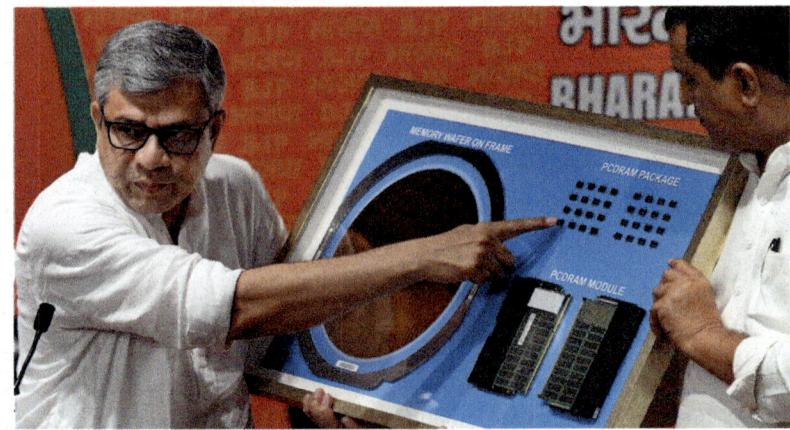

Indian Minister of Railways Ashwini Vaishnaw demonstrates a model of the precision semiconductor technology being imported under the US–India Initiative on Critical and Emerging Technology during a press conference, New Delhi, India, 26 June 2023

(Arvind Yadav/Hindustan Times via Getty Images)

rationale to expand and deepen the engagement across bilateral and minilateral platforms such as the Quad. The United States' diplomatic, military and intelligence cooperation with India has strengthened New Delhi's regional posture. India's regional presence has also been strengthened by its participation in the aforementioned minilateral groupings.

Joining forces with Japan

Shared concerns between India and Japan over China's growing regional presence have been a catalyst for their increased defence and security ties. Japan's geographical location and its willingness to work closely with India to strengthen their regional postures against China provides India with a deeper maritime presence and defence force in the Pacific Ocean. Their stronger collaboration under the Quad umbrella has also led to closer cooperation on maritime-security, cyber and intelligence issues.

In September 2020, three months after the Galwan clash, India and Japan signed an acquisition and cross-servicing agreement for the reciprocal provision of supplies and services, creating a framework for closer cooperation between their armed forces. The agreement came into force in July 2021 and enables mutual logistics support during joint exercises and training. They also held a '2+2' defence- and foreign-ministerial dialogue. India's Chief of Defence Staff, General Anil Chauhan, visited Japan in December 2023 – his only bilateral visit that year – highlighting the importance of defence ties with Japan. The two countries also held their first strategic and security dialogue in April 2022, attended by their deputy national-security advisers.[11]

Renewed focus with Australia

India was initially concerned about Australia's close relationship with China and was hesitant to engage Canberra on sensitive defence and security issues. However, the Galwan clash renewed India's focus on Australia, whose relationship with China has also deteriorated since April 2020 and through the COVID-19 pandemic. The two countries established a Comprehensive Strategic Partnership in June 2020, which included a Joint Declaration on a Shared Vision for Maritime Cooperation in the Indo Pacific, as well as a mutual logistics-support arrangement.[12]

In October 2020, India accepted Australia's long-standing request to join the *Malabar* naval exercise. India and Australia's defence partnership has grown significantly since then. The AUKUS agreement in 2021 showed New Delhi that Canberra was taking China seriously as a security threat. India also views Australia as a key Indian Ocean partner.

Maritime security therefore became a key focus. Australia even hosted *Malabar* for the first time in 2023. In July 2023, an Indian Navy Dornier maritime-patrol aircraft and

A member of the Indian Navy stands alongside naval personnel from Australia, Japan and the US during a review of visit, board, search and seizure procedures conducted during the annual *Malabar* quadrilateral field-training exercise, 7 November 2022

(Operation 2022 via Alamy Stock Photo)

an Indian Air Force C-130 transport aircraft undertook their first deployment to Australia's Cocos (Keeling) Islands, highlighting reciprocal access to their military facilities in the Indian Ocean. This was followed by the maiden visit by an Indian Navy submarine, INS *Vagir*, to Australia in August 2023. More broadly, their defence cooperation is monitored through the two countries' foreign and defence ministers' 2+2 ministerial meeting.

LOVE THY NEIGHBOUR

While countering China became a shared concern for Quad members, India has an additional goal for the Indian Ocean, Southeast Asia and the Gulf – presenting itself as an alternative to China and as a reliable and effective regional partner. Defence and security cooperation, in particular, became a useful means for India to strengthen relations with regional governments while drawing its South Asian neighbours closer and thus away from Beijing.[13] After all, India views its competition with China in the Indian Ocean and over the regional littoral and island states as zero-sum in the aftermath of Galwan.

One important platform for this effort is the Colombo Security Conclave (CSC), the most active security-focused minilateral group formed with Indian Ocean island countries. Held at the national-security adviser (NSA) level, the CSC brings together India, the Maldives, Mauritius and Sri Lanka, along with Bangladesh and the Seychelles as observers. The CSC's remit includes maritime security, countering terrorism and cyber security.

The CSC provides a platform for members to mutually and simultaneously address their strategic concerns and challenges in the Indian Ocean. The group held its sixth NSA-level meeting in December 2023. However, the meeting was not attended by the Maldives, whose vice-president, Hussain Mohamed Latheef, visited China instead. This signalled that the Maldivian government elected in September 2023 wanted to engage with China more closely than with India.[14]

In Southeast Asia, meanwhile, India has moved away from its previous reluctance to engage regional states over security matters for fear of antagonising Beijing. Since Galwan, India has sought to become a more consistent and reliable partner to Southeast Asian states to counter China's influence and presence. India also views Southeast Asia as a potential market for Indian-made arms and equipment and as burgeoning exercise and maritime-security partners.

India's key partners here are Indonesia, the Philippines, Singapore, Thailand and Vietnam. Notably, in January 2022, India signed its first major defence-export deal when it agreed to export three batteries of the *BrahMos* cruise missile to the Philippine Marine Corps. The first Association of Southeast Asian Nations (ASEAN)–India Defence Ministers' Informal Meeting was then held in Cambodia on the sidelines of the ASEAN Defence Ministers' Meeting-Plus (ADMM-Plus) in November 2022 to highlight

Indian Army and Royal Army of Oman soldiers practise cooperation during the joint military exercise *Al Najah-IV* at Mahajan Field Firing Range in Bikaner, Rajasthan, India, 12 August 2022

(Abaca Press via Alamy Stock Photo)

areas in which to strengthen collaboration. Subsequently, the inaugural ASEAN–India Maritime Exercise took place in May 2023.

India has also conducted maritime-security and defence engagements with the Gulf and western Indian Ocean countries. Under Modi, India has diversified its relationship with the Gulf, which was traditionally focused on energy, trade and expatriate issues, into defence and security cooperation, including counter-terrorism, maritime-security and naval cooperation. This focus highlights India's regional security concerns and enhances its regional presence and influence in the Gulf.[15]

India has sought to deepen these engagements further by establishing new military exercises in the Gulf. The Indian Navy established bilateral exercises with the United Arab Emirates in 2018, with Qatar in 2019, and with both Bahrain and Saudi Arabia, separately, in 2021. The Indian Army held its first exercises with the UAE and Saudi Arabia in January and February 2024. As a sign of growing strategic trust, India and the UAE have started trilateral military cooperation with France, including through a maritime exercise in 2023 and an air-force exercise in 2024.

As India seeks to become a reliable and credible regional partner, it will continue to try to strengthen defence engagement with Indian Ocean, Southeast Asian and Gulf countries.[16] The challenge is how to do so consistently across a wide range of countries – stretching from the Gulf to Southeast Asia – in order to counter China's presence and influence without overstretching its limited military, diplomatic and economic capacity and budget. In the Indian Ocean region, India's relationships also remain vulnerable to domestic political changes, unless it can better institutionalise these. India's influence on its neighbours, after all, also depends on the governments in power wanting to cooperate with it rather than with China.

BIGGER TOOLBOX

India hopes to increase its regional presence and influence by cooperating on sensitive defence and security issues with Asia-Pacific partners. India's defence diplomacy in the region comes in a variety of means. These include ministerial and service-chief visits, arms exports, defence LoCs, and participation in trilateral, minilateral and multilateral groupings. The Indian military also conducts a growing number of combined military exercises, port calls and coordinated patrols with Asia-Pacific militaries. Each of these defence-diplomatic and military tools is used to demonstrate India's presence. The combined military exercises provide a recurring means to cooperate and engage with different partners, as seen in Figure 3.1.

Preferential treatment

As noted above, India has increased its defence-diplomatic focus on Southeast Asia and the Pacific islands since the Galwan clash. Southeast Asia is geographically proximate to India and there is substantial room for growth in India–Southeast Asia defence relations. This is why Indian Minister of Defence Rajnath Singh made seven visits (out of a total 15 abroad) to Southeast Asia and the Pacific islands in 2022 and 2023. These stops included Indonesia, Japan, Malaysia, Singapore and Vietnam, as well as the Maldives. While each is

Figure 3.1: **India: number of bilateral exercises with selected partners, 2014–24**

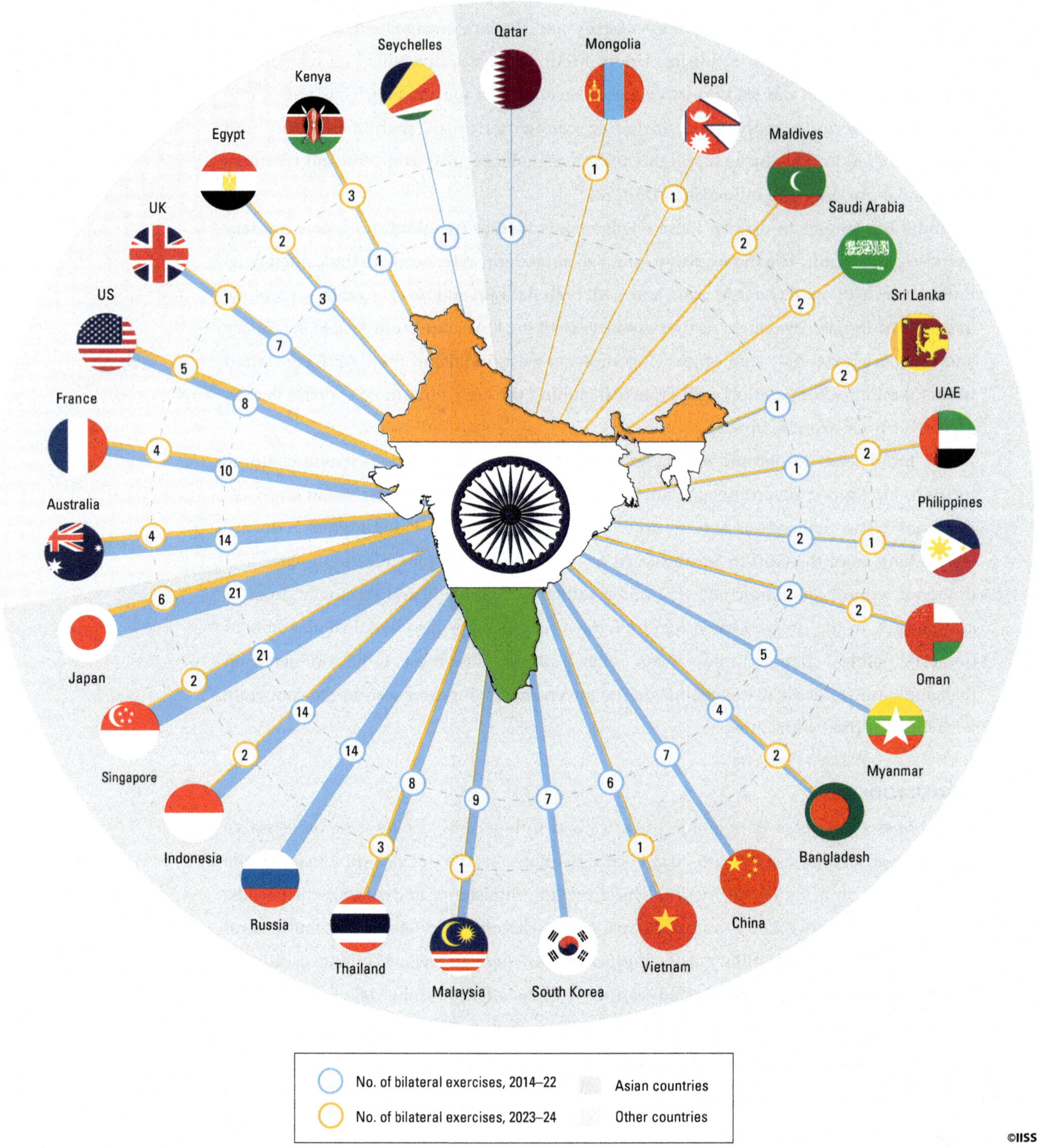

Country	No. of bilateral exercises, 2014–22	No. of bilateral exercises, 2023–24
Qatar		1
Seychelles	1	1
Kenya		3
Mongolia		1
Nepal		1
Egypt		2
Maldives	2	2
UK	1	3
Saudi Arabia		2
US	7	5
Sri Lanka	2	2
France	4	8
UAE	1	2
Australia	4	10
Philippines	1	1
	14	6
Oman	2	2
Japan	21	2
Myanmar	5	2
Singapore	21	2
	14	4
Indonesia	14	2
Bangladesh	7	
Russia	8	3
China	6	
Thailand	9	1
Vietnam	7	1
Malaysia		
South Korea		

Legend:
- No. of bilateral exercises, 2014–22 (blue)
- No. of bilateral exercises, 2023–24 (yellow)
- Asian countries
- Other countries

Source: IISS research; Indian Ministry of Defence, pib.gov.in

a key regional defence partner, a defence-ministerial visit highlights their elevated importance. It also sends a domestic signal to the Indian defence ministry and armed services to prioritise relations with that country.

High-level visits by Indian service chiefs and NSAs are another set of platforms in India's expanding defence-diplomatic toolbox. The Indian Navy chief, Radhakrishnan

Kumar, made numerous trips to the Asia-Pacific in 2022 and 2023, including Australia, Japan, New Zealand, Oman, the Seychelles, Singapore, Sri Lanka, Thailand and Vietnam. Visits by NSA Ajit Doval reinforce India's security priorities and whole-of-government focus. In March 2022, Doval visited Indonesia for the 2nd India–Indonesia Security Dialogue, which included a focus on maritime and defence cooperation. Doval also visited the Maldives in March 2022 and Mauritius in December 2023 for the CSC, emphasising India's focus on the Indian Ocean island states.

Doval at the signing of an MoU between Modi and Maldivian then-president Ibrahim Mohamed Solih in New Delhi, India, 2 August 2022

(Sonu Mehta/Hindustan Times via Getty Images)

Minilateral and multilateral groupings in the Asia-Pacific are also an increasingly important part of defence diplomacy for India, as they allow it to engage with multiple partners at once and to address common challenges. The Quad is the key regional group that India focuses on. India is also a member of the Indian Ocean Rim Association, the Indian Ocean Naval Symposium, the CSC and the Combined Maritime Forces in Bahrain, as well as an observer of the Indian Ocean Commission. Additionally, India is a member of ADMM-Plus, which resulted in the first ASEAN–India Defence Ministers' Informal Meeting in November 2022.

However, these mechanisms have limitations and defence engagement cannot be conducted through diplomacy alone. The Indian government should choose the countries its defence minister and service chiefs visit and prioritise carefully. Although visits are often catalysts for further engagement, by themselves they do not automatically translate into practical defence cooperation, and they require official and consistent engagement. India's capacity constraints also mean it must be selective about which groups to prioritise.

Sales pitch

India seeks to increase exports of its defence equipment to South and Southeast Asia – partly to demonstrate that it can be an alternative partner to China and partly to offset its broader defence-diplomatic limitations. Growing India's arms market also supports its military-modernisation goals, which include the need to reduce its reliance on imported Russian arms and prioritise domestic arms production, as well as research and development via the 'Make in India' initiative. This initiative seeks to foster defence-industrial collaboration through technology co-development, co-production and potential co-creation, with the intention of meeting the Indian government's ambitious policy of manufacturing in India and exporting to the world.

As these policies result in a greater intent for increased arms exports, Southeast Asia has become a viable potential market to develop. The region has a burgeoning military-modernisation requirement that New Delhi believes it can fulfil as an alternative to Beijing and Moscow. For several Southeast Asian states, India could be an alternative partner for providing maintenance for certain Russian-made arms and equipment, some complex platforms like supersonic cruise missiles and a possible industrial collaborative partner.[17]

Indeed, India's first major defence export was an agreement in January 2022 to export three batteries of the *BrahMos* cruise missile to the Philippines marines, with the delivery of the batteries beginning in late April 2024. The Philippine Army has also selected the *BrahMos* coastal-defence missile and will buy two batteries. India has also been in discussion about *BrahMos* sales with Vietnam since 2014, with Thailand since 2019 and with Indonesia since 2023.[18] But India has not finalised *BrahMos* sales to other Southeast Asian countries or exports of other equipment since, giving some idea of the difficulty that India faces in breaking into the regional arms market.

In the Indian Ocean region, India's primary form of defence exports is not through sales but through donations to the Maldives, Mauritius, the Seychelles and Sri Lanka. These include offshore-patrol vessels, advanced light helicopters and Dornier 228 maritime-patrol aircraft. India's donations to its Indian Ocean neighbours have enhanced their defence capabilities and demonstrated its own utility as a defence partner (see Table 3.1).

India also provides defence LoCs to partner countries to entice and enable procurement of Indian defence equipment. In Southeast Asia, India has focused on increasing arms sales to the Philippines and Vietnam, as they have demonstrated the most interest in Indian equipment, as noted above.[19] In June 2023, the Indian government reiterated its offer of a defence LoC to the Philippines – first made in 2018 – to enhance its defence-modernisation programme.[20] In June 2022, under a USD100m LoC, India handed over 12 high-speed guard boats to Vietnam. Additionally, Modi announced a second defence LoC to Vietnam worth USD500m in September 2016 for defence-industry cooperation, although this is yet to be finalised.[21]

For Indian Ocean nations, India's defence LoCs gives them the financial ability to expand their defence capacity beyond what it is willing to donate. India has sought to provide defence LoCs to each of its neighbours, underscoring the importance it places on ensuring that they each view New Delhi as a credible and trustworthy defence partner. Sri Lanka had utilised USD100m out of a USD150m defence LoC as of June 2023.[22] India has also approved a USD500m defence LoC with Bangladesh, a USD100m LoC with the Seychelles and with Mauritius and a USD50m LoC with the Maldives, primarily focused on enhancing these countries' maritime capacity, although these projects are not yet finalised.[23]

However, LoCs have their limits. India is still developing its domestic arms production, having been one of the world's largest arms importers. Unless it starts using its indigenous equipment more frequently and demonstrating its effectiveness, it will not be able to convince potential buyers, including Southeast Asian governments, to procure them. The fact that countries are not finalising or fully utilising India's defence LoCs, even with prices lower than other suppliers, suggests some of the challenges of convincing a country to procure arms from New Delhi. Consistent and perhaps bespoke sales pitches to each potential buyer are needed to convince them to procure Indian equipment.

Table 3.1: **India: arms exports to South and Southeast Asia, 2010–24**

Recipient(s)	Classification	Designation	Qty	Prime contractor(s)	Value (USD)	Order date
Afghanistan	Multi-role helicopter	*Cheetal*	3	Hindustan Aeronautics (HAL)	Donation	c. 2015
	Attack helicopter	Mi-24 *Hind*	4	India government surplus	Donation	Nov 2015
Maldives	Multi-role helicopter	*Dhruv*	1	India government surplus	Donation	2010
	Multi-role helicopter	*Dhruv* MkIII	1	HAL	Donation	Dec 2013
	Fast patrol boat	*Kaamiyab* (ex-IND C-401)	1	India government surplus	Donation	c. 2019
	Light transport aircraft	Do-228	1	India government surplus	Donation	Jun 2020
	Fast patrol craft	*Huravee* (ex-IND *Tarmugli*)	1	India government surplus	Donation	c. 2023
Mauritius	Oceangoing patrol craft	*Barracuda* (IND *Vikram* mod)	1	Garden Reach Shipbuilders & Engineers (GRSE)	58.5 million	Mar 2011
	Fast patrol boat	Fast Interceptor Boat	10	Goa Shipyard (GSL)	6m	Apr 2014
	Coastal patrol craft	*Victory* (IND *Sarojini Naidu*)	2	GSL	ε41m	May 2014
	Maritime patrol aircraft	Do-228-101	1	HAL	16.4m	Nov 2014
	Multi-role helicopter	*Dhruv*	1	India government surplus	Donation	c. 2020
	Light transport aircraft	Do-228	1	HAL	11.6m	c. 2021
	Light transport aircraft	Do-228-201	1	India government surplus	n.k.	2021
	Multi-role helicopter	*Dhruv* MkIII	1	HAL	17.7m	Jan 2022
Myanmar	Attack submarine	*Min Ye Thein Kha Thu* (Ex-IND *Sindhughosh* (Project 877EKM (*Kilo*)))	1	India government surplus	n.k.	2019
Nepal	Multi-role helicopter	*Dhruv* MkIII	1	HAL	7.6m	c. 2014
Philippines	Land-based anti-ship missile launcher	PJ-10 *BrahMos*	9	BrahMos Aerospace	375.0m	Jan 2022
Seychelles	Maritime patrol aircraft	Do-228	1	HAL	Donation	2012
	Coastal patrol craft	*Topaz* (ex-IND *Trinkat*)	1	India government surplus	Donation	c. 2013
	Fast patrol boat	*Hermes* (ex-IND C-401)	1	India government surplus	Donation	c. 2015
	Maritime patrol aircraft	Do-228	1	HAL	Donation	Mar 2017
	Coastal patrol craft	*Zoroaster* (IND *Car Nicobar* mod)	1	GRSE	Donation	c. 2020
Sri Lanka	Offshore-patrol ship with a hangar	*Sayurala* (IND *Samarth*)	2	GSL	n.k.	Apr 2013
	Oceangoing patrol craft	*Sagara* (IND *Vikram*)	1	India government surplus	Donation	c. 2015
	Oceangoing patrol craft	*Suraksha* (ex-IND *Vikram*)	1	India government surplus	Donation	c. 2016
	Maritime patrol aircraft	Do-228-101	1	India government surplus	Donation	c. 2022
Vietnam	Fast patrol boat	L&T 35m	12	Larsen & Toubro	99.7m	Sep 2016
	Corvette	*Khukri*	1	India government surplus	Donation	Jun 2023

Source: IISS, Military Balance+, milbalplus.iiss.org

Indian Minister of Defence Rajnath Singh inspects a guard of honour while visiting his British counterpart Grant Shapps in London, 9 January 2024

Training partners

Combined military exercises are the most critical element of India's defence engagement in the Asia-Pacific. They form the biggest part of India's preferred security-partner strategy and signal its inclusive approach towards military cooperation. Building inter-operability and mutual understanding, as well as sharing best practices, through combined exercises also allows the Indian armed forces to improve their proficiency and agility. Combined military exercises could also act as a gateway to possible Indian military exports down the line. Finally, some of these exercises could be litmus tests as to how far China is willing to entertain certain types of military engagement by India with regional countries, or whether it considered 'red lines' to have been crossed.

Taken together, India views combined military exercises with regional partners as a useful tool not only to improve cooperation, but also to grow their comfort level with New Delhi and simultaneously challenge China's regional posture. India thus conducts a wide array of combined military exercises. Bilaterally, these include air-force, army and naval exercises, as well as tri-service exercises, along with a supplementary category of maritime-partnership exercises, conducted on the sidelines of Indian Navy port calls to other countries. Additionally, the Indian military increasingly participates in trilateral, minilateral and multilateral exercises with Asia-Pacific militaries, as shown in Figure 3.1.

The Indian military conducted a total of 75 combined military exercises with partner countries in 2023 (see Figure 3.1). This included 55 bilateral, 16 multilateral and four minilateral exercises. This trend continued the year-on-year increase of 45 exercises conducted in 2022, 39 in 2021, 29 in 2019 and 40 in 2018. As India has sought to substantially grow its regional presence, it has aimed to increase the number of exercise partner countries, as well as developing new formats. In 2023, India's military exercises in the Asia-Pacific

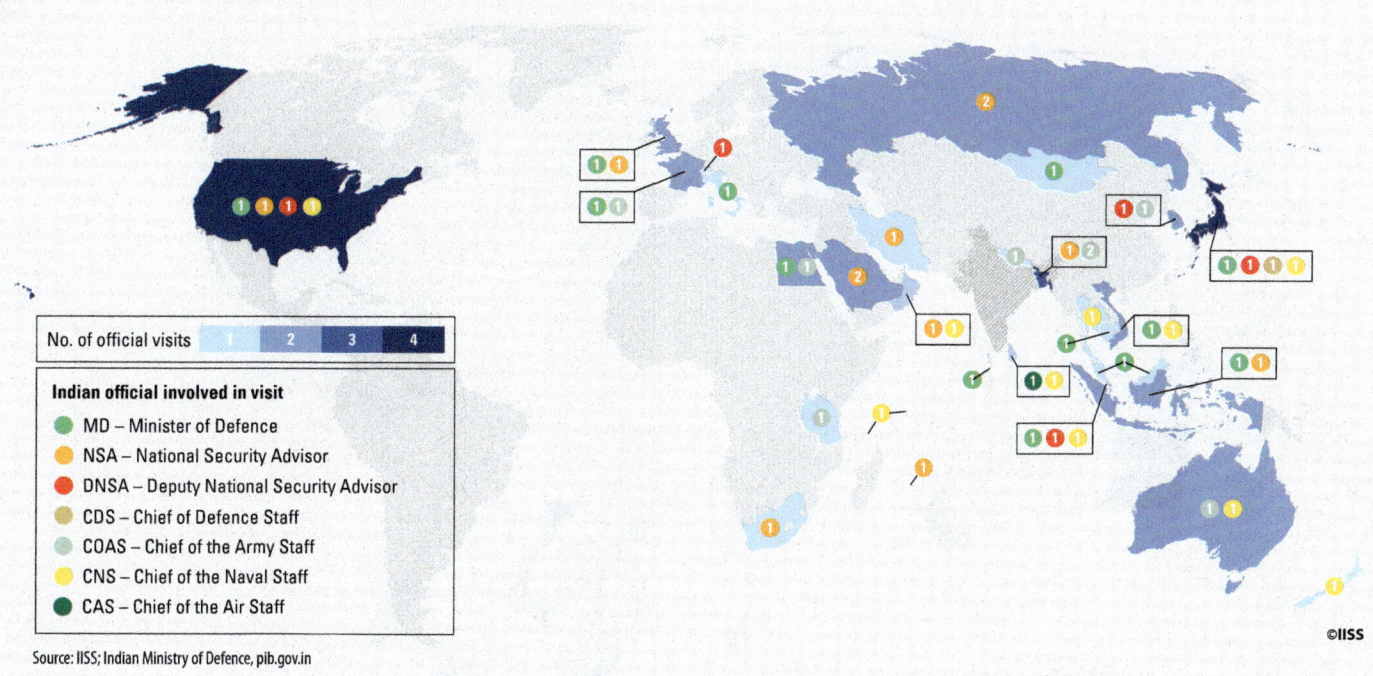

Map 3.1: **India: location and number of high-level defence-related official visits, 2022–24**

Source: IISS; Indian Ministry of Defence, pib.gov.in

included their first naval exercises with the Royal Thai Navy, as well as with ASEAN and European Union member-state naval assets, and the first India–Indonesia–Australia and India–France–UAE maritime-partnership exercises.

The growing frequency of India's combined exercises and presence in the Indian Ocean and in Southeast Asia demonstrates the Indian Navy's priority to strengthen defence relations within these regions. In 2023, India's military exercised with a large group of countries, ranging from Australia to the Maldives, the US and Vietnam, demonstrating the wide focus of India's Asia-Pacific military engagement. New Delhi views each of these countries as key regional defence partners, with the attendant military exercises improving cooperation with these nations.

The Indian Navy also uses port calls to display its presence, often though not exclusively as an ancillary to the military exercises. As with the exercises, the Indian Navy made significantly more port calls in 2023 – 51 – compared to 39 in 2022, 24 in 2021 and 25 in 2019. India's port calls in 2023 took place primarily in Indian Ocean and Pacific Ocean island and littoral countries, highlighting New Delhi's targeted display of its presence, as we can see in Map 3.2.

Notably, as New Delhi has become more willing to take risks in its Southeast Asia and Asia-Pacific policies, it has increased what used to be seen as 'sensitive' defence engagements such as submarine visits. This included the first deployment of an Indian submarine to Australia in August 2023, following the first visit by an Indian submarine to Indonesia in February 2023. An Indian submarine also visited Singapore as part of the *Singapore–India Maritime Bilateral Exercise* (SIMBEX) in September 2023.

With China's growing activity in the Indian Ocean, India has also conducted joint patrols with Australia and France and increased cooperation with both on maritime

Map 3.2: **India: location and number of naval port calls, 2014–24**

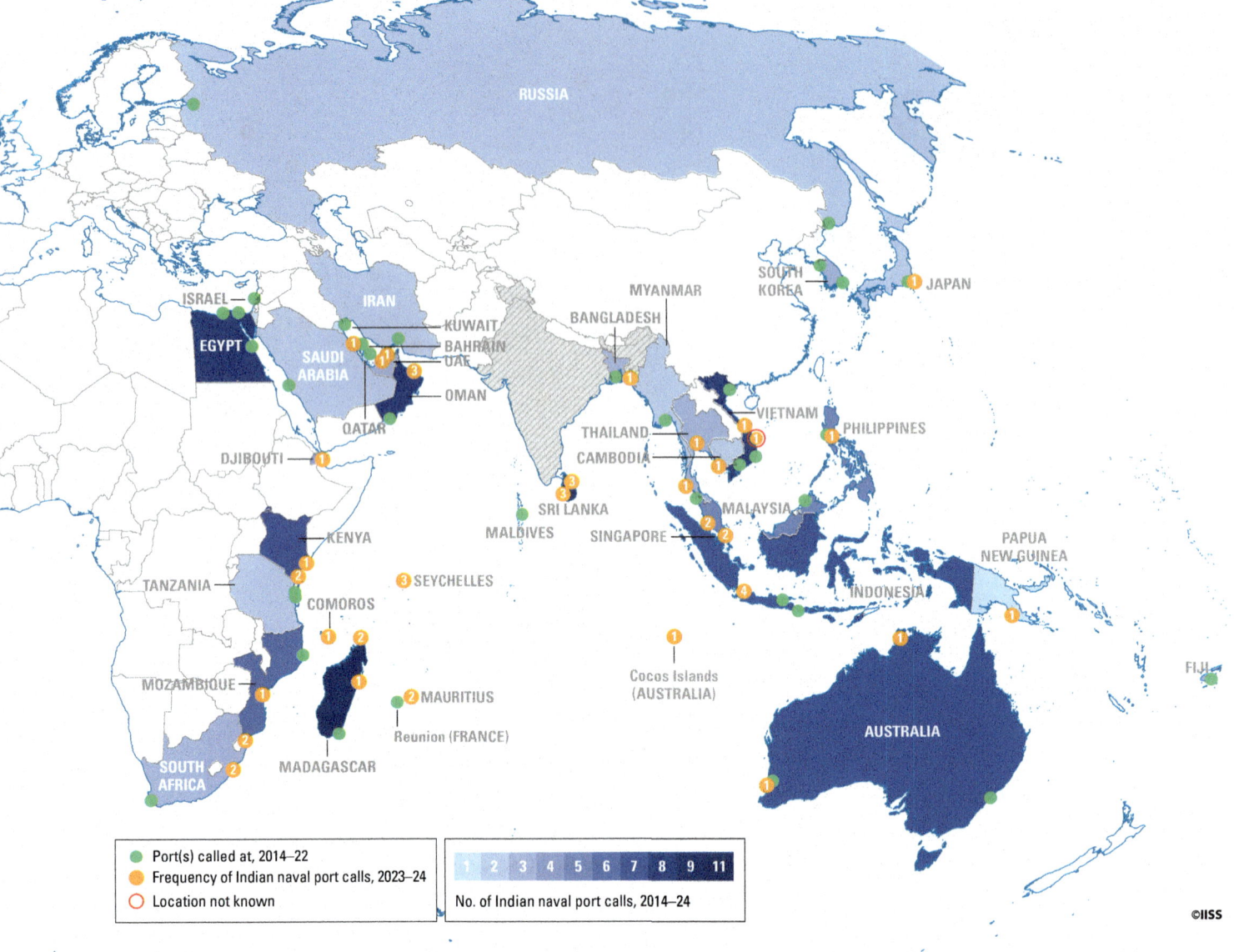

Source: IISS; Indian Ministry of Defence, pib.gov.in

surveillance and anti-submarine warfare. Indian and Australian maritime-patrol aircraft have also conducted at least four extended visits to one another's naval-air facilities for joint exercises and coordinated patrols between early 2022 and mid-2023.[24] India had also conducted two joint patrols with France since March 2020.

The Indian Navy also conducted broader coordinated patrols along the international maritime boundary line with the Bangladeshi, Indonesian and Thai navies. The goal of these activities was centred around mutual understanding and inter-operability and to put measures in place to 'prevent and suppress unlawful activities like illegal, unreported and unregulated fishing, drug trafficking, maritime terrorism, armed robbery and piracy'.[25]

India's maritime exercises and activities also focused on enhancing maritime domain awareness (MDA). This helps India address both non-traditional issues and traditional security challenges without appearing to overtly resist China. India conducts joint exclusive economic zone (EEZ) surveillance with Indian Ocean island and littoral nations, including Mozambique, the Seychelles and Tanzania. New Delhi has also provided coastal radar surveillance systems to the Maldives, Mauritius, the Seychelles and Sri Lanka to enhance their joint EEZ surveillance, which in turn provides India with a better maritime picture of its neighbourhood.

As new autonomous and networked sensors have increasingly become standard inventories among blue-water navies, India and its partners have begun to focus more on underwater and seabed domain awareness in the Indian Ocean. India is also keen for its partners to share increasingly sensitive information on 'grey' and 'dark' shipping (vessels whose identities are deceptively manipulated), although this would require higher levels of trust. Finally, to enhance maritime security and MDA, the Indian Navy has conducted 'mission-based deployments' in the Indian Ocean region since 2017, with a constant presence in the 'Gulf of Aden, Persian Gulf and Gulf of Oman, Approaches to Malacca Strait, Central and South Indian Ocean'.[26]

As India seeks to grow its military presence in the Asia-Pacific, there are questions raised surrounding its capabilities. These primarily revolve around whether the Indian Navy could consistently conduct a growing number of combined exercises, port calls, coordinated and joint patrols and EEZ surveillance, as well as a greater focus on MDA. India has for now leveraged its engagement in various minilateral and multilateral exercises. As India continues to prioritise being a reliable regional partner, these practices will only become more commonplace.

TAILORED ENGAGEMENT

There is a gap between India's perceived primary challenge of China and its secondary ones of terrorism and Pakistan. This gap has never been so wide in the minds of the Indian security establishment and is only expected to further widen over the next decade. For India, being a preferred security partner through defence partnerships increases its regional presence and enhances its influence and trust with Asia-Pacific countries and counters China's own presence.

India's most strategically effective defence-diplomacy tool will continue to be ministerial and service-chief visits. However, as noted above, these visits in themselves do not automatically translate into practical defence cooperation. New Delhi, after all, continues to focus on defence engagement which best suits its limited resources. This includes a focus on trilateral and minilateral platforms as India seeks to become a reliable regional partner while addressing its own capacity issues. India will continue to balance its engagement with as many partners in the region as possible while also engaging China in multilateral groups.

India's combined military exercises and port calls in the Asia-Pacific have been anchored on maritime-security challenges. They also form an important part of India's maritime-security strategy to build its role as a preferred regional security partner. The number of India's combined military exercises in the Indian Ocean and in Southeast Asia highlights that these regions are a defence-diplomatic priority.

Managing resources will be an important consideration for India going forward. India's 75 military exercises in 2023 belies the perception that India does not have the capacity for defence engagement. But India achieved this by optimising the allocation of its resources, such as ships, across its annual defence-diplomacy and exercise cycles, while allowing for new initiatives and features to gradually develop. This greater focus on delivery could be improved even further if India undertook more joint patrols and regional 'divisions of labour' with partners to ensure an effective and efficient use of their resources.

This may bear fruit in the next decade if India and its partners develop a common understanding based on trust, capabilities and advanced inter-operability. Another element of that partnership – economic ties – could also grow as more partners are interested in accessing India's markets in an era of global economic decoupling and de-risking from China. New Delhi could therefore potentially better set its terms of engagement with its growing number of partners.

Although tensions with China are unlikely to subside, India will seek to avoid being drawn into any Taiwan conflict. However, as US–China strategic competition grows, India's role as an alternative defence partner to both the US and China will grow as well. That said, India and its partners are all equally likely to remain highly sensitive to changes they each initiate in their respective mix of deterrence, defence, containment and engagement towards and with China. As India–China relations continue to suffer from a lack of trust and engagement, their relationship will likely remain antagonistic for the foreseeable future.

India's growing defence role and partnerships in the Asia-Pacific have broader implications for regional security. Its growing engagement with Australia, Japan and the US, both bilaterally and minilaterally, alongside states in the Indian Ocean region and in Southeast Asia, highlights a growing regional divide between India and China. The Indian foreign-policy and security tilt towards the US and its allies and partners will continue, and as US–China tensions worsen, the India–US engagement will likely add more fuel to the competitive India–China fire.

The main security concern for India is if China increases its defence engagement with India's neighbouring countries. India wants to be the primary security and defence partner in the Indian Ocean region, and it will seek to prevent China from operating regularly with its neighbours. For New Delhi to prevent this, it will need to become the preferred regional security partner.

NOTES

1 See 'Powers in the Middle: Japan, India, Russia, Australia, South Korea', in *Regional Security Assessment 2014* (London: International Institute for Strategic Studies, 2014), p. 43.

2 Rahul Roy-Chaudhury, 'From "Net Security Provider" to "Preferred Security Partnerships": The Rhetoric, Reality and Result of India's Maritime Security Cooperation', *Journal of the Indian Ocean Region*, vol. 18, no. 2, September 2022, pp. 87–8, https://www.tandfonline.com/doi/full/10.1080/19480881.2022.2118191.

3 'India–China Border Tensions: What Are the Strategic Implications for the Indo-Pacific', IISS, *Strategic Survey 2021* (Abingdon: Routledge for the IISS, 2021), pp. 162–76, https://www.tandfonline.com/doi/full/10.1080/04597230.2021.1984115.

4 Antoine Levesques, 'India–China Tensions: What Next for India?', IISS Online Analysis, 30 July 2020, https://www.iiss.org/online-analysis/online-analysis//2020/07/sasia-india-china-tensions.

5 Antoine Levesques and Viraj Solanki, 'South Asia', in *China's Belt and Road Initiative: A Geopolitical and Geo-economic Assessment* (Abingdon: Routledge for the IISS, 2023), pp. 108–32, https://www.tandfonline.com/doi/full/10.1080/28377710.2023.2293362.

6 Tanvi Madan, 'China Has Lost India', *Foreign Affairs*, 4 October 2022, https://www.foreignaffairs.com/china/china-has-lost-india.

7 Antoine Levesques and Viraj Solanki, 'India–US Relations in the Age of Modi and Trump', IISS Online Analysis, 27 March 2020, https://www.iiss.org/online-analysis/online-analysis/2020/03/sasia---us-india-relations-trump-and-modi/.

8 US Department of State, 'Integrated Country Strategy: India', 27 May 2022, https://www.state.gov/wp-content/uploads/2022/07/ICS_SCA_India_Public.pdf.

9 For artificial intelligence, see Antoine Levesques, 'Early Steps in India's Use of AI for Defence', IISS Online Analysis, 20 July 2023, https://www.iiss.org/online-analysis/online-analysis/2024/01/early-steps-in-indias-use-of-ai-for-defence/.

10 Antoine Levesques, 'US–India Defence and Technology Cooperation', IISS Online Analysis, 20 July 2023, https://www.iiss.org/online-analysis/online-analysis/2023/07/us-india-defence-and-technology-cooperation/.

11 Viraj Solanki and Mariko Togashi, 'India and Japan Enhance Cooperation Despite Their Differences', IISS Online Analysis, 23 May 2022, https://www.iiss.org/online-analysis/online-analysis/2022/05/india-and-japan-enhance-cooperation-despite-their-differences/.

12 Australian Department of Foreign Affairs and Trade, 'Joint Declaration on a Shared Vision for Maritime Cooperation in the Indo-Pacific Between the Republic of India and the Government of Australia', 4 June 2020, https://www.dfat.gov.au/geo/india/joint-declaration-shared-vision-maritime-cooperation-indo-pacific-between-republic-india-and-government-australia.

13 Antoine Levesques and Viraj Solanki, 'The State of Defence Cooperation in the Indian Ocean Region', IISS Online Analysis, 2 June 2023, https://www.iiss.org/online-analysis/online-analysis/2023/05/the-state-of-defence-cooperation-in-the-indian-ocean-region/.

14 Viraj Solanki, 'The Colombo Security Conclave: What Is It and What Does It Mean for Australia?', Observer Research Foundation, 16 May 2023, https://www.orfonline.org/expert-speak/the-colombo-security-conclave.

15 Hasan Alhasan and Viraj Solanki, 'The I2U2 Minilateral Group', IISS Online Analysis, 11 November 2022, https://www.iiss.org/online-analysis/online-analysis/2022/11/the-minilateral-i2u2-group/; Viraj Solanki, 'The Gulf Region's Growing Importance for India', IISS Online Analysis, 21 February 2024, https://www.iiss.org/online-analysis/online-analysis/2024/02/the-gulf-regions-growing-importance-for-india/.

16 To help counter China's regional presence and influence, India's engagement with France, Russia and the United Kingdom is also important, in providing India with arms equipment and diplomatic support and to enhance India's regional capacity and presence.

17 Curie Maharani Savitri, 'Go East or North? Recalibrating Defence Modernization in a Post-Russia Southeast Asia', *Contemporary Southeast Asia*, vol. 45, no. 2, 2023, pp. 166–92.

18 Dinakar Peri, 'Thailand in Talks with India to Buy BrahMos Cruise Missiles', *Hindu*, 31 July 2019, https://www.thehindu.com/news/national/thailand-in-talks-with-india-to-buy-brahmos-cruise-missiles/article28775607.ece; Devjyot Ghoshal, 'India–Russia Defence Firm Eyes $200 Mln Missile Deal with Indonesia', Reuters, 15 March 2023, https://www.reuters.com/business/aerospace-defense/india-russia-defence-firm-eyes-200-mln-missile-deal-with-indonesia-2023-03-15/; and Viraj Solanki, 'India–Vietnam Defence and Security Cooperation', *India Quarterly*, vol. 77, no. 2, April 2021, pp. 219–37, https://journals.sagepub.com/doi/10.1177/09749284211004982.

19 Other plans have made Vietnam a prominent defence partner for India in Southeast Asia. Since 2016, India and Vietnam have discussed the possible sale of India's *Akash* surface-to-air missile system to Vietnam, under the USD500m LoC. Hanoi has also expressed interest in procuring India's indigenously developed *Dhruv* advanced light helicopter; and India has also offered the possible sale of the *Varunastra* anti-submarine torpedo. However, no agreement had been finalised, despite extended talks.

20 Joyce Ann L. Rocamora, 'India Reiterates Loan Offer for PH Defense Modernization', Philippine News Agency, 30 June 2023, https://

www.pna.gov.ph/articles/1204618#:~:text=MA-NILA%20%E2%80%93%20The%20Indian%20government%20has,fund%20its%20defense%20modernization%20program.

21 Ministry of Defence, 'Raksha Mantri Shri Rajnath Singh Hands Over 12 High Speed Guard Boats, Constructed Under India's $US 100 Million Line of Credit, to Vietnam', Government of India, 9 June 2022, https://www.pib.gov.in/PressReleasePage.aspx?PRID=1832495#:~:text=Raksha%20Mantri%20Shri%20Rajnath%20Singh%20handed%20over%2012%20High%20Speed,Line%20of%20Credit%20to%20Vietnam; and Ho Binh Min, 'India Offers $500 Million Defence Credit as Vietnam Seeks Arms Boost', Reuters, 3 September 2016, https://www.reuters.com/article/idUSKCN11905X/.

22 Ministry of Defence, 'India Is Committed to Ensure Capacity & Capability Building of Sri Lankan Armed Forces, Says Defence Secretary in a Video Message at "India – Sri Lanka Defence Seminar cum Exhibition" in Colombo', Government of India, 7 June 2023, https://www.pib.gov.in/PressReleasePage.aspx?PRID=1930530#:~:text=Sri%20Lanka%20is%20one%20of,million%20credit%20has%20been%20utilised.

23 'Bangladesh–India Sign First Defence Contract Under $500 Million LoC', *Dhaka Tribune*, 7 September 2022, https://www.dhakatribune.com/bangladesh/foreign-affairs/293699/bangladesh-india-sign-first-defence-contract-under; Rezaul H. Laskar, 'India Extends $100 Mn Line of Credit for Defence Equipment to Mauritius', *Hindustan Times*, 22 February 2021, https://www.hindustantimes.com/india-news/india-extends-100-mn-line-of-credit-for-defence-equipment-to-mauritius-101613992341175.html; Ministry of External Affairs, 'Joint Press Statement on Official Visit of External Affairs Minister of India to the Maldives', Government of India, 21 February 2021, https://www.mea.gov.in/bilateral-documents.htm?dtl/33556/joint+press+statement+on+official+visit+of+external+affairs+minister+of+india+to+the+maldives; and 'India Offers Seychelles $ 100 Million Line of Credit for Defence, Infrastructure', Seychelles News Agency, 26 June 2018, http://www.seychellesnewsagency.com/articles/9350/India+offers+Seychelles+++million+line+of+credit+for+defence%2C+infrastructure.

24 See Tom Corben, 'The Quad Is Edging Closer to Collective Maritime Defense', *Nikkei Review Asia*, 8 August 2023, https://asia.nikkei.com/Opinion/The-Quad-is-edging-closer-to-collective-maritime-defense.

25 Ministry of Defence, '32nd Edition of Indo-Thai Coordinated Patrol (CORPAT)', Government of India, 12 November 2021, https://pib.gov.in/PressReleasePage.aspx?PRID=1771263.

26 Ministry of Defence, 'Maritime Cooperation with Regional Partners', Government of India, 21 March 2022, https://pib.gov.in/Pressreleaseshare.aspx?PRID=1807607.

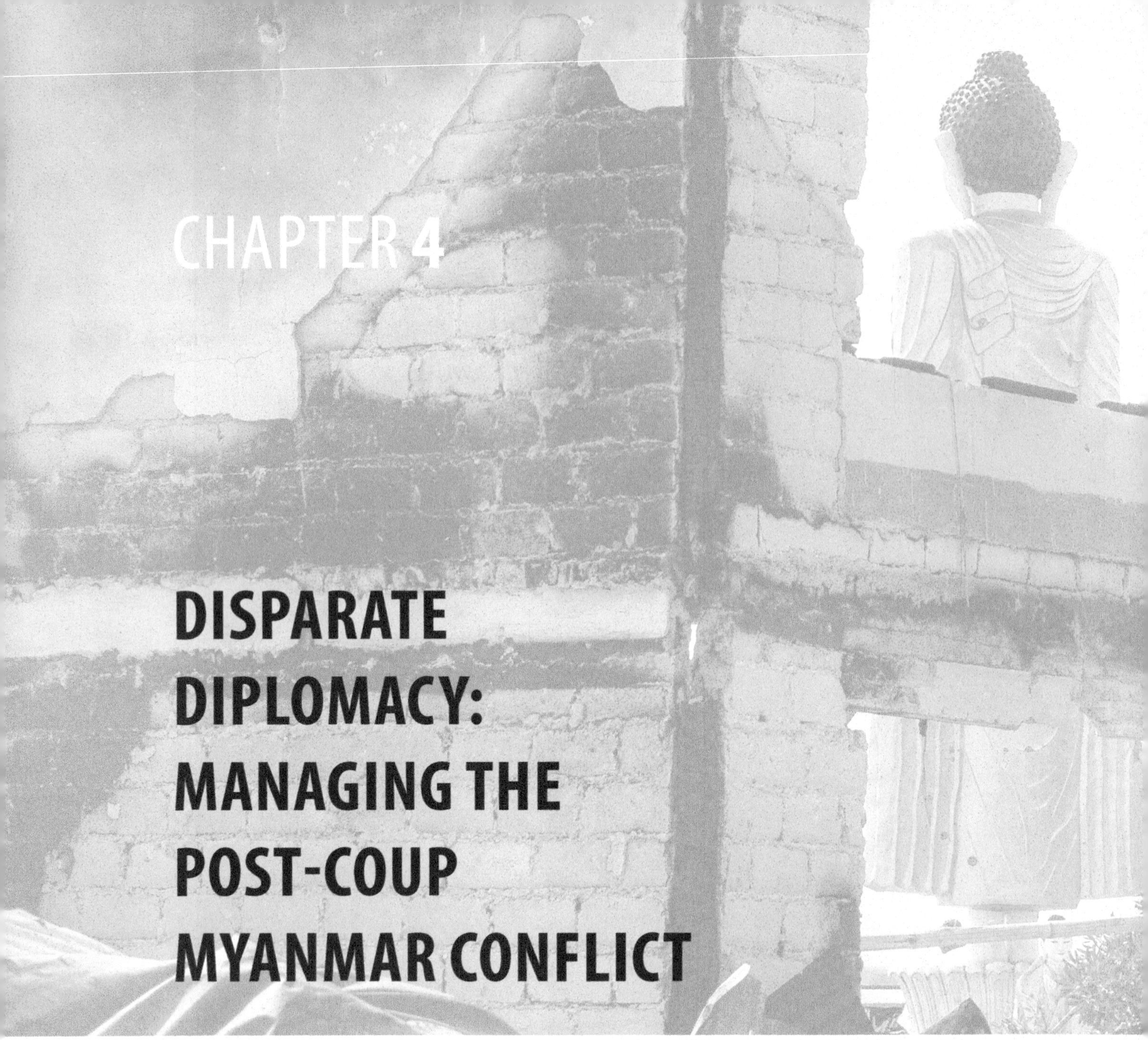

CHAPTER 4

DISPARATE DIPLOMACY: MANAGING THE POST-COUP MYANMAR CONFLICT

AARON CONNELLY

Shangri-La Dialogue Senior Fellow for
Southeast Asian Politics and Foreign Policy, IISS

MORGAN MICHAELS

Research Fellow for Southeast Asian
Politics and Foreign Policy, IISS

A destroyed building and a damaged statue of Buddha following fighting between Myanmar's military and the Kachin Independence Army (KIA) in Nam Hpat Kai, 4 February 2024. (STR/AFP via Getty Images)

OBJECTIVE:
The chapter will analyse the different diplomatic approaches of the West, China and the Association of Southeast Asian Nations (ASEAN) as well as Thailand's separate engagement in managing the ongoing conflict in Myanmar following the February 2021 coup.

ARGUMENTS AND FINDINGS:

Diplomacy around the post-coup conflict in Myanmar has proceeded along four distinct tracks. Firstly, Western countries have used economic sanctions and symbolic engagement with ousted lawmakers to seek to reverse the coup, while otherwise deferring to ASEAN to manage the crisis. Secondly, ASEAN has downgraded Myanmar's representation at key meetings in response to its failure to implement the group's 'Five Point Consensus' but has struggled to find ways to de-escalate the conflict and foster dialogue. Thirdly, Myanmar's neighbours, led by Thailand, have sought to create a diplomatic channel outside of ASEAN more sympathetic to engagement with the junta. Finally, China has become the most influential external actor in Myanmar, influencing developments on the battlefield and in negotiations among parties to the conflict.

REGIONAL SECURITY IMPLICATIONS:

The post-coup conflict holds significant implications for Myanmar's 55 million inhabitants, the majority of whom have been exposed to violence, but also for the broader Asia-Pacific region. Given its strategic location between China, India and the Indian Ocean, the conflict will naturally attract the attention of outside powers. The conflict has also led to more prosaic concerns for the region, including growth in transnational organised crime, from illegal drugs and human trafficking to online-scam centres.

While Myanmar has experienced numerous internecine conflicts since independence in 1948, the ongoing war sparked by the 2021 coup is distinct. For the first time in decades, the mainstream movement opposed to military rule has abandoned non-violence and endorsed armed struggle, helping to fuel the rapid proliferation of grassroots militias across Bamar-majority areas. Armed violence has now touched 317 of Myanmar's 330 townships.

The recent emergence of a widespread armed movement in the country's heartland has lent new-found legitimacy to ethnic armed organisations (EAOs), which have fought in the borderlands against Bamar-dominated central regimes for decades. In some areas, EAOs have offered support or found recruits among these newly formed local militias, usually referred to as People's Defence Forces (PDFs). The Myanmar military has thus been confronted with widespread armed resistance from the general population, as well as revitalised insurgent movements in geographically peripheral areas where ethnic minorities reside in greater numbers.

Unlike in previous decades, Myanmar's current conflict involves a higher level of combat intensity, a trend driven by the regime's expanded use of aerial firepower, in addition to the proliferation of new technologies, such as drones, in the hands of opposition forces. This dynamic has combined with generalised violence against civilians to devastating effect. Of Myanmar's estimated 55 million people, 68% have been exposed to armed violence since the coup.[1]

The immense human costs, however, have done little to advance a sense of urgency or generate a unified approach to conflict management among the various regional and international actors interested in Myanmar. Instead, diplomacy around the conflict has proceeded along separate tracks led by Western countries, ASEAN, China and Myanmar's other neighbours, respectively. The structure of these tracks reflects the preference of each sponsor. They have intersected at times but have otherwise remained mostly distinct.

COUP COUNTER-CURRENTS

The Myanmar armed forces launched a *coup d'état* in the early hours of 1 February 2021, overthrowing the elected government led by state counsellor Aung San Suu Kyi. Protests against the coup erupted around the country several days later, which security forces initially permitted for several weeks and then suppressed by force.

Beginning in April 2021, tens of thousands of citizens of various ethnicities, including the majority Bamar, responded by taking up arms against the junta in what they labelled the Spring Revolution. These so-called 'local defence forces' (LDFs) joined the four ethnic-minority armed groups known as K3C – Kachin Independence Organization (KIO), Karen National Union (KNU), Karenni National Progressive Party (KNPP) and Chin National Front (CNF) – who initially mobilised in response to the coup.[2]

Myanmar citizens hold up homemade shields as the police crack down on a demonstration against the military coup in Yangon, Myanmar, 16 March 2021

(STR/AFP via Getty Images)

Candidates from the ruling National League for Democracy who had won seats in the November 2020 election soon formed an opposition National Unity Government (NUG) with ethnic-minority allies. In September 2021, the NUG lent its legitimacy to the incipient uprising, calling for a 'people's defensive war' against the junta. This energised armed resistance against the new regime. Violence spiked, particularly in the Bamar-majority Dry Zone in the centre of the country, where LDFs attacked junta convoys and installations.

The junta's armed forces retaliated against population centres in an attempt to deny the LDFs the support that they required to carry on an insurgency. Many LDFs pledged their allegiance to the NUG – often renaming themselves as PDFs to demonstrate their affiliation with the shadow government. But the NUG has struggled to exercise control over PDF activities and has no relationship with hundreds of other LDFs who have refused to accept its authority.

Around the periphery of the country, the NUG initially sought to form a broad coalition with EAOs also fighting the junta. Some groups have been more open to partnership with the NUG than others. The NUG's strongest relationships presently are with the K3C grouping noted above. These groups have maintained their autonomy even as they align themselves with the NUG in the fight to expel the junta's armed forces from their respective ethnic homelands.

And yet groups with few connections to the NUG have made the biggest impact on the battlefield. On 27 October 2023, the Myanmar National Democratic Alliance Army (MNDAA) launched a massive assault on junta positions in northern Shan State, the homeland of the ethnic Kokang people, among whom the MNDAA recruits.[3] Their allies in the so-called Three Brotherhood Alliance, the Arakan Army (AA) and the Ta'ang National Liberation Army (TNLA), followed by attacking junta positions in their home areas.

After weeks of fierce fighting, Chinese diplomats facilitated the signing of a truce in Kunming between the junta, the MNDAA and the TNLA, although

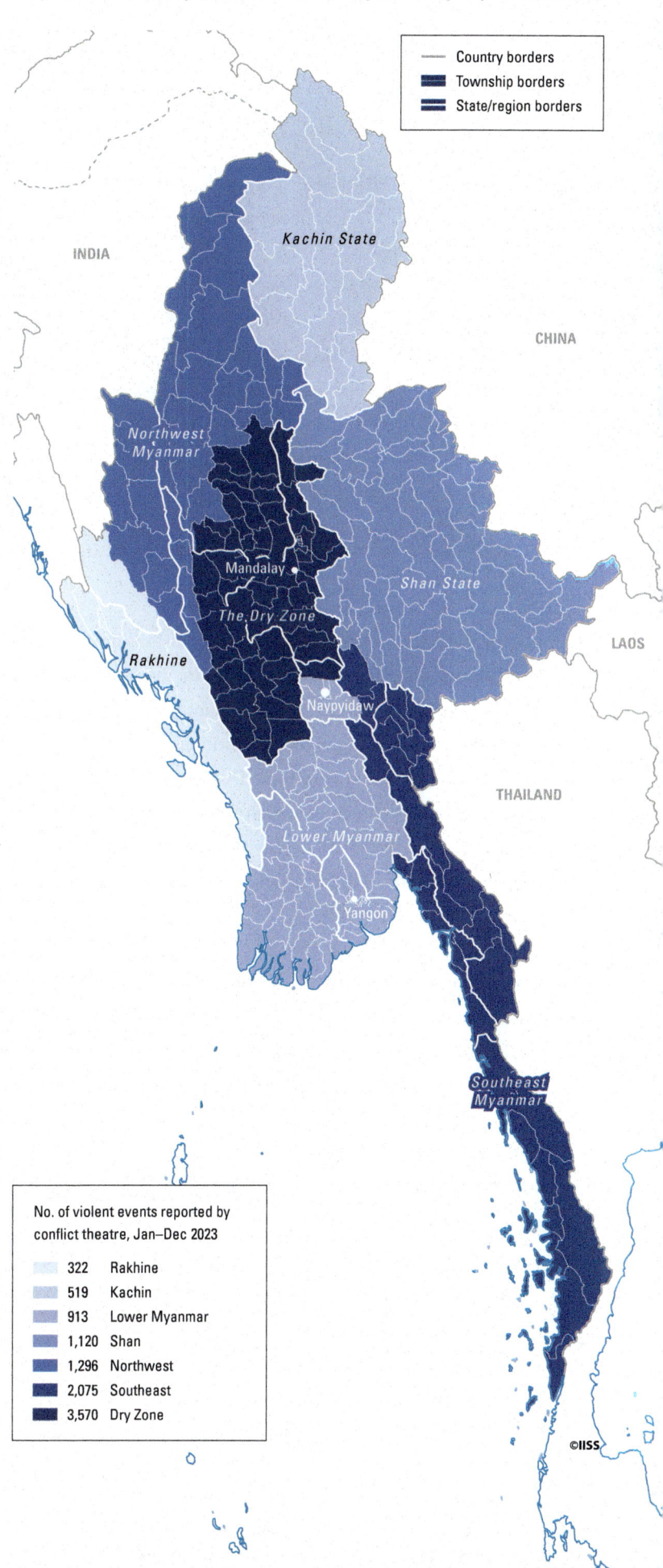

Map 4.1: **Violence by conflict theatre in post-coup Myanmar, 2023**

No. of violent events reported by conflict theatre, Jan–Dec 2023

322	Rakhine
519	Kachin
913	Lower Myanmar
1,120	Shan
1,296	Northwest
2,075	Southeast
3,570	Dry Zone

Members of ethnic-minority armed group TNLA standing guard in a temple area of a hill camp seized from Myanmar's military in Namhsan Township in Myanmar's northern Shan State, 13 December 2023

not the AA.[4] Under the truce, the Myanmar military withdrew from most of the Kokang and Palaung special administrative zones, the respective homelands of the MNDAA and TNLA. The AA has become the dominant force throughout much of Rakhine State, where, as of the time of writing, fighting continues.[5]

But groups aligned with the NUG have made progress against the junta as well, with the KNPP seizing much of Kayah State, its homeland, including large parts of the state capital, Loikaw. In Chin State, the Myanmar military appears to have abandoned efforts to contest large parts of it, increasingly allowing a new 'Chinland Council' affiliated with the CNF to govern much of it.

The KNU and PDFs in the Dry Zone have been less successful. Joint offensives between the KNU and PDFs in Karen State and Bago have yet to yield any major territorial gains. In the central Dry Zone, PDFs ostensibly affiliated with the NUG have claimed several towns since the beginning of the offensive, known as *Operation 1027*, but have ceded back two while others remain contested.

PERFORMATIVE PRESSURE

Western countries, especially the United States, have been focused above all on reversing the coup while avoiding deeper entanglement in the crisis. In this they have been broadly supportive of the NUG, though unwilling to supply it with lethal assistance in its fight against the State Administration Council (SAC). Support has been limited to diplomatic engagement with the NUG, advocacy for its representation in international fora and encouragement of its efforts to be more inclusive. For example, the US, Canada, the European Union and many of its member states have regularly met with representatives of the NUG, especially its foreign minister, Zin Mar Aung.

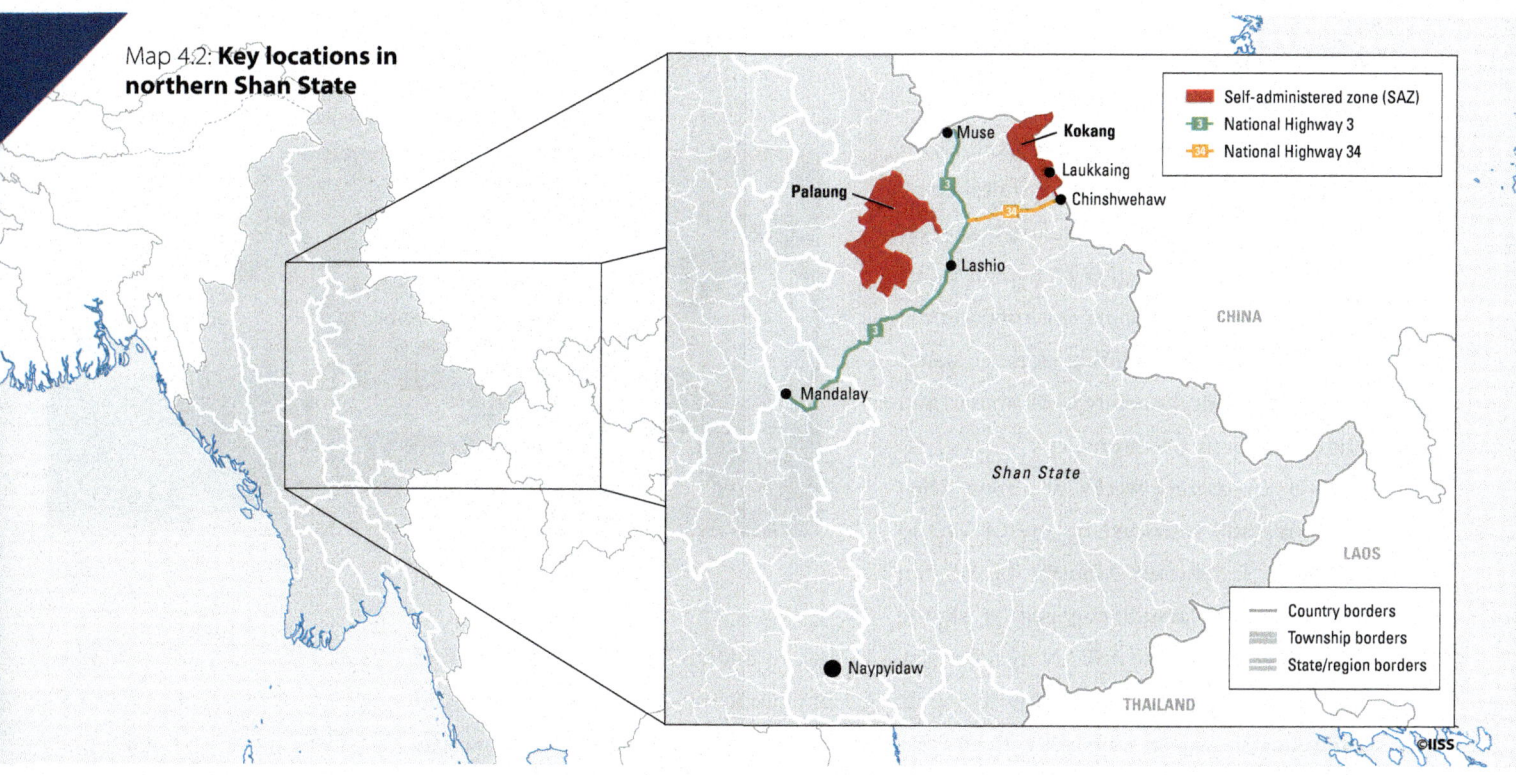

Map 4.2: **Key locations in northern Shan State**

These meetings give the appearance of support for the NUG's claim to be the legitimate government of Myanmar, despite having no control of the state bureaucracy or most of Myanmar's territory. Western diplomats have also encouraged other countries, especially those in Asia, to openly engage with the NUG. Likewise, Western countries have ensured that the United Nations General Assembly's credentials committee does not transfer Myanmar's representation at the UN in New York to the junta.[6]

In its engagement with the NUG, Western countries have generally encouraged it to do more to build support among the country's main ethnic-minority groups. Diplomats have also urged the NUG to consolidate command and control of forces aligned with it, whether EAOs or PDFs and LDFs. Western officials hope that, through these efforts, the junta's adversaries will become stronger, thus putting them in a better position to negotiate a favourable end to the conflict at some later date.

In the weeks after the *coup d'état*, multilateral organisations, including the G7 and the UN Security Council (UNSC), met to discuss the developing crisis and issued statements condemning the military's seizure of power.[7] After the military began to suppress the domestic protests, however, Western countries began to defer to ASEAN to lead diplomacy on the crisis.

In doing so, Western governments are seeking to avoid deeper engagement in a conflict to which they see no easy resolution. They also wish to avoid the appearance that they are fomenting a 'proxy war' in the region, which would damage relations with ASEAN members, risk diminishing regional support for the NUG and prompt a negative reaction from Beijing. Moreover, by deferring to ASEAN, Western countries have placed the organisation's leaders under pressure to take a more active role in diplomacy around the conflict, and to take a harder line than they otherwise would have done.

FAMILY FALLOUT

Brunei issued a statement on the evening of the coup in its capacity as the chair of ASEAN on behalf of the other nine member states, citing 'the principles of democracy, rule of law, good governance, and protection of human rights and fundamental freedoms' enshrined in the ASEAN charter, highlighting member states' interests in political stability in Myanmar, and calling for a 'return to normalcy'.[8]

Over the coming weeks, at a time when travel was still restricted by the COVID-19 pandemic, Indonesian Minister of Foreign Affairs Retno Marsudi engaged in shuttle diplomacy with fellow ASEAN member states to seek to build a consensus which would de-escalate the crisis and prevent further violence. Her plans to travel to Myanmar at the end of the effort, however, were met with an outcry from Myanmar people opposed to the coup, who saw such a meeting as legitimising the junta. Retno instead met SAC Minister of Foreign Affairs Wunna Maung Lwin at Don Mueang Airport in Bangkok on 24 February, where he effectively refused Retno's requests that the junta negotiate a de-escalation.[9]

Indonesian Foreign Minister Retno Marsudi and her Thai counterpart Don Pramudwinai meet Myanmar's military-appointed Wunna Maung Lwin at Don Mueang Airport in Bangkok, Thailand, 24 February 2021

(Indonesian Foreign Ministry/Handout/Anadolu Agency via Getty Images)

The junta first began to fire on protesters in Yangon on 28 February 2021.[10] ASEAN foreign ministers met via videoconference two days later and urged the junta to refrain from violence and engage in dialogue with the pro-democracy movement, with some members also calling on the junta to release political detainees.[11] The junta refused to heed these calls, repeatedly ordering its forces to fire on non-violent demonstrations over the course of the next several weeks.

On 27 March 2021, for example, as the junta celebrated Armed Forces Day in Naypyidaw, troops killed 114 protesters around the country.[12] The following day, in Kalay, a town in Sagaing Region, protesters fired back for the first time, using homemade hunting rifles. Four died on each side.[13] On 9 April, troops killed at least 82 civilians in the city of Bago, at that time the deadliest single incident of the crisis.[14]

As the scale of demonstrations slowed following violence against protesters in April 2021, Chairman of the SAC Min Aung Hlaing agreed to attend a special meeting of ASEAN leaders at the organisation's Secretariat in Jakarta on 24 April. By this point, an estimated 748 civilians had been killed by the junta.[15] At the meeting, the leaders agreed to a 'Five Point Consensus' with Min Aung Hlaing, which would become the basis of the organisation's approach to the crisis going forward.[16] The Consensus included the following points:

- First, there shall be immediate cessation of violence in Myanmar and all parties shall exercise utmost restraint.
- Second, constructive dialogue among all parties concerned shall commence to seek a peaceful solution in the interests of the people.
- Third, a special envoy of the ASEAN Chair shall facilitate mediation of the dialogue process, with the assistance of the Secretary-General of ASEAN.

- Fourth, ASEAN shall provide humanitarian assistance through the ASEAN Coordinating Centre for Humanitarian Assistance Centre.
- Fifth, the special envoy and delegation shall visit Myanmar to meet with all parties concerned.[17]

In agreeing to the Five Point Consensus, some of the leaders of ASEAN member states who were present, including Singapore and Malaysia, made it clear that they did not consider the meeting an official ASEAN summit, but rather a leaders' meeting. A summit would have required the attendance of all ten leaders, and they did not wish to confer legitimacy on Min Aung Hlaing by accepting him as the leader of Myanmar.

Min Aung Hlaing quickly disassociated himself from the Five Point Consensus, treating it as merely advisory. The junta refused to allow the special envoy of the ASEAN Chair, Bruneian Second Minister of Foreign Affairs Erywan Yusof, to travel to Myanmar in that capacity to 'meet with all parties concerned', and escalated violence against its opponents rather than entering into dialogue with them.[18]

As no progress on the points enumerated in the Consensus had been made by October 2021, Brunei took the decision to not invite Min Aung Hlaing to attend the virtual summit to be held later that month. Brunei instead invited Myanmar to send a 'non-political representative', such as a permanent secretary or other civil servant.[19] This decision was supported by eight of the other ASEAN member states; Thailand objected but did not boycott the summit in response.

Although framed as a neutral response to the dispute between the junta and the NUG over the identity of the legitimate government, the decision effectively downgraded the junta's membership of ASEAN in response to frustrations among the other members at its refusal to de-escalate the situation. The junta refused to accept the decision and declined to send a non-political representative. In January 2022, the precedent was extended to the meeting of ASEAN's foreign ministers when the next chair, Cambodia, under Malaysian pressure, invited a non-political representative to attend the ASEAN Foreign Ministers' Retreat held in Siem Reap, rather than junta Minister of Foreign Affairs Wunna Maung Lwin.[20]

In November of that year, Cambodia also excluded SAC Minister of Defence Mya Tun Oo from the ASEAN Defence Ministers' Meeting Plus, concerned that if he were invited then several of ASEAN's dialogue partners, like the US, would boycott the meeting. Indonesia continued this practice throughout its chairmanship year in 2023. Only in January 2024, after suffering a series of battlefield setbacks, did the SAC accept the convention of non-political representation at ASEAN meetings, sending the permanent secretary of the foreign ministry to attend the ASEAN Foreign Ministers' Retreat.[21]

The individual member states of ASEAN have adopted a range of attitudes towards the post-coup junta and the subsequent domestic

Representatives from the Philippines, Singapore, Thailand and Vietnam, as well as Myanmar Permanent Secretary of the Foreign Ministry and non-political representative, Marlar Than Htaik, prepare for a group photo at the ASEAN Foreign Ministers' Retreat in Luang Prabang, Laos, 29 January 2024

(Tang Chhin Sothy/AFP via Getty Images)

resistance to it. In general, the countries of maritime Southeast Asia, led by Indonesia and also including Brunei, Malaysia, the Philippines and Singapore, have supported taking a harder line on the junta. These countries have demanded that the junta do more to stop the violence, have been more willing to exclude it from ASEAN meetings for its failure to do so and are more willing to engage with the NUG.

The countries of mainland Southeast Asia, led by Thailand and also including Cambodia, Laos and Vietnam, have been at times more reluctant to take these steps. They have tended to argue that the junta is more likely to cooperate as a result of engagement and been more sensitive to the possibility that a negative bilateral relationship with the junta could affect their interests.

REFERENCE POINT

The Five Point Consensus is often referred to in the international media as a 'peace plan' for Myanmar, and against that standard it cannot be considered a success, given the intensity of the ongoing conflict.[22] But the primary utility of the Five Point Consensus has been to hold ASEAN member states together in addressing the crisis, enabling them to repeatedly reach consensus on Myanmar despite significant differences between them.

It would be difficult to negotiate a new consensus at the leader level, upon which ASEAN diplomacy could be based. As a result, the Five Point Consensus remains ASEAN's 'main reference' in dealing with the crisis.[23] Yet it is clear in the way that ASEAN diplomats speak about the Consensus that they understand its character differently. Mainland Southeast Asian countries generally treat it as an agenda for dialogue with the SAC, while some maritime countries appear to regard it as an ultimatum that the SAC must fulfil before it can be fully embraced by its fellow member states.

At the same time, ASEAN's engagement in diplomacy on Myanmar has pulled the mainland countries closer to the centre of the bloc than their interests would have otherwise led them. The mainland states have a greater interest in a good relationship with the SAC, but they have been unable to fully embrace the junta because they must take into account the interests of the maritime states.

If ASEAN were not the primary locus for diplomacy around the conflict, the maritime states might otherwise disassociate from the conflict, given that it is more peripheral to their interests. But because the world has looked to ASEAN to handle the conflict, the maritime states have insisted that the junta's actions not be allowed to interfere in their ability to engage ASEAN's dialogue partners, particularly the EU and the US. The effect of this has been to distance many Southeast Asian states from the Myanmar military.

While chair of ASEAN, Indonesia sought to create an 'all-inclusive dialogue' which would bring together the SAC, the NUG and EAOs. In November 2023, all three groups flew to Jakarta, where they held proximity talks; while officials from each side were present in Jakarta, they were placed at different sites around the capital and messages were carried between them by Indonesian diplomats.[24]

Following the meeting, the NUG distanced itself from the talks. The prospect of dialogue with the junta remains deeply unpopular among the NUG's supporters in Myanmar and abroad, so NUG officials fear a loss of popular support, or even retaliatory attacks against the families of officials who parley with the junta.

At the same time, the Indonesian format offers the NUG the best prospect of securing the status of being a key negotiating party, based on its claim to domestic and international legitimacy. Its limited impact on the battlefield would not otherwise merit such a role in talks to resolve the conflict. The future of the Indonesian format for all-inclusive dialogue remains unclear under the chairmanship of Laos in 2024.

GOOD FENCES

Myanmar's immediate neighbours have occasionally chafed at ASEAN's refusal to fully embrace the junta. Diplomats from these countries, particularly Thailand and India, appear to believe that the junta will ultimately prevail over all but the strongest EAOs. Their interests in peace and stability across their border, they believe, are therefore best served by ASEAN and the international community normalising relations with the junta as quickly as possible.

To this end, in March 2022 Prayuth Chan-o-cha's government in Thailand sought to organise a series of track 1.5 dialogues which included the SAC, some less powerful EAOs and many of Myanmar's neighbours, but which excluded the NUG.[25] Though these discussions focused on humanitarian assistance and conflict resolution, little progress was made on these issues and the talks had the effect of helping to legitimise the junta. The first of the track 1.5 dialogues was held in Bangkok in March 2023, with a second in New Delhi in April 2023.[26] A third was held in Laos in September 2023.

Alongside these dialogues, Thailand and India also sought to engage the SAC at a high level on a bilateral basis. The then-Thai foreign minister Don Pramudwinai had visited Myanmar after the coup and met with Min Aung Hlaing on two occasions. In July 2023, after the Prayuth government in which he served had been voted out of office but while it was still acting as a caretaker government, he claimed to have travelled to Naypyidaw to meet with Aung San Suu Kyi.[27] Don would have been the first foreign diplomat to be granted such access, though he furnished no evidence of the meeting. He claimed that Aung San Suu Kyi urged peace and dialogue.[28]

Map 4.3: **Refugees and internally displaced persons (IDPs) in southeast Myanmar and border areas with Thailand, 2023**

Note: IDPs since Feb 2021 (as of 25 Dec 2023).
*IDP figure is for eastern Bago Region only: Taungoo, Nyaunglebin and Bago Districts.
**As of 30 June 2023.

Source: IISS; UN Office for the Coordination of Humanitarian Affairs, Reliefweb, reliefweb.int

Don had not shared his plans to visit Naypyidaw or meet Aung San Suu Kyi with his ASEAN counterparts beforehand. His visit came two days before he was to meet them and counterparts from around the region at the annual ASEAN Regional Forum in Jakarta. When he shared the news of his visit with the assembled ministers, Retno regarded it as undermining her efforts to facilitate an all-inclusive dialogue. In an implicit rebuke, the ministers agreed that the chair should lead future efforts. Don stepped down as foreign minister weeks later.

Despite this, the new Thai government has pursued similar policies, albeit in less confrontational ways. At the initiative of Vice Minister for Foreign Affairs Sihasak Phuangketkeow, Thailand has proposed a humanitarian corridor to allow aid to flow into Myanmar as part of an arrangement between the Thai Red Cross and the Myanmar Red Cross.[29] But it is unlikely that the Myanmar Red Cross will distribute the aid in accordance with humanitarian principles, given the junta's interference in the organisation and the junta's track record in using humanitarian assistance as leverage over civilian populations.

Displaced people of the Karen ethnic-minority group transport donated meals from a designated aid pick-up site in Mae Sot district, Thailand, across the Moei River to their temporary campsite in Myanmar, 1 January 2022

(Phobthum Yingpaiboonsuk/SOPA Images/LightRocket via Getty Images)

It is also unclear what the corridor would add to a much larger, ongoing large-scale aid-distribution complex operating out of Thailand with the Thai government's knowledge and tacit consent, which involves a much broader range of actors, including EAOs and resistance groups. Despite these concerns, ASEAN endorsed the plan at its Foreign Ministers' Retreat in Luang Prabang in January 2024, demonstrating that the new Thai government's more consultative style had paid dividends.

Such a 'neighbour track' is appealing to the junta because it shifts the centre of gravity for diplomacy surrounding the conflict from ASEAN to a grouping centred on Myanmar. By excluding ASEAN's maritime states and instead incorporating those states that are geographically closest, the SAC is likely to receive a more sympathetic hearing. As a result, the junta can be expected to continue to look for opportunities to redirect diplomacy towards this track in a way that undermines ASEAN consensus around the conflict, for example by providing or teasing access to Aung San Suu Kyi, as it did with Don.

BIG BROTHER

China is the most influential external actor in Myanmar today. Beijing has significant influence with the junta as an economic partner and a shield against unwanted scrutiny at the UNSC. It also has influence on EAOs, who likewise rely upon China as an economic partner, a source of arms and equipment and a strategic hinterland. Unlike Myanmar's other neighbours, however, China does not appear to be using its influence in Myanmar to achieve an overarching objective, such as the victory of either the junta or the NUG.[30]

China's diplomatic interventions instead appear to be narrowly focused on protecting its interests in Myanmar. Long-standing Chinese interests include stability along its long, shared border and the security of its investments and trade, particularly the Sino-Myanmar oil and gas pipelines and the planned deep-sea port at Kyaukpyu, key components of the China–Myanmar Economic Corridor.

Over the first six months of 2023, Beijing appeared to be primarily focused on securing a peaceful and stable border. To achieve this, it pressured EAOs along the border to negotiate with the junta. These negotiations were unsuccessful, however. In July 2023, the Myanmar military launched an operation against the Kachin Independence Army (KIA), particularly near its headquarters at Laiza, which appeared to be designed to bring a stop to cooperation and joint operations between the KIA and Bamar PDFs in the Dry Zone. This is a goal that Beijing likely shared, seeing the PDFs as too pro-democracy.

Members of the TNLA patrol a hill camp seized from Myanmar's military government during *Operation 1027* in Namhsan Township, northern Shan State, 12 December 2023

(TSTR/AFP via Getty Images)

In the second half of 2023, however, an additional interest came to the fore – the elimination of scam centres based along the border, which are often controlled by Border Guard Forces, the ethnic militias which serve as junta proxy forces. Beijing seeks to free its citizens who have been trafficked into the scam centres and held against their will, and shut down their operations defrauding Chinese citizens of their savings.

Despite repeated demands that the junta order its confederates to shut down the centres, the SAC was unable or unwilling to do so. This may have led China to authorise the Three Brotherhood Alliance offensive – *Operation 1027* – which has led to the most significant territorial losses that the Myanmar military has suffered in decades, as noted above.[31]

If it was a Chinese green light that launched *Operation 1027*, it was also Chinese-led negotiations which brought a near stop to the fighting in northern Shan State in January 2024. The Myanmar military withdrew significant forces who were hunkered down in the Kokang city of Laukkaing on the border with China before it signed a ceasefire with the Three Brotherhood Alliance. The agreement followed the arrest and extradition to China of the most-wanted scam-centre operators, including Border Guard Force commanders, and the achievement of long-standing MNDAA and TNLA territorial objectives.

Beijing has notably refused entreaties by ASEAN to use its influence to coerce the junta into honouring the Five Point Consensus.[32] It has also turned down opportunities to engage more deeply with the 'neighbour track' noted above. Furthermore, it has criticised Western efforts to sanction and isolate the junta.[33] Given China's influence on both sides of the conflict, however, if it were to intervene with the intention of pushing the conflict in one direction or another, or put its energies firmly behind another diplomatic track, it could be dispositive.

Despite significant differences between the diplomatic tracks described above – Western-led, ASEAN-anchored, Thai-driven and Chinese-backed – they have intersected at times. UNSC Resolution 2669 was passed in December 2022 with 12 votes in favour, no votes against, and abstentions from China, India and Russia.[34] The resolution represented a compromise between Western and Asian countries on the Council, but its passage – the first UNSC resolution on Myanmar since the country was admitted to the UN as Burma in 1948 – represents a generational failure for Myanmar diplomats, whose topmost goal at the UN for decades has been to prevent the internationalisation of the conflicts in their country through a UNSC resolution.

STEPS TO NOWHERE

After three years of grinding stalemate, Myanmar's conflict was thrust into a violent new reality following *Operation 1027* and the various opposition offensives it instigated around the country. Overstretched and facing a shortage in manpower, Myanmar's regime has begun to recede from the geographic peripheries even as the intensity of violence and its impact on the population worsen. Having already struggled to understand and respond to the deeply complex crisis, by early 2024 few external actors appeared to fully appreciate the seismic shifts happening across Myanmar – with one exception.

Brokered by Beijing, the ceasefire in northern Shan State, signed on 11 January 2024, involved multiple firsts. Never before had the Myanmar armed forces ended a battle by conceding territory in a ceasefire, and never before had they signed a written agreement mediated by a foreign power. The enormous escalation brought on by *Operation 1027*, an offensive fought primarily with Chinese weapons and munitions, and the sudden de-escalation that followed at Beijing's behest, were clear indications of China's ability to reshape the trajectory of Myanmar's future. But whether leaders in Beijing are concerned with how these decisions affect the contest between the junta and its opponents, rather than merely its own interests in the country, remains unclear.

With that said, the fundamental barrier to conflict resolution is not lack of interest, disparate diplomatic approaches or divergent regional interests. As of early 2024, both the Myanmar regime and the NUG continued to publicly maintain maximalist aims of destroying one another. While some early signs point toward the possibility of softened demands, neither appears ready to begin laying the groundwork for dialogue. And though current international approaches could help to shape the course of the conflict or a future peace process, the decision to initiate dialogue will remain in the hands of parties to the conflict in Myanmar.

NOTES

1 'Conflict Exposure', The Armed Conflict Location & Event Data Project, https://acleddata.com/conflict-exposure/#overview.

2 Andrew Ong, 'Ethnic Armed Organisations in Post-Coup Myanmar: New Conversations Needed', *ISEAS Perspective*, vol. 79, 11 June 2021, https://www.iseas.edu.sg/articles-commentaries/iseas-perspective/2021-79-ethnic-armed-organisations-in-post-coup-myanmar-new-conversations-needed-by-andrew-ong/.

3 Morgan Michaels, 'Operation 1027 Reshapes Myanmar's Post-coup War', Myanmar Conflict Update, November 2023, https://myanmar.iiss.org/updates/2023-11.

4 Al-Jazeera Staff, 'Myanmar's Military, Ethnic Armed Groups Agree to China-mediated Truce', Al-Jazeera, 12 January 2024, https://www.aljazeera.com/news/2024/1/12/myanmars-military-ethnic-armed-groups-agree-to-china-mediated-truce.

5 Kyaw Hsan Hlaing, 'New Battlefront Emerging in Western Myanmar', Fulcrum, 19 February 2024, https://fulcrum.sg/new-battlefront-emerging-in-western-myanmar/.

6 Colum Lynch, Robbie Gramer and Jack Detsch, 'U.S. and China Reach Deal to Block Myanmar's Junta From U.N.', *Foreign Policy*, 13 September 2021, https://foreignpolicy.com/2021/09/13/myanmar-united-nations-china-biden-general-assembly/.

7 US Department of State, 'G7 Foreign Ministers' Statement on the Myanmar Military Junta's Executions', 28 July 2022, https://www.state.gov/g7-foreign-ministers-statement-on-the-myanmar-military-juntas-executions/; The White House, 'Quad Leaders' Joint Statement: "The Spirit of the Quad"', 12 March 2021, https://www.whitehouse.gov/briefing-room/statements-releases/2023/05/20/quad-leaders-joint-statement/; and United Nations Security Council, 'Security Council Press Statement on Situation in Myanmar', 4 February 2021, https://press.un.org/en/2021/sc14430.doc.htm.

8 ASEAN, 'ASEAN Chairman's Statement on The Developments in The Republic of The Union of Myanmar', 1 February 2021, https://asean.org/asean-chairmans-statement-on-the-developments-in-the-republic-of-the-union-of-myanmar-2/.

9 Emma Connors and Natalia Santi, 'Myanmar Needs to Engage with ASEAN, Says Indonesia's Foreign Minister', *Asian Financial Review*, 3 March 2021, https://www.afr.com/world/asia/myanmar-needs-to-engage-with-asean-says-indonesia-s-foreign-minister-20210303-p577h7.

10 Andrew Nachemson, 'Myanmar Security Forces Open Fire on Protesters, Killing at Least 18, According to U.N.', *Washington Post*, 28 February 2021, https://www.washingtonpost.com/world/2021/02/28/myanmar-security-forces-open-fire-protesters-killing-least-5/.

11 ASEAN, 'Chair's Statement on the Informal ASEAN Ministerial Meeting (IAMM)', 2 March 2021, https://asean.org/wp-content/uploads/2021/03/30.pdf.

12 Reuters Staff, 'Myanmar Security Forces Kill over 100 Protesters in "Horrifying" Day of Bloodshed', Reuters, 27 March 2021, https://www.reuters.com/world/asia-pacific/myanmars-junta-says-will-strive-democracy-after-warning-anti-coup-protesters-2021-03-27/.

13 Myanmar Now Staff, 'Greatly Outgunned but Determined to Defend Themselves, Kalay Protesters Manage to Even the Score', Myanmar Now, 6 April 2021, https://myanmar-now.org/en/news/greatly-outgunned-but-determined-to-defend-themselves-kalay-protesters-manage-to-even-the-score/.

14 Joyce Sohyun Lee et al., 'Anatomy of a Crackdown: How Myanmar's Military Terrorized Its People with Weapons of War', *Washington Post*, 25 August 2021, https://www.washingtonpost.com/world/interactive/2021/myanmar-crackdown-military-coup/.

15 Assistance Association for Political Prisoners, 'Daily Briefing in Relation to the Military Coup', 24 April 2021, https://aappb.org/?p=14567.

16 ASEAN, 'Chairman's Statement on the ASEAN Leaders' Meeting', 24 April 2021, https://asean.org/wp-content/uploads/Chairmans-Statement-on-ALM-Five-Point-Consensus-24-April-2021-FINAL-a-1.pdf.

17 *Ibid*.

18 Sebastian Strangio, 'ASEAN Envoy Cancels Planned Myanmar Trip Due to Junta Stonewalling', *Diplomat*, 15 October 2021, https://thediplomat.com/2021/10/asean-envoy-cancels-planned-myanmar-trip-due-to-junta-stonewalling/.

19 Kentaro Iwamoto, 'Myanmar Military Chief to Be Excluded From ASEAN Summit', Nikkei Asia, 16 October 2021, https://asia.nikkei.com/

Spotlight/Myanmar-Crisis/Myanmar-military-chief-to-be-excluded-from-ASEAN-summit.
20 Reuters Staff, 'ASEAN to Exclude Myanmar Foreign Minister From Meeting, Says Cambodia', Reuters, 3 February 2022, https://www.reuters.com/world/asia-pacific/cambodia-says-non-political-myanmar-rep-invited-asean-meeting-2022-02-03/.
21 Amanda Teresia, 'ASEAN Foreign Ministers Back "Myanmar-owned and Led" Solution to Crisis', Reuters, 29 January 2024, https://www.reuters.com/world/asia-pacific/with-generals-barred-myanmar-junta-sends-bureaucrat-asean-meeting-2024-01-29/.
22 Kiki Siregar, 'ASEAN Foreign Ministers Assert Five-point Consensus Remains Main Peace Plan for Myanmar Crisis', Channel News Asia, 14 July 2023, https://www.channelnewsasia.com/asia/asean-foreign-ministers-meeting-five-point-consensus-peace-plan-myanmar-crisis-3628391.
23 ASEAN, 'ASEAN Leaders' Review and Decision on the Implementation of the Five-point Consensus', 5 September 2023, https://asean.org/wp-content/uploads/2023/09/01.FINAL-ASEAN-LEADERS-REVIEW-AND-DECISION-ON-THE-IMPLEMENTATION-OF-THE-5PC-1.pdf.
24 Ministry of Foreign Affairs of the Republic of Indonesia, 'Office of the Special Envoy Engagements with Myanmar Stakeholders Jakarta, 20–22 November 2023', 24 November 2023, https://kemlu.go.id/portal/en/read/5545/berita/office-of-the-special-envoy-engagements-with-myanmar-stakeholders-jakarta-20-22-november-2023.
25 Ministry of Foreign Affairs of Kingdom of Thailand, 'Thailand Hosts an Informal Meeting Among Countries Affected by the Situation in Myanmar', 18 June 2023, https://www.mfa.go.th/en/content/informal-discussion-myanmar-2?cate=5d5bcb4e15e39c306000683e; and Zachary Abuza, 'Myanmar, Neighbors Including Thailand Hold Track 1.5 Dialogue Without ASEAN Members', Radio Free Asia, 29 April 2023, https://www.rfa.org/english/commentaries/myanmar-asean-04282023140153.html.
26 Nirmala Ganapathy, 'India Hosts Dialogue, Seeks to Play a Role to Ease Myanmar Crisis Which Complements Asean's Efforts', *Straits Times*, 1 May 2023, https://www.straitstimes.com/asia/south-asia/india-hosts-dialogue-seeks-to-play-a-role-to-ease-myanmar-crisis-which-complements-asean-s-efforts.
27 Al-Jazeera Staff, 'Thai Foreign Minister Met Aung San Suu Kyi on Secret Myanmar Trip', Al-Jazeera, 12 July 2023, https://www.aljazeera.com/news/2023/7/12/thai-foreign-minister-met-aung-san-suu-kyi-on-secret-myanmar-trip.
28 *Ibid*.
29 Bangkok Post Staff, 'Govt Plans "Aid Corridor"', *Bangkok Post*, 10 February 2024, https://www.bangkokpost.com/thailand/general/2739501.
30 Jason Tower, 'The Limits of Beijing's Support for Myanmar's Military', United States Institute of Peace, 24 February 2023, https://www.usip.org/publications/2023/02/limits-beijings-support-myanmars-military.
31 Priscilla A. Clapp and Jason Tower, 'China's Influence Increases Amid Myanmar's Instability', United States Institute of Peace, 20 December 2023, https://www.usip.org/publications/2023/12/chinas-influence-increases-amid-myanmars-instability.
32 Shotaro Tani, 'ASEAN Meets with China as Progress on Myanmar Consensus Stalls', Nikkei Asia, 7 June 2021, https://asia.nikkei.com/Spotlight/Myanmar-Crisis/ASEAN-meets-with-China-as-progress-on-Myanmar-consensus-stalls.
33 Teddy Ng, 'Chinese Foreign Minister Wang Yi Warns Asean to Be Alert to External Forces Interfering in Myanmar', *South China Morning Post*, 5 April 2021, https://www.scmp.com/news/china/diplomacy/article/3128371/chinese-foreign-minister-wang-yi-warns-asean-be-alert-external?module=perpetual_scroll_0&pgtype=article&campaign=3128371.
34 United Nations Security Council, 'Resolution 2669: The Situation in Myanmar', 21 December 2022, http://unscr.com/en/resolutions/2669.

CHAPTER 5

DRIVING WEDGES: CHINA'S DISINFORMATION CAMPAIGNS IN THE ASIA-PACIFIC

JULIA VOO

Senior Fellow for Cyber Power and Future Conflict, IISS

Protesters raise signs with messages stating 'reject red media' and 'safeguard the nation's democracy' during a rally against Chinese media influence in front of the Presidential Office in Taipei, 23 June 2019 (Hsu Tsun-Hsu/AFP via Getty Images)

OBJECTIVE:
This chapter examines how information operations are being used alongside other tools to negatively impact regional stability in the Asia-Pacific, focusing on China's disinformation operations against Taiwan and the Philippines.

ARGUMENTS AND FINDINGS:

China uses disinformation operations to discredit political leaders and to deter the Taiwanese electorate who may be supportive of Taiwan proclaiming *de jure* independence. In the Philippines, China has pushed the narrative of it being a positive regional actor and has cast doubt on the United States' leadership in an attempt to drive a wedge in US–Philippine relations. Governments must work with experts and platforms equipped with the tools to monitor, identify, debunk or take down this inauthentic information. They must also take steps to disincentivise disinformation-for-hire operations and build national digital literacy throughout all segments of the population.

REGIONAL SECURITY IMPLICATIONS:

While the impact of information operations alone is insufficient for China to achieve its regional strategic objectives, the additional resources and growing sophistication of China's information operations suggests that these sorts of information operations will increase in frequency. It is likely that with US–China geopolitical tensions set to remain elevated and with wider conflicts being waged in Ukraine and across the Middle East, the importance of the information domain as a place for all parties to tell their story, persuade, broaden their influence and reach populations in the Asia-Pacific is going to grow.

Information operations have been deployed by states throughout history, during periods of both peace and war, to sow narratives in support of their national objectives. Government-driven efforts at shaping the information space cover a range of activities: from the overt and legitimate use of strategic communications channels to keep citizens well informed, to covert operations aiming to anonymously influence the perspectives and actions of targeted audiences. As societies are more digitised, it is now easier for the latter to proliferate and be adapted to reach target audiences online.

But the online information ecosystem from which most populations in Asia retrieve their information and through which they communicate is an increasingly contested space. Governments now recognise the deteriorating integrity of the online information ecosystem as a key challenge, to the extent that 34 countries (including Australia, Japan, New Zealand and South Korea in the Asia-Pacific) signed the Global Declaration on Information Integrity Online in September 2023.[1]

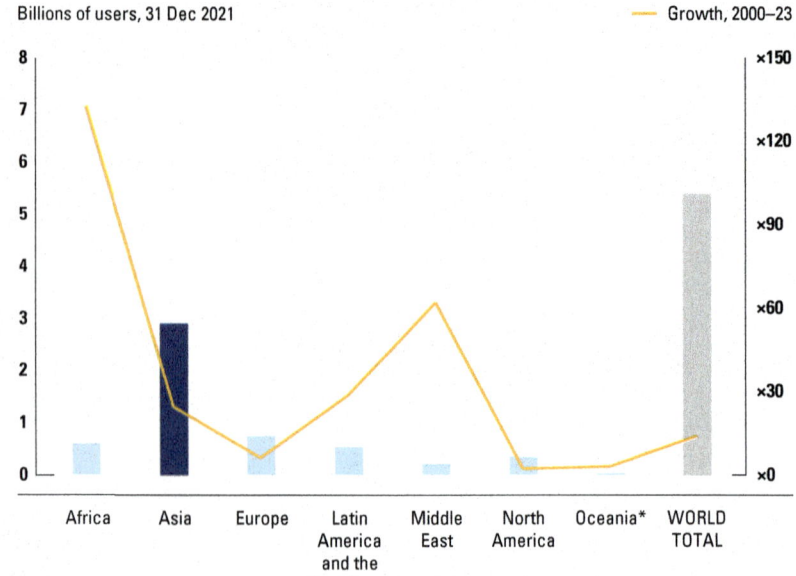

Figure 5.1: **Internet usage by world region**

*Includes Australia, New Zealand and the Pacific Islands.

Source: Internet World Stats, www.internetworldstats.com

INFORMATION IS STILL POWER

Information operations have always existed. But the use of the internet and, in particular, social media as means of running information operations has grown prominently over the past decade. Today, the internet is seen as a force multiplier for these operations.[2] Indeed, the advantages of the internet – namely, speed, scale, its low cost and anonymity – make the truth difficult to discern.

The scope and impact of information operations are not yet well understood. Much of what is known about information operations comes from public reporting on the largest American social-media platforms. Some governments, primarily those of the US and its allies, have also attributed a selection of information operations to state actors. What we know about information operations should, therefore, be considered a selectively disclosed snapshot rather than the overall picture.

State actors who carry out information-operation campaigns use both disinformation and misinformation. Their campaigns benefit from the social-media algorithms which privilege content that generates engagement. Since 2019, there has been an uptick in the number of operations that have used profile photos generated using artificial intelligence (AI) techniques.[3]

Advances in technology, such as AI-generated fake videos and photos (also known as deepfakes), voice cloning and AI chatbots like ChatGPT could also enhance the quality and, crucially, the apparent authenticity of disinformation campaigns. The increase in quality, across multiple languages, of completely fabricated personas, voice cloning and generated text, which may have previously given away content as inauthentic, is now harder to identify.

This feature, combined with a majority of humans' predilection to believe narratives that reinforce their existing beliefs, makes counteracting information operations more difficult and polarisation more likely.[4] Actors who conduct information operations via social-media platforms can gauge how effective their campaigns are through the number of likes, views and shares. The immediacy of the feedback loop assists potentially malicious actors to refine their campaigns and to reach their desired audience in real time.

Table 5.1: **Key definitions**

Definition	Description
Disinformation	Deliberately spreading false or inaccurate information to manipulate the opinions and actions of others
Misinformation	False or inaccurate information spread without malicious intent, although its effects can still be harmful
Propaganda	Information designed to manipulate a specific target audience toward a particular behaviour or belief, either overtly or covertly, often as part of a prolonged campaign by a state actor with a political agenda

Source: NATO, www.nato.int/cps/en/natohq/topics_219728.htm

The growing number of takedowns of various accounts or pages by social-media platforms for what they view as inauthentic state-backed behaviour demonstrates how a range of state and non-state actors are increasingly using social-media platforms to target the general public.[5] Adversaries are using, and will continue to use, the internet to covertly target overseas audiences.

Defending against these increasingly sophisticated campaigns using technical means alone is difficult. While it is possible to conduct reverse-image searching to identify whether a profile picture has been stolen or artificially generated, the technology to identify AI-generated content needs to keep up or with or, better yet, stay ahead of the trends in the rapidly improving technology that creates it. As the proliferation of potentially inauthentic content across multiple platforms is immense, the technical tools need to operate at scale. Inter-operability between the platforms and tools is also essential.

Information operations undermine trust in information more broadly. Studies have shown that exposure to falsehoods online, even if they have low levels of credibility, can affect perceptions of truth over time.[6] With trust in information eroding, democracies which draw their authority from an informed public could be further destabilised. Information operations that go viral can also indirectly affect national security when they pressure governments towards policies and actions that may not align with their best interests but have caught the public's attention.

Information operations destabilise populations that have a fragile relationship with the state. In the case of the Rohingya in Myanmar, online disinformation inflamed an existing situation and led to violence.[7] Information operations having real-world effects was also seen during the COVID-19 pandemic, where online misinformation resulted in panic buying of food and other essential items and affected public-health responses worldwide.

Taken together, while information operations are just one tool used by states alongside others, such as cyber operations or economic coercion, and are unlikely to be decisive on their own, they could divide and coerce targeted societies and challenge national and regional security.

Hundreds of Buddhist monks attend a nationalist rally in support of the Myanmar military's actions against the country's Rohingya Muslim minority group, Yangon, 14 October 2018

SUBVERTING THE POWER

The Chinese Communist Party (CCP) and, by extension, the People's Liberation Army (PLA) conduct information operations for political power.[8] The creation of political power in Chinese military strategy can be summed up as the 'Three Warfares': public-opinion warfare, psychological warfare and legal warfare, where all three contribute to the 'perceptual preparation of the battlefield that is ... critical to advancing [the Party's] interests during both peace and war'.[9]

According to a 2001 issue of the Chinese journal *The Science of Military Strategy*, public-opinion warfare involves using public opinion as a weapon by propagandising through various forms of media to weaken the adversary's 'will to fight', while ensuring strength of will and unity among China's civilian and military views.[10] Psychological warfare aims to undermine an adversary's combat power, resolve and decision-making, while exacerbating internal disputes to divide the adversary into factions. Legal warfare envisions the use of national law, international law and the laws of war to seize 'legal principle superiority' and delegitimise an adversary.

The CCP considers each of these warfare methods to have the potential to establish favourable conditions for battlefield success and eventual victory.[11] China's disinformation operations can be considered part of its public-opinion and psychological warfare, wherein it seeks to weaken Taiwan's will to announce *de jure* independence and also undermine the Philippines' maritime claims in the South China Sea.

China's information operations are conducted by a range of actors: the PLA's Strategic Support Force, which conducts cyber operations as part of the PLA's political warfare; the Ministry of State Security, which conducts covert operations for national security; the Central Propaganda Department, which oversees China's domestic and foreign propaganda efforts; and the Ministry of Public Security, which enforces China's internet laws.[12]

Table 5.2: **China: strategic objectives and disinformation operations regarding the Philippines and Taiwan**

China's objectives	China's disinformation operations/narratives
Achieving the 'great rejuvenation of the Chinese nation' by 2049 includes safeguarding China's sovereignty through asserting control over its territorial claims in the South China Sea and reunification with Taiwan.	
2023 In response to Philippines' foreign minister celebrating the seventh anniversary of the South China Sea arbitration, China's foreign ministry spokesperson Wang Wenbin states that: 'the award is illegal, null and void. China does not accept or recognize it, and will never accept any claim or action based on that award'.	▸ **Operation Naval Gazing** Focused on: 1. Critiquing US military presence in the Asia-Pacific 2. Applauding China's naval accomplishments in the South China Sea 3. Promoting Philippine political figures who do not oppose China's position in the region
2022 At a meeting with US Secretary of Defense Lloyd Austin, China's then-defence minister Wei Fenghe describes Taiwan as the core of China's core interests and a 'red-line' that must not be crossed.	▸ **DRAGONBRIDGE** Operation focused on: 1. Discrediting US political leaders 2. Discrediting pro-independence Taiwanese political leaders

Source: Ministry of Foreign Affairs of the People's Republic of China, www.mfa.gov.cn/eng; Reuters, www.reuters.com; Graphika, www.graphika.com

China's state-media outlets and Ministry of Foreign Affairs officials are also running covert operations to amplify their open propaganda efforts. And increasingly, as demonstrated by takedown reports from major platforms, China's government agencies are conducting information operations in collaboration or outsourcing to Chinese companies as well as non-state actors such as hacktivist groups (those breaking into secure networks for social or political goals).

Muddying the waters
China has employed overt military manoeuvres, foreign-influence operations and disinformation against the Philippines in pursuit of its strategic objectives in the South China Sea. Following the Scarborough Shoal stand-off in 2012, relations between the Philippines and China have deteriorated noticeably. China's use of grey-zone tactics (non-military means below the threshold of war), including economic coercion in the form of imposing bans on banana exports from the Philippines (causing many banana traders to file for bankruptcy), building artificial islands and military installations, and activities by maritime militia and cyber operations for espionage and disruptive purposes to intimidate, have been widely reported.[13]

The CCP also continues to dispute the 2016 ruling of an international tribunal convened under the United Nations Convention on the Law of the Sea, of which China is a ratifying party, which effectively deemed China's nine-dash line claims to be illegal.[14] The Ministry of Foreign Affairs has recently stated that 'the award is illegal, null and void. China does not accept or recognise it and will never accept any claim or action based on that award.'[15]

More recently, China has used its own coastguard vessels to harass and block the regular resupply missions, run by government-chartered civilian vessels escorted by the Philippine

Coast Guard, to Philippine marines living aboard the BRP *Sierra Madre* outpost on Second Thomas Shoal. In December 2023, the China Coast Guard (CCG) used water cannons against three Philippine vessels, with dangerous manoeuvres leading to a collision. Civilian and coastguard vessels are intentionally used around the disputed shoal to present the CCG's activities as non-military.[16] In addition to these coercive maritime efforts, China has conducted extensive cyber operations against its rival South China Sea claimants as well as information operations against the Philippines.[17]

One such covert information operation, named *Operation Naval Gazing* by social-media analysis firm Graphika, originated in the province of Fujian and was dismantled only two years after the suspected activity started.[18] Graphika found that the operation used a mixture of stolen pictures from authentic individuals and AI-generated profile pictures in an attempt to disguise itself.

Protesters raise signs with messages stating 'reject red media' and 'safeguard the nation's democracy' during a rally against Chinese media influence in front of the Presidential Office in Taipei, 23 June 2019

(Hsu Tsun-Hsu/AFP via Getty Images)

Furthermore, while *Operation Naval Gazing* started posting about Taiwan in 2016, in early 2018 it started posting about the Philippines with content that supported president Rodrigo Duterte's arguments that favoured Chinese regional influence. At the same time, it created a number of Facebook pages that focused more broadly on the South China Sea and defending China's policies there.[19]

Whilst it is challenging to link these disinformation operations directly to the CCP, it is notable that the content of the posts relevant to China–Philippine relations in the South China Sea can be roughly grouped into three narratives: 1) opposition to US presence in the Asia-Pacific; 2) applauding China's naval accomplishments in the South China Sea; and 3) promoting figures who are not opposed to China's position in the area. These are key pro-CCP narratives that support its interests in the region.

Whilst it is difficult to comprehensively assess the impact of information operations, and whilst engagement does not necessarily directly translate to impact or influence, *Operation Naval Gazing* managed to garner some engagement in the Philippines via Facebook. For example, one Facebook group backing Philippine Senator Imee Marcos attracted over 50,000 followers, and despite only being active since January 2019, a group named Solid Sarah Z Duterte 2022 (referring to Sara Duterte's potential presidential bid) made 115,000 posts and generated over 9.1 million interactions.[20] This operation started in 2018, around the time that then-US secretary of state Mike Pompeo reaffirmed US defence commitments to the Philippines in the South China Sea.[21] Based on the timing and the content of the post, it could be inferred that part of the intention behind *Operation*

Naval Gazing was to undermine the US–Philippine alliance.

Other regional countries also continue to challenge China's maritime claims and behaviour, and the range of tactics that China employs in return spans the full range of tools available to states.

Breaking the resolve

The Chinese government has increased pressure on Taiwan through both direct and indirect means of coercion at least since 2016.[22] This has taken the form of increased military activities, including the August 2022 large-scale joint military exercises by the PLA in the Taiwan Strait. The exercises included firing ballistic missiles over Taiwan, deploying more than a dozen naval patrols and launching hundreds of flights into Taiwan's air defence identification zone.[23] China has also employed economic coercion by suspending People's Republic of China (PRC) tourist visas to Taiwan as well as the import of Taiwanese goods into the mainland.[24]

A television at an electrical repair store broadcasts news about a live-fire drill conducted by China off the coast of Taiwan following US speaker of the house Nancy Pelosi's visit in Taipei, Taiwan, 4 August 2022

(Annabelle Chih via Getty Images)

This follows on from a history of China conducting cyber operations against Taiwan, including espionage, intellectual-property (IP) theft and defacement/intimidation, with reports detailing operations as early as 1996 – around the time of Taiwan's first presidential election.[25] Ahead of Taiwan's presidential election in January 2024, China mounted a barrage of distributed denial of service (DDoS) campaigns, registering at 3370% growth, to disrupt services in Taiwan.[26] Alongside these acts, China has also conducted information operations to deter Taiwan from announcing *de jure* independence.

Taiwan can be viewed as a testing ground for China's information warfare during both the COVID-19 pandemic and its presidential elections.[27] During the then-speaker of the house Nancy Pelosi's visit to Taiwan, the first visit by a high-ranking US official to the island in 25 years, China's information operations included broadcasting to television screens in 7-Eleven supermarkets with the messages 'the old witch's visit to Taiwan is a grave challenge to the sovereignty of the Chinese motherlands; those who actively support (her visit) will face reprimand from the people of China' and 'warmonger Pelosi get out of Taiwan'.[28]

China has also conducted disinformation campaigns in Taiwan. One China-linked disinformation actor named *DRAGONBRIDGE*, also known as *Spamouflage Dragon*, began its activity in 2019 and was described by Google's Threat Analysis Group in 2022 as the most prolific information-operations actor it has tracked.[29] During this period, *DRAGONBRIDGE* created and amplified content that was supportive of China's rise and critical of the US. According to Google, while the number of accounts related to *DRAGONBRIDGE* across its platforms and X (formerly Twitter) was over 100,000 during its lifetime, posting in both Chinese and English, pre-2022 the activity was of low quality, with blurry visuals, poor audio, weak translations, mispronunciations and no explicit political message.

In 2022, following the announcement in April of Pelosi's possible visit to Taipei in late July, DRAGONBRIDGE shifted some of its focus towards criticising Pelosi, her family and finances, in line with the usual DRAGONBRIDGE activity of deploying narratives to discredit US political leadership.[30] In August 2022, during and after the PLA's military drills around Taiwan, DRAGONBRIDGE escalated its rhetoric with content including militaristic videos of the PLA, as well as with videos calling for Taiwanese President Tsai Ing-wen and her allies to 'surrender'. Google observed that DRAGONBRIDGE's behaviour became more coherent with the use of uniform hashtags and titles across channels, as well as more responsive, repeatedly uploading topical, high-production-value content.[31]

CCG personnel film Philippine ships conducting a resupply mission to the BRP *Sierra Madre* on Second Thomas Shoal in the South China Sea, 5 March 2024

(Ezra Acayan/Getty Images)

This behaviour suggests that DRAGONBRIDGE's objectives in Taiwan were to negatively affect perceptions of the latter's relationship with the US and to deter support for *de jure* independence and its proponents.

While DRAGONBRIDGE's activity has not reached a significant enough audience to compel major political upheavals, its content was amplified in 2021 by senior politicians and figures as well as four YouTube channels primarily aimed at Chinese viewers, each with tens of thousands of followers. Chinese diplomats have also been known to amplify their contents. While it is not clear that they knew they were promoting content from fake accounts, analysts deduce that it increasingly resembles a state-aligned propaganda network that boosts, and is boosted by, the Chinese government.[32]

An interesting characteristic of DRAGONBRIDGE is the account infrastructure that it utilises to amplify its content. The majority of the 100,000 accounts associated with DRAGONBRIDGE were obtained through bulk account sellers who create and sell accounts for profit.[33] The incorporation of a potential profit-making industry, alongside state-backed disinformation operations, is of further concern.

Ahead of the 2024 presidential elections in Taiwan, Joseph Wu, Taiwan's foreign minister, revealed that 'the PRC has been making unprecedented efforts to meddle in the democratic process in Taiwan'.[34] The elections on 13 January 2024 resulted in a win for the independence-leaning Democratic Progressive Party. While it is still too early to confidently assess the extent of China's cyber and information operations against Taiwan during this period, initial reports suggest that there is evidence that the CCP conducted a broad range of information operations, including disinformation, against Taiwan during this period.[35]

Democracies, which rely on an informed electorate, are particularly vulnerable to disinformation operations. However, a number of studies have shown that China's coercive-information operations will likely have limited long-term success in Taiwan vis-à-vis its reunification bid.[36] Instead, the assessment is that the short-term effect of China's threats towards Taiwan has been an increase in Taiwanese public support for external balancing against China by allying with the US and Japan, rather than retaliation or a declaration of *de jure* independence. While this maintenance of the status quo is in some ways a win for China, it does not necessarily mean that in the long term China's efforts will contribute to its abiding aims of advancing reunification.

FAKE-PROOFING THE ECOSYSTEM

Fake news is 70% more likely to be retweeted than true stories.[37] China is conducting targeted disinformation campaigns across social-media platforms in the Asia-Pacific, alongside other operations, to achieve its strategic objectives. While it is difficult to assess the impact and influence of an operation such as DRAGONBRIDGE, the overt and covert proliferation of narratives designed to reinforce China's sovereignty claims in the Asia-Pacific and to favourably shape opinions online in its favour should encourage regional governments to limit this spread, enhance the debunking of false narratives, de-incentivise a blooming disinformation industry and improve the digital literacy of their populations.

Fast takedowns

Studies show that first impressions leave a lasting mark. Therefore, disinformation and broader malicious-information operations need to be monitored and removed before they reach the tipping point of becoming widely accepted. Governments need to establish a firm understanding of how their populations could be manipulated into furthering other parties' strategic objectives, and have near-real-time collaboration with the platforms in question, which also need to have the necessary tools to identify what is likely to be a growing wave of inauthentic content and behaviour.

Some disinformation operations cross platforms; the activities of DRAGONBRIDGE were seen on Meta, X, Telegram, TikTok, Blogspot and YouTube.[38] Actors behind information operations do not restrict their activity to one platform. To defend against cross-platform disinformation operations, collaboration will be needed across platforms to remove damaging content.

Disinformation campaigns also occur on less well-known platforms, as well as on encrypted messaging apps like WhatsApp and Telegram, where only the sender and the receiver, and not even the provider, can access the information exchanged. The trade-off for

A commuter walks past a government-sponsored poster advertisement against disinformation with the slogan 'Sharing a Lie Makes You a Liar' in downtown Kuala Lumpur, 26 March 2018

(MOHD RASFAN/AFP via Getty Images)

Figure 5.2: **Top five social-media platforms and messaging apps in selected Asia-Pacific markets**

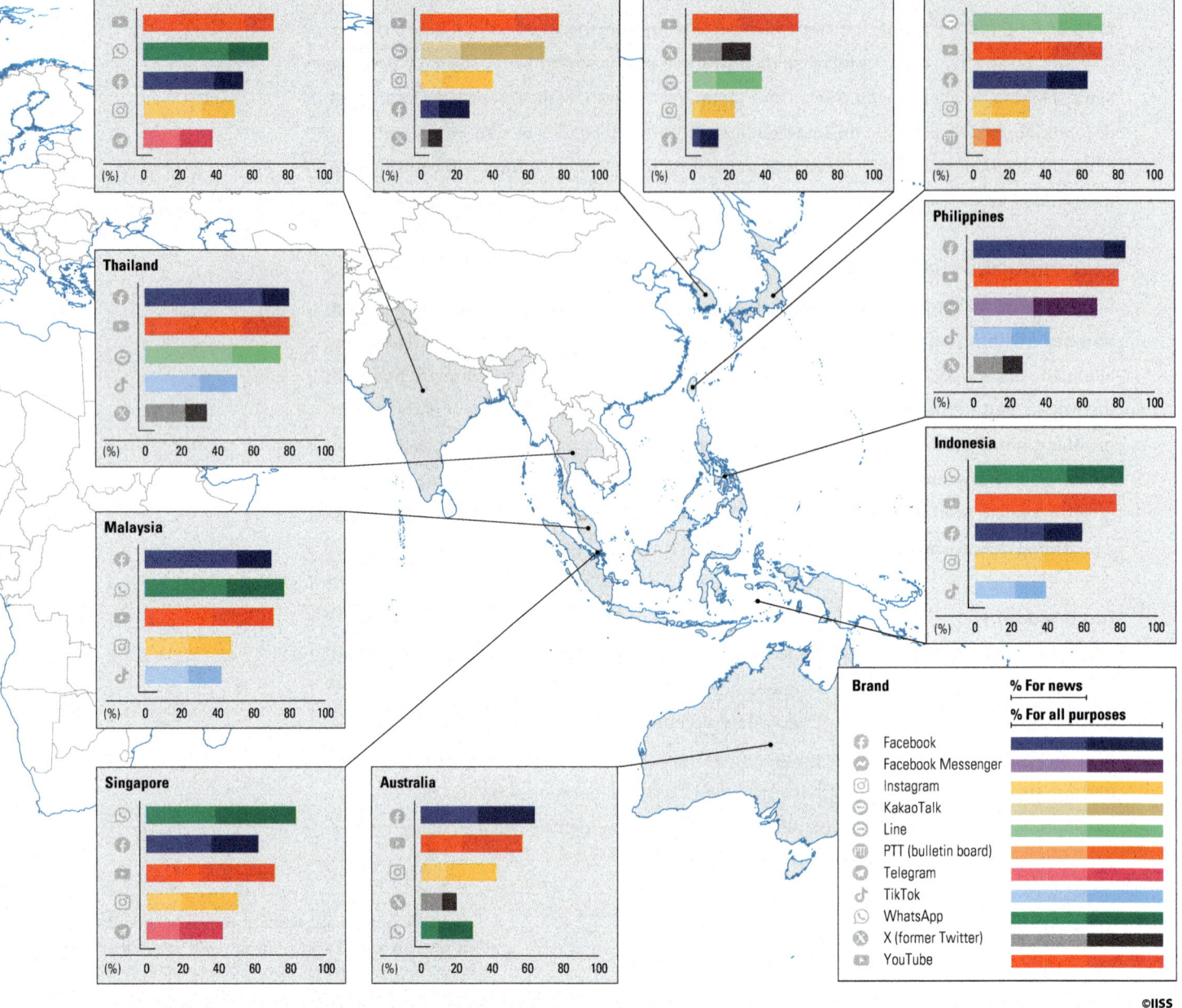

privacy in this case is that disinformation on these platforms can easily spread undetected. It is therefore important that wider actions are synchronised with fast takedowns and debunking and are used to disincentivise a burgeoning disinformation industry.

Discouraging disinformation-for-hire

There is increasing evidence of disinformation-for-hire operations.[39] This can come in the form of state-sponsored propagandists, click armies, troll farms, commercially motivated data-analytics firms selling toolkits to politicians, fake-news factories, as well as content farms (content designed to be clickbait and highly ranked on search engines).[40] The hiring of private entities to carry out inauthentic behaviour on behalf of a state makes it harder to identify the

Source: Reuters Institute for the Study of Journalism, reutersinstitute.politics.ox.ac.uk

source of their funding and thereby more difficult to hold the hiring actor to account.

Disinformation-for-hire as an industry exists and is increasingly lucrative, with evidence of a private entity in one country accepting customers from overseas. This evidence shows that China's disinformation campaigns take their material directly from content farms in Malaysia, which has been described as the epicentre of Chinese-language disinformation campaigns likely orchestrated by the Chinese state.[41] This is one example of how the disinformation industry is transnational and will require a regional – for example, by the Association of Southeast Asian Nations (ASEAN) – or an international response to limit its reach.

An unidentified man watches a video on misinformation shared by a Vietnamese law firm on the social-media platform TikTok, 6 October 2023

(NHAC NGUYEN/AFP via Getty Images)

Fact checking

Governments do not currently possess the expertise or resources to counter the disinformation targeted at their populations, as is also the case for social-media platforms. An effective fact-checking network is crucial to any national effort to counter information operations and to identify and debunk false narratives. While many countries have vibrant, often volunteer-staffed fact-checking communities, it is a Sisyphean task to parse the millions of potential posts that are malicious, and even more unfeasible to do so as a volunteer. While the fact-checking community is an indispensable part of national defence against disinformation, it is not an effective defensive tool alone.

Digital literacy

Digital literacy, in the context of disinformation and misinformation, is the ability to evaluate the quality of information encountered online.[42] Asia has become wealthier, more connected and increasingly dependent on digital technologies. Since 2000, the internet penetration rate has soared, growing by 1,392% to 67.9% internet penetration worldwide in 2022. Sixty-seven per cent of the population of Asia now has access to the internet, growing by 2,452% since 2000. However, as the pace of digitalisation in the Asia-Pacific has risen, digital literacy, as elsewhere in the world, has lagged behind. Some studies show that even 'highly educated' users struggle to differentiate between truths and untruths. To nurture an informed public and to enhance societal resilience against an information ecosystem that varies hugely in accuracy, national-education initiatives aimed at all age groups should be a key tenet of digital literacy.

IT TAKES A VILLAGE

The *Regional Security Assessment 2014* (hereafter RSA 2014) focused on the large range of cyber capabilities across the region and the diversity of doctrines. This divergence not only hinders domestic efforts towards building cyber resilience, but also limits the scope for effective intra-regional cooperation in areas of crisis management and for the de-escalation of threats in cyberspace. The evidence base for attributed cyber attacks highlights that only a few governments conducted cyber operations overseas to achieve their national objectives; more countries, instead, used cyber capabilities to conduct domestic surveillance operations. The RSA 2014 also foresaw that regional governments would need to develop cyber-security strategies that sit within wider national-security strategies.[43]

A decade later, cyber security is now considered a national-security priority for all Asia-Pacific governments. According to the UN Global Cybersecurity Index, five Asian countries – Indonesia, Japan, Malaysia, Singapore and South Korea – rank in the top ten countries committed to enhancing cyber security worldwide. In fact, all countries in Asia (except Myanmar) have demonstrated a growing commitment to cyber security.[44] However, there remains significant regional disparity, with some countries, such as Laos and Cambodia, ranking at 131st and 132nd in the UN Global Cybersecurity Index, respectively. While the baseline of understanding and implementation of measures has grown, the divergence in resources and capabilities remains the same.

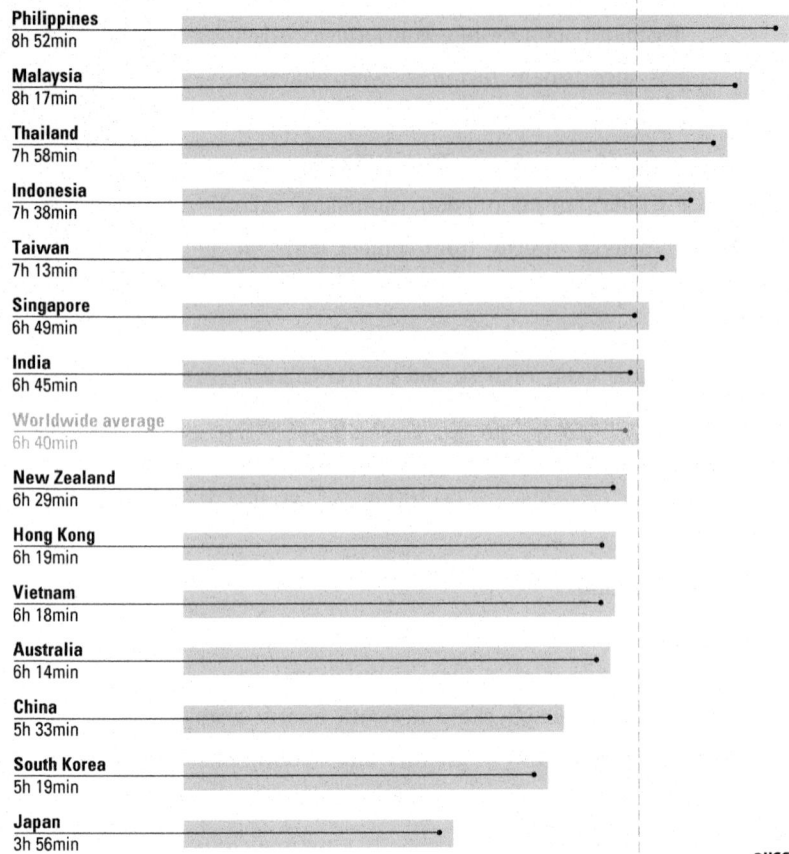

Figure 5.3: **Asia-Pacific: average daily time spent online, 2023**

Source: Data Reportal, datareportal.com

Cyberspace is, however, now central to inter-state conflict and competition and since 2014 has been recognised as a domain of military operations.[45] Many regional states have been attributed as being behind state-backed cyber operations, and a few are even considered to have significant global cyber capabilities.[46] While cyber operations conducted for espionage, IP theft, or criminal or destructive purposes remain a threat to the region, the use of the cyber domain for information operations at the scale observed today was not predicted a decade ago.

However, in recent years regional states have identified information operations as a threat and have introduced various measures domestically and regionally to strengthen collective security. For example, ASEAN member states established the ADMM Cybersecurity and Information Centre of Excellence in 2021 to '(i) share information, research and analyse cyber, information and other threats relevant to the defence sector; and (ii) promote cooperation against cyber and information threats'.[47] As the divergence in capability and resources remains a significant barrier to inter-regional collaboration on cyber security, the same is likely to be true for defending against information operations, which requires significant expertise, resources and partnerships with industry, as well as advanced technological capabilities, to identify inauthentic behaviour in the tide of online information.

A further potential complicating factor is that some Asia-Pacific governments have deployed similar tools of disinformation and misinformation domestically to discredit political competitors and amplify their own political messages, and may even benefit from the disinformation campaigns conducted by foreign actors.[48] It is likely that the already challenging task of building a society resilient to outside information operations could be obstructed by domestic political self-interest. It would perhaps be beneficial for regional countries to also build relationships with experienced information-operation defenders outside of the Asia-Pacific who have the interest and capabilities to share information.

Continuous and systematic monitoring of the information ecosystem and an understanding of potential targets requires a deep and broad base of expertise and resources. The use of information operations alongside other means will inevitably continue to be used in the region. China's strategic objectives in Asia do not only involve Taiwan and the Philippines, but possibly also other countries it has maritime and border disputes with, including Brunei, India, Japan, Malaysia, Nepal and Vietnam.[49]

Further studies are needed to better understand the strategic objectives and tactics used in these disputes. The scope should also be widened to other potential actors who seek to covertly coerce countries in the Asia-Pacific. A number of China-linked disputes are possible flashpoints for a major-power conflict, which would draw in the US. With broader US–China geopolitical tensions set to remain elevated and with wider conflicts being waged in Ukraine and the Middle East, the information domain is going to grow in importance as a place for all parties to broaden their influence overtly and, increasingly, covertly.

Globally, more work should be done to measure the impact of information operations, as without clear evidence of its impact, the defence against it may be deprioritised. Much of what we know about information operations is because of public reporting from YouTube, X and Meta sharing evidence of inauthentic operations on their platforms, as well as certain governments attributing operations to certain actors. However, these exposures only represent a fraction of the platforms in use, illustrate only the operations detected and are a reflection of the disinformation operations that these platforms and governments choose to disclose. It is likely that the most successful information operations will remain undetected and that publicly revealed information on who is conducting information operations against who is only the tip of the iceberg.

NOTES

1. Global Affairs Canada, 'Global Declaration on Information Integrity Online', Government of Canada, 27 October 2023, https://www.international.gc.ca/world-monde/issues_development-enjeux_developpement/peace_security-paix_securite/declaration_information_integrity-integrite.aspx?lang=eng.
2. Catherine Theohary, 'Defense Primer: Operations in the Information Environment', US Congressional Research Service, 14 December 2023, https://crsreports.congress.gov/product/details?prodcode=IF10771.
3. Ben Nimmo and David Agranovich, 'Recapping our 2022 Coordinated Inauthentic Behaviour Enforcements', Meta, 15 December 2022, https://about.fb.com/news/2022/12/metas-2022-coordinated-inauthentic-behavior-enforcements/.
4. Gordon Pennycook and David Rand, 'The Psychology of Fake News', *Trends in Cognitive Sciences*, vol. 25, no. 5, May 2021, pp. 388–402, https://www.sciencedirect.com/science/article/pii/S1364661321000516.
5. NATO, 'NATO's Approach to Countering Disinformation'., NATO, 8 November

2023, https://www.nato.int/cps/en/natohq/topics_219728.htm

6 Gordon Pennycook, Tyrone Cannon and David Rand, 'Prior Exposure Increases Perceived Accuracy of Fake News', *Journal of Experimental Psychology*, vol. 147, no. 12, September 2018, pp. 1865–80, https://pubmed.ncbi.nlm.nih.gov/30247057/.

7 Amnesty International, 'The Social Atrocity: Meta and the Right to Remedy for the Rohingya', 29 September 2022, https://www.amnesty.org/en/documents/ASA16/5933/2022/en/.

8 Peter Mattis, 'China's "Three Warfares" in Perspective', War on the Rocks, 30 January 2018, https://warontherocks.com/2018/01/chinas-three-warfares-perspective/.

9 Elsa Kania, 'The PLA's Latest Strategic Thinking on the Three Warfares', *China Brief*, vol. 16, no. 13, 22 August 2016, https://jamestown.org/program/the-plas-latest-strategic-thinking-on-the-three-warfares/.

10 See Timothy Thomas, Dragon Bytes: *Chinese Information-war Theory and Practice from 1995–2001* (Leavenworth, KS: US Army Foreign Military Studies Office, 2004).

11 Kania, 'The PLA's Latest Strategic Thinking on the Three Warfares'.

12 US Department of Defense, 'Annual Report to Congress: Military and Security Developments Involving the People's Republic of China', 19 October 2023, https://media.defense.gov/2023/Oct/19/2003323409/-1/-1/1/2023-MILITARY-AND-SECURITY-DEVELOPMENTS-INVOLVING-THE-PEOPLES-REPUBLIC-OF-CHINA.PDF; and Albert Zhang, Tilla Hoja and Jasmine Latimore, 'Gaming Public Opinion', Australian Strategic Policy Institute, April 2023, https://ad-aspi.s3.ap-southeast-2.amazonaws.com/2023-04/Gaming%20public%20opinion.pdf?VersionId=QA5PdhJujZo_UpHZu.24STMjJfTr.lJB.

13 Greg Austin, Kai Lin Tay and Munish Sharma, 'Great-power Offensive Cyber Campaigns: Experiments in Strategy', IISS, February 2022, https://www.iiss.org/globalassets/media-library---content--migration/files/research-papers/2022/02/great-power-offensive-cyber-campaigns-experiments-in-strategy.pdf.

14 Permanent Court of Arbitration, 'The South China Sea Arbitration (The Republic of Philippines v. The People's Republic of China)', 22 January 2013, https://pca-cpa.org/en/cases/7/.

15 Ministry of Foreign Affairs of the People's Republic of China, 'Foreign Ministry Spokesperson Wang Wenbin's Regular Press Conference'.

16 Dean Cheng, 'Rising Tensions Between China and the Philippines in the South China Sea', United States Institute for Peace, 14 December 2023, https://www.usip.org/publications/2023/12/rising-tensions-between-china-and-philippines-south-china-sea.

17 Austin, Tay and Sharma, 'Great-power Offensive Cyber Campaigns: Experiments in Strategy'.

18 Nathaniel Gleicher, 'Removed Coordinated Inauthentic Behaviour', Meta, 22 September 2020, https://about.fb.com/news/2020/09/removing-coordinated-inauthentic-behavior-china-philippines/.

19 Ben Nimmo, C. Shawn Eib and Léa Ronzaud, 'Operation Naval Gazing', Graphika, 22 September 2020, https://graphika.com/reports/operation-naval-gazing.

20 Gregory Winger, 'China's Disinformation Campaign in the Philippines', *Diplomat*, 6 October 2020, https://thediplomat.com/2020/10/chinas-disinformation-campaign-in-the-philippines/.

21 *Ibid*.

22 Ja Ian Chong, David W.F. Huan and Wen-China Wu, '"Stand Up Like the Taiwanese!": PRC Coercion and Public Preferences for Resistance', *Japanese Journal of Political Science*, vol. 24, no. 2, June 2023, 208–29.

23 Yvette Tan, 'Taiwan and China Will "Surely Be Reunified" Says Xi in New Year's Eve Address', BBC News, 1 January 2024, https://www.bbc.com/news/world-asia-china-67855477.

24 Chong, Huan and Wu, '"Stand Up Like the Taiwanese!": PRC Coercion and Public Preferences for Resistance'.

25 Austin, Tay and Sharma, 'Great-power Offensive Cyber Campaigns: Experiments in Strategy'.

26 Omer Yoachimik and Jorge Pacheco, 'DDoS Threat Report for 2023 Q4', Cloudflare Blog, 1 September 2024, https://blog.cloudflare.com/ddos-threat-report-2023-q4.

27 Double Think Lab, 'Deafening Whispers: China's Information Operations and Taiwan's 2020

Election', 24 October 2020, https://medium.com/doublethinklab/deafening-whispers-f9b1d773f6cd.

28 Jonathan Greig, 'Cyberattacks on Taiwan Started Several Days Before Pelosi Arrival: Report', The Record, 30 September 2022, https://therecord.media/cyberattacks-on-taiwan-started-several-days-before-pelosi-arrival-report.

29 Zac Butler and Jonas Taege, 'Over 50,000 Instances of DRAGONBRIDGE Activity Disrupted in 2022', Google Threat Analysis Group, 26 January 2023, https://blog.google/threat-analysis-group/over-50000-instances-of-dragonbridge-activity-disrupted-in-2022/.

30 Nathaniel Gleicher, 'Removing Coordinated Inauthentic Behaviour from China', Meta, 19 August 2019, https://about.fb.com/news/2019/08/removing-cib-china/.

31 Butler and Taege, 'Over 50,000 Instances of DRAGONBRIDGE Activity Disrupted in 2022'.

32 Ben Nimmo, Ira Hubert and Yang Cheng, 'Spamouflage Breakout', Graphika, 4 February 2021, https://graphika.com/reports/spamouflage-breakout.

33 Butler and Taege, 'Over 50,000 Instances of DRAGONBRIDGE Activity Disrupted in 2022'.

34 Joseph Wu, 'Taiwan's Foreign Minister on What's at Stake in the Coming Election', *The Economist*, 3 January 2024, https://www.economist.com/by-invitation/2024/01/03/taiwans-foreign-minister-on-whats-at-stake-in-the-coming-election.

35 Global Taiwan Institute, 'A Preliminary Assessment of CCP Political Warfare in Taiwan's 2024 Elections', *Global Taiwan Institute*, vol. 9, no. 1, 10 January 2024, https://globaltaiwan.org/issues/vol-9-issue-1/.

36 Chong, Huan and Wu, '"Stand Up Like the Taiwanese!": PRC Coercion and Public Preferences for Resistance'.

37 Sorough Vosoughi, Deb Roy and Sinan Aral, 'The Spread of True and False News Online', *Science*, vol. 359, no. 6380, 9 March 2018, pp. 1146–51, https://www.science.org/doi/10.1126/science.aap9559.

38 Nimmo and Agranovich, 'Recapping Our 2022 Coordinated Inauthentic Behaviour Enforcements'.

39 Ben Nimmo, 'Meta's Adversarial Threat Report, First Quarter 2023', Meta, 3 May 2023, https://about.fb.com/news/2023/05/metas-adversarial-threat-report-first-quarter-2023/.

40 Rafael Grohmann and Jonathan Corpus Ong, 'Disinformation-for-hire as Everyday Digital Labor: Introduction to the Special Issue', *Social Media + Society*, vol. 10, no. 1, 20 January 2024, https://journals.sagepub.com/doi/full/10.1177/20563051231224723.

41 Freedom House and Atlantic Council, 'Descendants of the Dragon: China Targets Its Citizens and Descendants Beyond the Mainland', December 2020, https://www.atlanticcouncil.org/wp-content/uploads/2020/12/China-Diaspora-FINAL-1.pdf.

42 Internet World Stats, 'World Internet Usage and Population Statistics: 2023 Year Estimates', 30 June 2022, https://www.internetworldstats.com/stats.htm.

43 IISS, 'Regional Security Assessment 2014', May 2014, https://www.iiss.org/en/publications/strategic-dossiers/regional-security-assessment-2014/.

44 UN International Telecommunications Union, 'Global Cybersecurity Index', 2020, https://www.itu.int/en/ITU-D/Cybersecurity/Pages/global-cybersecurity-index.aspx.

45 'Nato Summit Updates Cyber Defence Policy', NATO Cooperative Cyber Defence Centre of Excellence, 4 September 2014, https://ccdcoe.org/incyder-articles/nato-summit-updates-cyber-defence-policy/.

46 Council on Foreign Relations, 'Cyber Operations Tracker', https://www.cfr.org/cyber-operations/.

47 Singapore Ministry of Defence, 'Fact Sheet: ASEAN Defence Ministers' Meeting (ADMM) Cybersecurity and Information Centre of Excellence (ACICE)', 18 July 2023, https://www.mindef.gov.sg/web/portal/mindef/news-and-events/latest-releases/article-detail/2023/July/18jul23_fs.

48 In the same report that identified China's disinformation operations against the Philippines and Southeast Asia, a disinformation operation traced back to the Philippine police and military targeting domestic audiences was also identified. See Gleicher, 'Removed Coordinated Inauthentic Behaviour', 22 September 2020. See also Nimmo and Agranovich, 'Recapping Our 2022 Coordinated Inauthentic Behaviour Enforcements'.

49 For an analysis of China's cyber and information operations in the Asia-Pacific, see Austin, Tay and Sharma, 'Great-power Offensive Cyber Campaigns: Experiments in Strategy'.

CHAPTER 6

WAITING IN THE WINGS: THE ASIA-PACIFIC AIR-TO-AIR CHALLENGE

DOUGLAS BARRIE

Senior Fellow for
Military Aerospace, IISS

BEN THORNLEY

Visiting Graduate Researcher, Defence
and Military Analysis Programme, IISS

J-20 multi-role fighter aircraft land at the PLAAF's Changchun Air Base during a rehearsal for the 2023 Changchun Air Show, Jilin province, China, 24 July 2023 (Zhou Guoqiang/VCG via Getty Images)

OBJECTIVE:

This chapter examines the continuing development of China's tactical airpower and explores the implications that an increasingly capable People's Liberation Army Air Force (PLAAF) has for the United States as well as other Asia-Pacific air powers.

ARGUMENTS AND FINDINGS:

Over the past decade the PLAAF has benefited from sustained and substantial investment, particularly in tactical-combat aircraft and air-to-air weapons, developments that will make the air force a yet more credible adversary in any peer-on-peer war. Complementing the introduction of new and upgraded combat aircraft, the PLAAF has also been acquiring advanced air-to-air missiles (AAMs) that are equivalent to, if not better than, the weapons currently fielded by the US and its allies in the Asia-Pacific.

REGIONAL SECURITY IMPLICATIONS:

A more capable, and therefore potentially more assertive, PLAAF will make the air domain a strongly contested environment in the eventuality of a peer-on-peer war. It also presents a challenge for other Asia-Pacific air powers that could conceivably be confronted by Chinese airpower.

Russia's war of aggression against Ukraine has offered lessons across all domains, but key among these is the importance of gaining air superiority, having the capacity to deny an adversary this, and the impact of its absence. Neither belligerent over the first two years of the war has been able to gain air superiority, even for a relatively short period, with a subsequent limitation on their respective air, ground and maritime operations.

The air domain, alongside the maritime realm, will be fundamental in a peer or near-peer state-on-state war in the Asia-Pacific. For some states, maritime airpower will be an additional yet key component in any air campaign. The US Department of Defense already considered the Asia-Pacific air domain important enough to begin on its Air-Sea Battle concept by 2009. This was to address what it termed the anti-access/area-denial (A2/AD) military problem set.[1] While the A2/AD rubric has received less consideration as of late, developments in the region over the past decade, combined with lessons offered from the war in Ukraine, serve only to further underscore how critical the air realm remains, along with its increasingly contested nature.

A decade on from the IISS's first *Regional Security Assessment* (RSA) in 2014, the challenge of a contested air domain in the Asia-Pacific is all the greater. Deteriorating relations between the US and China continue to be compounded by the latter's ever-growing military capabilities. The PLAAF has received substantial and sustained investment that has transformed its equipment inventory. In 2014 the PLAAF had yet to field its first low-observable fighter aircraft; by the end of 2023, it had an estimated 200 Chengdu J-20 multi-role fighter aircraft.

Since the launch of the RSA, the PLAAF has also introduced the Chengdu J-10C *Firebird* and J-16 *Flanker* N multi-role fighter aircraft in significant numbers. These multi-role planes have been complemented by the introduction of new generations of air-to-air and air-to-surface weapons and a growing focus on more realistic training. The PLAAF's inventory of multi-role fighters has more than doubled since 2014, providing the service with greater

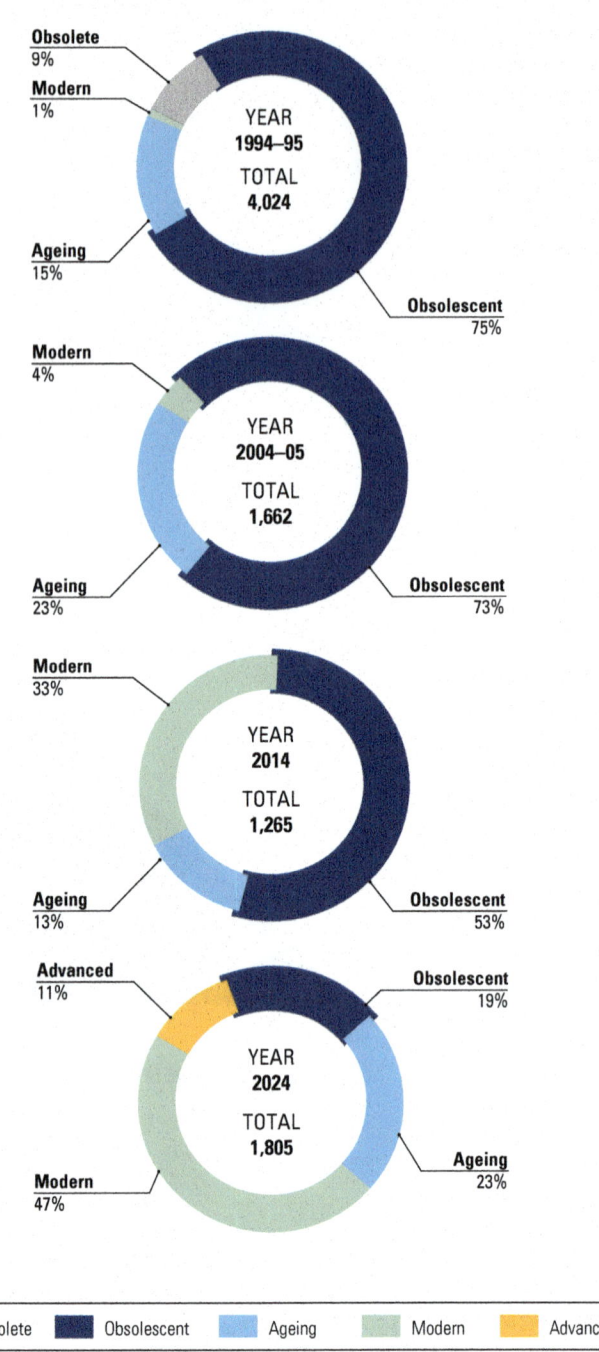

Figure 6.1: **PLAAF: percentage of combat fixed-wing aircraft by capability level, 1994–2024**

Source: *The Military Balance 1994–95, 2004–05, 2014* and *2024*

flexibility as well as more capable aircraft. For the US and other regional air powers, the PLAAF's progress cannot be ignored.

PERILS OF PARITY

China is now the pacing threat for the US and its regional allies, with the PLAAF near transformed from the service that entered the twenty-first century. Simultaneously, Beijing looks to US capabilities and plans as the metric for its own forces' continuing development. China's tactical-combat aircraft fleets and the associated air-launched weapons now pose a far greater challenge to any adversary than they did 20 years ago.[2]

The PLAAF, additionally, continues to pursue a wide-ranging modernisation, acting to further force the recapitalisation and development plans of the US and regional allies. The key regional powers' acquisition and development programmes, as well as those of Australia, already go beyond combat-aircraft fleet-recapitalisation needs, but are concerned by an increasingly capable PLAAF, along with Chinese naval aviation.

China's air force entered the twenty-first century reliant on mainly obsolescent tactical-combat aircraft designs, supplemented by a small number of considerably more capable aircraft acquired from Russia during the 1990s (see Figure 6.1). Today, more than half of the PLAAF's multi-role fighter aircraft are either modern or advanced. The former consists of the Chengdu J-10C and the Shenyang J-16, alongside the Chengdu J-20A, the most advanced tactical-combat aircraft in the PLAAF inventory. All three of these types are fitted with an active electronically scanned array (AESA) radar, rather than the traditional mechanical antenna. AESA radars perform better and are more reliable than traditional designs and are less vulnerable to jamming countermeasures.

The J-10C, J-16 and J-20A have all been fielded with a missile fitted with an AESA seeker. The J-10C and J-16 are modern combat aircraft, while the J-20 is the PLAAF's first fighter aircraft designed with signature management – or stealth – from the outset. The J-20 is almost certainly not as low-observable as the US equivalent, the Lockheed Martin

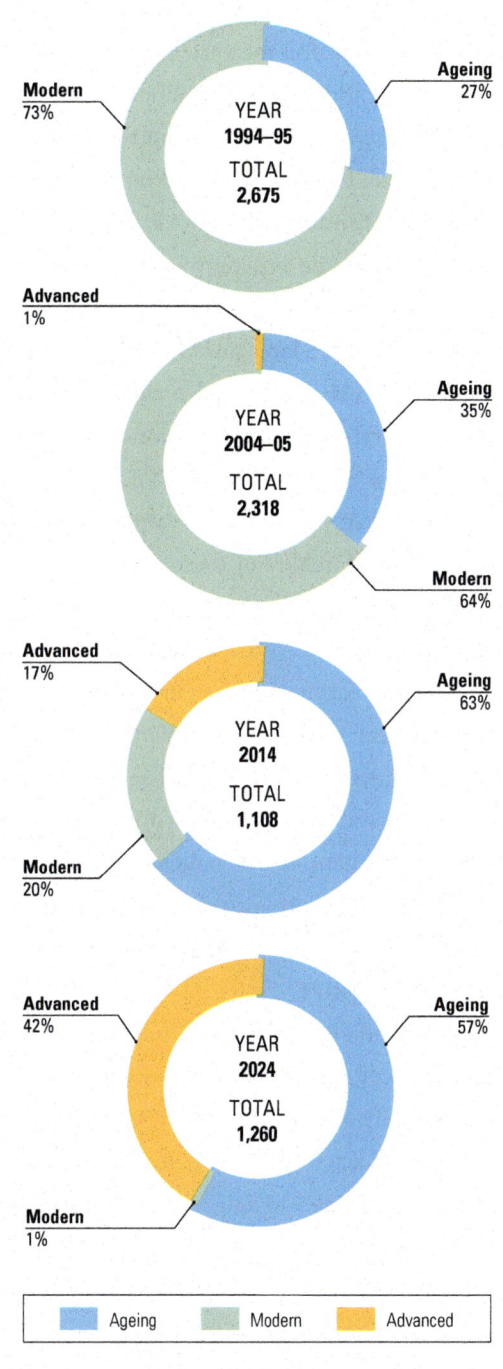

Figure 6.2: **US Air Force: percentage of combat fixed-wing aircraft by capability level, 1994–2024**

Source: *The Military Balance 1994–95, 2004–05, 2014 and 2024*

F-22 *Raptor*. As such, in terms of combat-aircraft design and performance, the PLAAF still lags behind the US Air Force (USAF), but the gap is far narrower than it was two decades ago. In the AAM realm – the primary weapon type for a modern or advanced fighter aircraft – the PLAAF is at the very least on par with the USAF, if not arguably ahead.[3]

The airpower that Beijing could now bring to bear in any peer-on-peer conflict would present a more credible challenge and threat than at any other time since the PLAAF's inception in 1949. The PLAAF would be a key element in any Taiwan contingency. In addition to negating Taiwan's capacity for air defence and its ability to mount offensive action, a further role would be to deter the US from intervening or, failing this, limit its ability to do so. With the PLAAF's most capable combat aircraft now on a near-technical par with those of the US, the US faces an evident risk of air parity.

Where the USAF does retain a clear advantage is in the depth of its recent combat experience, operating in joint-force constructs and in the complex training that underpins the development and sustainment of its combat capabilities at all operational levels. The United States' ability to execute coalition campaigns in the Asia-Pacific is underpinned by the growth and quality of its combined military exercises with allies and partners, as chapter 1 of this year's *Asia-Pacific Regional Security Assessment* (APRSA) attests.

Meanwhile, the PLAAF's most recent combat experience, and one that was very limited, was the February 1979 Sino-Vietnamese War. During the three-month conflict, Beijing limited air activities to 'defensive patrols and reconnaissance'.[4] In the ensuing decades Beijing has not just replaced ageing types, but has instead rebuilt and remodelled its airpower to be able to contest the domain and at the very least attempt to deny air superiority to an opponent. It is a challenge that the US and its allies have not had to confront in any military operation since the beginning of the 1990s.

SEEKING SUPERIORITY

The US and its allies have enjoyed freedom of action in the air in almost all combat operations since the collapse of the Soviet Union and the end of the Cold War. Described in 2020 as an 'historically anomalous period' by then-USAF chief of staff General Charles Brown, such freedom of action is no longer a given.[5] The US and its allies are now re-equipping and retraining to be able to fight and prevail in a highly contested air domain against a peer or near-peer rival.

The USAF defines air superiority as 'that degree of control of the air by one force that permits the conduct of its operations at a given time and place without prohibitive interference from air and missile threats'.[6] While the phrase 'air dominance' continues to be used and, indeed, is enshrined in the eponymous Next-Generation Air Dominance (NGAD) (the USAF's future combat air project), notably it is absent from 'Air Force Joint Doctrine 3-01 Counter-Air Operations'.

The term 'air supremacy' continues to be preferred to 'air dominance' and is widely recognised in doctrinal terms. This is described as 'the highest level of control of the air that air forces can pursue. Air supremacy may be difficult to achieve in a peer or near-peer conflict.'[7] The term 'air dominance' came to prominence in discussions of US airpower post-Cold War, reflecting the extent to which the US lacked a peer rival in the

1990s and early 2000s, with the result that it could operate in the air environment generally uncontested.[8]

How to ensure air superiority, if confronted by a peer rival, has become the USAF's priority. The primary rival for the foreseeable future is, of course, China. The USAF has also been able to respond more quickly to the PLAAF's pace of development than it previously envisaged. When it began what was dubbed F-X in 2015 – the intent to create a fighter-aircraft successor to the Lockheed Martin F-22 *Raptor* – funding constraints and the likely development timeline anticipated a circa 2040 entry into service.[9]

For the USAF, this has raised doubts as to its ability to ensure air superiority in a peer-on-peer war in the 2030s. Studies resulted in the 'Air Superiority 2030 Flight Plan', which included a 'penetrating counterair' capability. The latter was the precursor to what is now known as the NGAD, a programme intended to field a successor to the F-22 *Raptor* fighter aircraft, likely from around the early 2030s.

Twenty-fifteen also marked the year the USAF began to publicly flag a key development in the China Airborne Missile Academy (CAMA)/Luoyang's PL-15 (CH-AA-10 *Abaddon*) extended-range radar-guided AAM. General Herbert 'Hawk' Carlisle, USAF Air Combat Command, pointed to the capabilities a weapon in the class of the PL-15 would bring to the 'high-end flight' in an address to the Center for Strategic and International Studies (CSIS).[10] Elsewhere he raised the spectre of the USAF being out-ranged in the beyond-visual-range (BVR) battle when faced with the PL-15.[11]

Air and space power will be central to any peer-on-peer war in the Asia-Pacific. The ability to gain air superiority remains key to US concepts of operation. For the USAF and the US Navy, this goal underpins the pillars of combat-aircraft procurement, the associated weaponry, and concepts of operation and training. The USAF's NGAD requirement is shaped by the operational demands in the Asia-Pacific theatre, as is the US Navy's equivalent programme (titled F/A-XX) for a next-generation combat aircraft.

For US allies, it will be necessary to ensure inter-operability and having broadly equivalent areas of capability in order to be able to operate alongside the US from 'day one' of a war. This, in turn, will possibly be reflected in the types of regional air exercises the US and its allies conduct, as covered in chapter 1 of this year's APRSA. In turn, the behaviour of the US and its allies continues to inform Chinese defence and aerospace development.

The key tools of an air campaign are the multi-role fighter aircraft and their respective armaments. As previously stated, the PLAAF has considerably narrowed the gap with the USAF in terms of the capabilities of its modern and advanced combat. This is even more the case with the primary air-to-air armaments. The PLAAF's latest BVR AAM, the PL-15, now drives the design of future US and US allies' AAMs.

General Herbert 'Hawk' Carlisle, then-commander of Air Combat Command, speaking at a promotion ceremony at Joint Base Anacostia-Bolling, Washington DC, 28 August 2015

(AB Forces News Collection via Alamy Stock Photo)

A Chengdu J-10C displayed at the 2023 Changchun Air Show, fitted with PL-10 and PL-15 training rounds

LONGER-RANGE MARCH

The PL-15 AAM entered service into the PLAAF around 2018 and now has one export customer – the Pakistan Air Force. This active radar-guided missile has a greater maximum-engagement range than even late models of Raytheon's AIM-120 Advanced Medium-Range AAM, while it is also faster than either the AIM-120D or the European *Meteor* rocket-ramjet-powered AAM. The PL-15 is believed to have a peak speed above Mach 5 if the fighter launch occurs at supersonic speed, with the missile sustaining this speed for much of the engagement. Time to target and the missile's remaining energy in the final stage of an engagement are important features of BVR-missile engagement.

The PL-15 is the current apex of Chinese in-service AAM development. Its development has been made feasible by three decades of sustained investment and research, initially with considerable support from Russia. Complementing the acquisition of the Sukhoi Su-27SK *Flanker* B in the early 1990s, China also looked to Russia's AAM-technology manufacturers to help it modernise its domestic capacity more rapidly.[12] By the early 1990s, the PLAAF already had a BVR capability in the shape of the PL-11. This, however, had a semi-active rather than active radar seeker, requiring the launch aircraft to use its air-intercept radar to illuminate the target for the whole of the missile's flight.

Work on an active-radar version of the PL-11 is believed to have been under way by the early 1990s, but development was a challenge. Beijing turned to Moscow for assistance. The key advantage of an active radar seeker is that it does not require the launch aircraft to continually illuminate the target, instead being able to use its own radar to lock on, while receiving target updates from the launch aircraft, if required, via datalink during the engagement.

What was to become the PL-12 (CH-AA-7 *Adze*) was associated with Project 129 and K-93/94 in the mid-1990s.[13] The latter was a Russian identifier, with the 'K' denoting a

Figure 6.3: **PLAAF: selected modern air-to-air missiles (AAMs)**

PL-10 (CH-AA-10) imaging infrared AAM	PL-12/PL-12A (CH-AA-7/7B *Adze*) active radar-guided AAM	PL-15 (CH-AA-10 *Abaddon*) extended-range active radar-guided AAM	PL-17 (CH-AA-X-12) active/passive radar-guided very-long-range AAM	PL-21 Ramjet A / PL-21 Ramjet B
Overall length c. 3 metres	Overall length c. 3.8 m	Overall length c. 4 m	Overall length c. 6 m	Overall length c. 4 m
In-service date c. 2015	In-service date 2007 (PL-12); c. 2016–17 (PL-12A)	In-service date 2018	In-service date 2024?	In-service date tbd
Associated aircraft J-10A/B/C, J-11B, J-16, JF-17 Block III (export), J-20	Associated aircraft J-8, J-10A/B, J-11B, J-15, JF-17 (PL-12) (export)	Associated aircraft J-10C, J-16, JF-17 Block III (export), J-20	Associated aircraft J-16	

Source: IISS

developmental programme, with the numerals possibly reflecting when the project began. The active seeker, inertial navigation and datalink technology were all based on Russian designs.[14] The PL-12 and the Russian Vympel R-77 (RS-AA-12A *Adder*) likely had very similar seekers with comparable performance and limitations. The PLAAF began to field the PL-12 around 2006–07, introducing it into service with the J-10A and J-11B.

While the PLAAF was initially reliant on Moscow for its radar-guided AAMs, either directly through the purchase of the R-77 or indirectly through reliance on major sub-systems for the PL-12, this was a period of transition only. Able to provide superior AAM technology in the 1990s, Moscow now lags considerably behind Beijing in this area.

By the time the PL-12 entered service, China was already working on a far more capable active radar-guided AAM – the PL-15 – while also looking to upgrade the basic PL-12. The improved variant of the PL-12, the PL-12A (CH-AA-7B *Adze*), was probably introduced into the inventory by the middle of the 2010s. The focus of the upgrade was on improving seeker performance, specifically its capacity to counter fighter-target escape manoeuvres.

Unlike the PL-12, it appears that the requirement for a longer-range AAM may have been competed between CAMA, Luoyang and at least one other Chinese guided-weapons manufacturer. The PL-15 is notable not only for its considerable range, likely in the order of 200 kilometres (more than double the basic PL-12), but as significant, if not more, is its use of an AESA radar rather than a mechanically scanned antenna.[15]

Senior design specialists from Luoyang had been writing scientific papers exploring the use and advantages of AESA seekers for AAMs since at least the early 2010s. AESA seekers can offer improved performance in terms of range detection, including against low-observable targets, and better resistance against countermeasures. While they are more expensive than mechanically scanned systems, they are also more reliable. The PL-15 likely began to enter service around 2018, was first fielded on the J-10C and J-16 and provided the primary AAM armament for the J-20 from its entry into service.[16]

The J-20 can carry four PL-15s in its main weapons bay, with the two shoulder bays each fitting a single PL-10 (CH-AA-9) imaging infrared short-range missile, but appear not be able to house the near four-metre-long PL-15. Imagery of the main internal bay suggests six weapon stations, and China's PL-16 (likely CH-AA-X-13)

A Chengdu J-20 on display during an airshow in Zhuhai, Guangdong, China, 8 November 2022

(CFOTO/Future Publishing via Getty Images)

programme is intended to provide a design in which six weapons can be carried internally by the J-20.[17] Like the PL-15, the PL-16 requirement could also be competitive. The requirement is assumed to provide a similar performance to that of the PL-15. Folding fins and a dual-pulse rocket motor may be elements of any contender.

Alongside the PL-16 programme, Chinese missile manufacturers are believed to have been testing at least two different rocket-ramjet AAM configurations. Two different missile designs – both unofficial – have been shown, but the status of any ongoing ramjet-sustainer AAM programme remains unknown.[18] Whether elements of these programmes were intended to provide an alternative to the PL-15 at the very least is also unclear.

The cumulative upshot of these efforts is that the air domain has become considerably more challenging not just for the US and its regional allies, but for any Asia-Pacific country that could directly or indirectly face such Chinese systems. In a Taiwan contingency, the improvements in the PLAAF's AAMs and its yet-greater capacity to contest the air domain pose capability challenges in the defence of the island.

AIM HIGH

The PL-15, and likely the PL-16, will be the baseline extended-range AAMs for the PLAAF throughout the 2030s and integrated with multiple aircraft. If the PL-15 follows the same path as the PL-12, the missile will then be upgraded over the course of its service life. The air force now also appears to be introducing an additional AAM into its inventory, the PL-17 (CH-AA-X-12). The PL-17 has been in development for over a decade, with imagery of the weapon first appearing in 2016.[19] The missile is almost six metres long, considerably larger and heavier than any other AAM now in service.

The requirement for the PL-17 almost certainly set out a small number but important target list, aircraft referred to by the US as high-value airborne assets (HVAAs). The PL-17 has been designed to be used to engage HVAAs, such as airborne early warning and control system (AEW&C) aircraft, and likely some classes of intelligence, surveillance and reconnaissance aircraft, tankers and signals-intelligence aircraft. Such engagements, furthermore, would be carried out at extreme range: the PL-17 may be able to be used to engage targets at up to 400 km.

The apparent approach to the PL-17 is in part analogous to the US Navy's 'Outer Air Battle' of the 1980s, or to late Soviet-era interest in very-long-range AAMs. In the late 1980s the US was working on the AIM-152, intended to replace the Raytheon AIM-54 *Phoenix*, with the former meant to have a range of over 270 km. The goal was to be able to engage threat systems – Soviet bombers equipped with long-range anti-ship missiles – before these aircraft reached their missile-launch point. In the case of the PLAAF, the intent is to be able to target those types or air platforms – sometimes known as enablers – at very long range in order to disrupt an enemy's ability to mount and sustain a successful air campaign.

A Northrop Grumman E-2 *Hawkeye*, used by the US as an AEW&C aircraft, sits on the deck of US Navy aircraft carrier USS *Nimitz* in Busan Naval Base in Busan, South Korea, 28 March 2023

(Woohae Cho/Getty Images)

The PL-17 missile was first seen on a J-16, and the first image of a training round appeared on social media in December 2023, again on a J-16. As such, it seems reasonable to infer that the PL-17 will be first introduced into service on this Chinese two-seat variant of the *Flanker* family. The missile's range, and the circa-1,300 km unrefuelled combat radius of the J-16, would require any opponent to be aware of this threat at notional ranges of up to 1,700 km from mainland China. Basing the J-16 from island runways, for example, in the disputed South China Sea, would expand the threat footprint yet further.

The designer of the PL-17 remains unknown. As such, it should not be assumed that it is another CAMA programme. The missile most likely uses dual-mode guidance, with an active radar seeker combined with additional sensors. When first observed in public, there was speculation that it might use a secondary-imaging infrared seeker, but given the target set, a passive radar homing capability is a distinct possibility. If a passive radio-frequency mode is indeed part of the guidance, this could be used by the missile to detect target radar emissions first, before switching to active radar guidance for the final stage of the engagement.

Targeting information and mid-course guidance could be provided by either the launch aircraft or third-party platforms, potentially including from satellites, during the missile fly-out.

The size of the PL-17 precludes the weapon being carried internally on the J-20, while carrying it externally on a wing station would significantly reduce the low observability of the aircraft. As such, the primary carrier for the missile will likely be the J-16.

The ability to target HVAAs at extended range and hold AEW&Cs and tanker aircraft

US tanker aircraft, such as the Boeing KC-46 *Pegasus*, seen here during the 2023 Dubai Air Show, would be a core element of the PL-17 target set

(Giuseppe Cacace/AFP via Getty Images)

at threat poses dilemmas for the latter's operator. A more defensive posture could be adopted by simply deploying these aircraft from a greater range from potential threats. This brings with it the penalties of reduced sensor coverage in the case of AEW&C aircraft, or longer transition flights for tactical aircraft to reach tanker aircraft, with an adverse impact on their operational radius. Alternatively, HVAAs could be the focus of greater protection using tactical aircraft, whether crewed or uninhabited, or indeed be the subject of signature-management designs intended to reduce platform detectability, thus improving survivability. A preference for a mix of these options may well emerge.

WITH FRIENDS LIKE THESE

The PLAAF's burgeoning counter-air capability and increasingly advanced AAM arsenal, as already mentioned, has provided impetus to the USAF's next-generation fighter-aircraft programme in the shape of the NGAD. The service's intended replacement for the Raytheon AIM-120 family, the Lockheed Martin AIM-260, is a counter to the PL-15. While the US has released scant information on the AIM-260, having disclosed little technical or performance detail, it is designed to have more range than the AIM-120.[20] The missile, however, does not use a ramjet sustainer, which suggests that it may utilise some form of dual-pulse motor configuration, possibly involving advanced propellants.[21]

The US was hoping to start production of the AIM-260 in 2023. When in service, it will provide the NGAD and the Lockheed Martin F-35 with their primary BVR AAM for carriage in their respective internal weapon bays. Given the sensitivity surrounding the AIM-260, it remains unclear to what extent the weapon, or even its less sophisticated version, will be made available for export.

The AIM-260 will also be integrated with non-crewed platforms. The weapon has already been earmarked for what the USAF now calls collaborative combat aircraft (CCA).[22] As of January 2024, five US companies (Anduril, Boeing, General Atomics, Lockheed Martin and Northrop Grumman) reportedly remained in contention to provide elements of the air force's CCA requirements.[23] CCAs are intended to provide additional combat mass, and, in any war with China, to help offset the United States' numerical disadvantage. Such platforms are intended to operate cooperatively with crewed aircraft in offensive and defensive roles. This could include using CCAs to help provide protection for HVAAs.

China's emergence as an air power continues to have implications for other Asia-Pacific countries, particularly those increasingly aligning with the US. Australia and Japan are at different stages of recapitalising their combat-aircraft fleets and associated weapons, but inter-operability with the USAF is of growing importance to both.

Any large-scale confrontation with China would likely see the Royal Australian

General Atomics was one of five companies bidding for the United States' collaborative combat-aircraft programme

(A rendering of the jet-powered Gambit drone via General Atomics Aeronautical Systems, Inc)

Air Force (RAAF) and the Japan Air Self-Defense Force operate alongside the USAF and US naval aviation. The RAAF continues to modernise its fighter/ground-attack fleet. It introduced the F/A-18F *Super Hornet* into service in December 2010 and placed its first order for the F-35A in 2009, with the last few of the 72 ordered due to be handed over in 2024.

The RAAF is yet to make a decision on a successor to its 24 F/A-18Fs. Further F-35As are an option, but not the only ones. The RAAF's original aim was to acquire 100 of the type, but having to pull the General Dynamics F-111C from service before its planned withdrawal date meant an interim capability was needed, resulting in the F/A-18F purchase. The RAAF now plans for the F/A-18F to remain in the inventory until the mid-2030s. This time frame widens the options for the RAAF.

The multi-role fighter being jointly developed by Italy, Japan and the United Kingdom in the Global Combat Air Programme (GCAP) is planned to enter service from 2035. The New Generation Fighter being designed by France, Germany and Spain is due to enter service from the early 2040s. The GCAP requirement is being shaped partly by the demands of the Asia-Pacific environment.

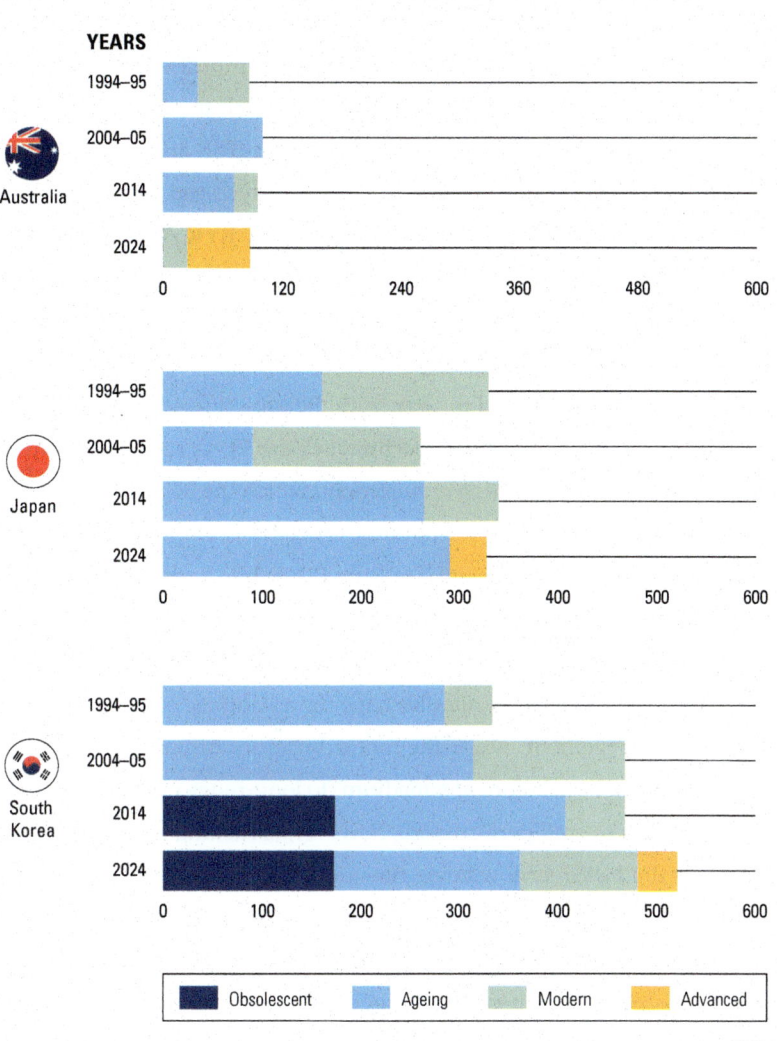

Figure 6.4: **Australian, Japanese and South Korean air forces: number of combat fixed-wing aircraft by capability level, 1994–2024**

Source: *The Military Balance 1994–95, 2004–05, 2014* and *2024*

The RAAF's AAM arsenal is also mainly procured from the US, although it does also include the British advanced short-range AAM as one of two short-range weapons. The other is the Raytheon AIM-9X *Sidewinder* II. The RAAF's primary BVR missile is the AIM-120, with the B, C-5, C-7 and D variants of the missile already acquired.

Phase 5 of Project Air 6000, the now 20-year-old programme to refresh the overall RAAF combat capability, with the F-35A at its core, covers the purchase of additional AIM-120D missiles, the most capable and longest-range version of the weapon. The AIM-120D provides the RAAF with the aircraft's BVR AAM. The air force is also exploring the utility of CCAs through its Boeing Australia MQ-28 *Ghost Bat* programme. The RAAF is looking at the potential of CCAs to support crewed aircraft and to provide additional combat mass.[24]

Alongside Australia, Japan and the Republic of Korea (RoK) are the two other Asia-Pacific operators of the F-35s. Unlike Australia, both countries also have domestic combat-aircraft projects under way, although at different stages. The Korea Aerospace

Industries' KF-21 *Boramae* is nearing initial production, while, as previously mentioned, Japan is a partner in the tri-national GCAP. Although with the KF-21 the RoK has begun to move away from dependence on the US for its fighter aircraft, its current AAM inventory is made up entirely of US systems. It compromises AIM-9 and AIM-9X *Sidewinder*, AIM-7 *Sparrow* and AIM-120 B, C-5 and C-7s. Both the KF-21 and the GCAP, however, will use missiles other than the AIM-120D as their BVR armament.

The KF-21 will carry the *Meteor* semi-recessed under the fuselage, while Japan's GCAP variant is intended to operate with a new BVR AAM. From 2014, Japan and the UK had worked jointly on what was known as the Joint New AAM (JNAAM). This design married the *Meteor*'s ramjet sustainer with a Japanese AESA seeker and had been anticipated, at least by some participants, to lead to an acquisition programme. The JNAAM was, however, concluded in 2023, with the project used to inform a follow-on project instead.[25]

The need to address the threat of the PL-15 may have contributed to Japan's decision. The mid-1990s British requirement, which the *Meteor* was designed to address, was likely based on the ability to counter projected developments of the Russia R-77, particularly its ramjet-sustainer variant, the R-77-PD. While a ramjet variant of the R-77 was tested in the 1990s, it never went into production.[26] This version of the R-77 likely had a speed between Mach 3 and Mach 4, while the PL-15, under optimised launch conditions, can achieve Mach 5. Ramjet-sustainer missiles have the advantage of still being powered in the final stage of an engagement, while the motor burn of current-generation solid-propellant designs is finished long before any medium- to long-range engagement. The peak speed of the PL-15, and its overall performance, however, is fuelling future requirements. A mid-life upgrade of the *Meteor* is now being considered, driven by the pacing threat of the PL-15.

Most Asia-Pacific nations have traditionally looked to Europe, Russia or the US for their combat aircraft and weapons. As China's capabilities continue to improve, however, this poses a challenge to many of them regarding the kinds of medium-range AAMs they may require in the future. Several of these air forces now use the AIM-120, but the variants available are inferior to the PL-15. The US weapon being developed as the AIM-120 successor, the AIM-260, is unlikely to be available for export to these countries, certainly in the near term. MBDA's *Meteor*, perhaps after a mid-life update, remains an alternative.

CONTESTED SKIES

The PLAAF's progress continues to force the US and its allies to focus on developing operational concepts, tactics and AAM technologies, with the intention of securing air superiority in any war with China. The United States' past qualitative advantage in the BVR realm now appears to be much closer to parity. Developments such as the NGAD, AIM-260 and CCAs are intended to redress this. For Washington's regional allies, using platforms and weapons systems that are inter-operable, and that are complementary and capable of confronting Chinese threat systems, will also be important. This, however, does not always mean buying American, as projects such as GCAP, KF-21 and Japan's new AAM demonstrate.

China's greater combat capability in the air domain, however unproven, only increases its confidence in the outcome of any Taiwan contingency, and in any wider conflict with the US and its allies. If Beijing perceives the risk of conflict to have lessened, then the possibility of actual hostilities will be greater. Conversely, the more credible the ability of the US and its allies to reinforce deterrence, and to cast in doubt any positive outcome for China, the more regional instability will be reduced. A greater confidence in its capabilities could also lead to yet more assertive behaviour from China, in both air and other domains. This brings with it the concomitant risk of incidents and inadvertent escalation.

When the APRSA was launched a decade ago, the PLAAF had yet to field the J-20, while the J-16 variant of the *Flanker* was only on the cusp of entering service. The IISS's *Military Balance 2024* records over 200 J-20s and 280 J-16s in service as of the end of 2023. In the same period, the PLAAF has introduced an improved version of the PL-12, fielded the PL-15 and, as of 2024, is on the brink of introducing the PL-17 AAM. Development of the PL-16, meanwhile, appears to continue. By any measure of capability development in the air-combat realm, the improvements are marked. Already a contested domain when the APRSA was first published, China's investment in its tactical airpower has made the Asia-Pacific only more so.

A two-seat version of the Republic of Korea's KF-21, now in development, was on show during the Seoul International Aerospace & Defense Exhibition (ADEX) at the Seoul Air Base, Seongnam, South Korea, held on 18 October 2023

(Chris Jung/NurPhoto via Getty Images)

NOTES

1. US Department of Defense, 'Air-Sea Battle: Service Collaboration to Address Anti-Access & Area Denial Challenges', May 2013, https://dod.defense.gov/Portals/1/Documents/pubs/ASB-ConceptImplementation-Summary-May-2013.pdf.
2. Charles Pope, 'Brown Says China's Challenge Must Be Met with Speed, Focus and Commitment', US Air Force, 6 August 2021, https://www.af.mil/News/Article-Display/Article/2723168/brown-says-chinas-challenge-must-be-met-with-speed-focus-and-commitment/.
3. John Tirpak, 'NEXTAAM', *Air & Space Forces Magazine*, 12 July 2016, https://www.airandspaceforces.com/nextaam/.
4. 'China: Military Options Against Vietnam', Directorate of Intelligence, 1 March 1984, p. 7, https://www.cia.gov/readingroom/document/cia-rdp84s00928r000300050006-0.
5. General Charles Q. Brown Jr, 'Accelerate Change or Lose', United States Air Force, August 2020, p. 3, https://www.af.mil/Portals/1/documents/2020SAF/ACOL_booklet_FINAL_13_Nov_1006_WEB.pdf.
6. 'Counterair Operations', US Air Force, Air Force Doctrine Publication 3-01, 15 June 2023, p. 2, https://www.doctrine.af.mil/Portals/61/documents/AFDP_3-01/3-01-AFDP-COUNTERAIR.pdf.
7. *Ibid.*, p. 2.
8. Rebecca Grant, 'Losing Air Dominance', *Air & Space Forces Magazine*, 1 December 2008, https://www.airandspaceforces.com/article/1208dominance/#:~:text=In%20the%20wake%20of%20the,advanced%20fighters%20for%20future%20needs.
9. Alex Grynkewich, 'The Future of Air Superiority Part II: The 2030 Problem', War on the Rocks, 5 January 2017, https://warontherocks.com; and Alex Grynkewich, 'The Future of Air Superiority, Part I: The Imperative', War on the Rocks, 3 January 2017, https://warontherocks.

com/2017/01/the-future-of-air-superiority-part-i-the-imperative/.
10   Center for Strategic and International Studies, 'Military Strategy Forum: General Herbert "Hawk" Carlisle on Air Combat Command: Today's Conflicts and Tomorrow's Threats', 18 September 2015, https://www.csis.org/events/military-strategy-forum-general-herbert-hawk-carlisle-air-combat-command-to-days-conflicts.
11   James Drew, 'USAF Seeks "Interim" CHAMP, Longer-range Air-to-air Missiles', Flight Global, 16 September 2015, https://www.flightglobal.com/usaf-seeks-interim-champ-longer-range-air-to-air-missiles/118220.article.
12   Andreas Rupprecht, *Red Dragon 'Flankers': China's Prolific 'Flanker' Family* (Vienna: Harpia Publishing, 22 October 2022), p. 141.
13   Robert Hewson and Duncan Lennox, *Jane's Air-launched Weapons*: Issue 53 (New York: Sterling Publishing, 2009), p. 55.
14   Ibid., p. 55.
15   Rupprecht, *'Red Dragon 'Flankers': China's Prolific 'Flanker' Family*, p. 142.
16   Chinese Military Aviation, 'Fighters II', https://chinese-military-aviation.blogspot.com/.
17   'Weapons Bay of China's J20 Fighter Revealed', People's Daily Online, 28 July 2013, en.people.cn/90786/8343530.html; and Douglas Barrie, 'Air-launched Missiles, a Low-observable Numbers Game', IISS Military Balance Blog, 24 April 2020, https://www.iiss.org/online-analysis//military-balance/2020/04/air-launched-missiles-china-plaaf-j-20-fighter.
18   Chinese Military Aviation, 'PL-21', https://chinese-military-aviation.blogspot.com/.
19   Chinese Military Aviation, 'PL-17', https://chinese-military-aviation.blogspot.com/.
20   Rachel S. Cohen, 'Air Force Developing AMRAAM Replacement to Counter China', *Air & Space Forces Magazine*, 20 June 2019, https://www.airandspaceforces.com/air-force-developing-amraam-replacement-to-counter-china-2/.
21   Joseph Trevithick, 'Meet the AIM-260, the Air Force and Navy's Future Long-range Air-to-air Missile', *Warzone*, 21 June 2019, https://www.thedrive.com/the-war-zone/28636/meet-the-aim-260-the-air-force-and-navys-future-long-range-air-to-air-missile.
22   Douglas Barrie, 'A Collaborative Response to US Aircraft and Aircrew Shortfalls', IISS Military Balance Blog, 12 May 2023, https://www.iiss.org/online-analysis/military-balance/2023/05/a-collaborative-response-to-us-aircraft-and-aircrew-shortfalls/.
23   Michael Marrow, '5 Companies in Early Running for Air Force's CCA Drone Wingmen', Breaking Defense, 15 December 2023, https://breakingdefense.com/2023/12/exclusive-5-companies-in-early-running-for-air-forces-cca-drone-wingmen/.
24   See 'The Chief of Air Staff's Global Air & Space Chiefs' Conference 2023', speech delivered by Robert Chipman, Global Air & Space Chiefs Conference 2023, 13 July 2023, https://www.airforce.gov.au/news-events/speeches-transcripts/chief-air-staffs-global-air-space-chiefs-conference-2023.
25   Akhil Kadidal, 'Japan to Develop New Medium-range Air-to-air Missile', Janes Defence Weekly, 27 September 2023, https://customer.janes.com/Janes/Display/BSP_63290-JDW.
26   Piotr Butowski, Russia's *Air-launched Weapons* (Houston, TX: Harpia Publishing, 2017), p. 53.

INDEX

A

A330 aircraft 34, *37*

A400M aircraft 34, 36, 37

Abe Shinzo 62, 67

active electronically scanned array (AESA) radar 127, 131, 136

Afghanistan War (2001–2021) 28

Agreement on the Establishment of a Secure Defense Telephone Link (2008) (United States and China) 56, 57, *60*

AIM-9X missiles 135–136

AIM-120 missiles 130, 134–136

AIM-260 missiles 134, 136

Anduril 134

anti-submarine warfare (ASW) 18–19, 31–33, *32*

Aquilino, John C. 26

Armitage, Richard 57

artificial intelligence (AI) 110, 114

Asia-Pacific Regional Security Assessment (2014) 6, 9, 39, 67–68, 74, 119, 126, 137

Association of Southeast Asian Nations (ASEAN) 7, 9, 12–13, *21*, 22, 39, 61–63, 66–67, *67*, 78, 81, 85, 93–94, 98, 102–104, 119–120
see also China–ASEAN Code of Conduct in the South China Sea
 ADMM Cybersecurity and Information Centre of Excellence 120
 ASEAN Defence Ministers' Meeting-Plus (ADMM-Plus) 6, 7, 67, 99
 ASEAN Foreign Ministers' Retreat 102
 ASEAN Regional Forum (ARF) (China, Japan, North Korea, Russia, South Korea and United States) 6, 7, 63, 67, 102

 Five Point Consensus 93, 98, 100, 103
 ASEAN Defence Ministers' Meeting Plus (ADMM-Plus) 63
 ASEAN Defence Ministers' Meeting-Plus (ADMM-Plus) 78, 81

Aung San Suu Kyi 94, 101–102

Austin, Lloyd 52, 58, 113

Australia 6, 10–11, 28, *37*, 57, 65, *65*, 66, 74, 78, 81, 85, 88, 110, *118*, *120*, 127
 military and naval exercises 17, 18, 22, *23*, 26, 29, 34, 40, *80*
 Royal Australian Air Force (RAAF) 134–135, *135*

B

Baden-Wurttemberg (German Navy) 34

Bahrain 79, 81

Bangladesh 6, 17, *23*, 66, 78, *80*, 82, 86

Bayern (German Navy) 34

Biden, Joe 6, 10, 12, 59, 61

Blue Sword (exercise) 40

Boeing 134–135

Bowditch (USNS) 54, 57

BrahMos missiles 82

Brown, Charles 128

Brunei 6, 17, *21*, *23*, 59, *60*, 66, 98–100, 121

C

Cambodia 6, 11, 17, *21*, 22, *23*, 59, *60*, 61, *67*, 99–100, 120

Canada *21*, *23*, 24, 54, 57, 65, *65*, 66, 96

Carlisle, Herbert Hawk 129

Cavour aircraft carrier 38

Chauhan, Anil 77

China 6, 6–7, 9–11, 13, *17*, 26, 28–29, 34, *57*, 65, 68, 79, 82, 84–86, 88, 93–95, 97, 104, *113*, *120*, 121, 136–137
- Belt and Road Initiative (BRI) 7, 30–31, 33
- China Airborne Missile Academy (CAMA) 129
- China Coast Guard (CCG) 113
- Chinese Communist Party (CCP) 67, 112–114
- defence spending 74
- Global Security Initiative 31
- military and naval exercises 15–16, *21*, 22–23, *23*, 25–26, *27*, 28, *32*, 33, 39–41, *80*
- Military Power Report (CMPR) (2023) 26, 28
- Ministry of National Defense 56
- *Operation Naval Gazing* 113, 115
- paramilitary forces 59
- People's Liberation Army (PLA) 23, 28–29, 32–33, 39, 112, 115–116
- People's Liberation Army Air Force (PLAAF) 12, 23, 29, 52, 54–55, 56, 58, 65, *126*, *127*, *130–131*, *137*
- People's Liberation Army Navy (PLAN) 29, 32–33, 53, 56–58, 65
- *The Science of Military Strategy* (TSMS) 30, 112

China–ASEAN Code of Conduct in the South China Sea 62, 68

China–Myanmar Economic Corridor 103

China–Pakistan Economic Corridor 32

China–Vietnam War (1979) 128

Chinese–Indian border skirmishes (2020–2021) 7, 74–78

Clinton, Bill 57

Cobra Gold (exercise) 19, *21*, 25, 26, *27*

Code for Unplanned Encounters at Sea (CUES) 58, 62

Colombo Security Conclave 78, 81

Comprehensive Strategic Partnership (India and Australia) 77

counter-terrorism 9, 15–16, 18, *24*, 23–26, 40, 59, 61–63, 66, 78–79, 86–87

COVID-19 pandemic 7, 77, 98, 111, 115

Cowpens (USS) 53, *54*

cyber security 24, 59, 63–64, 67, 120

D

Djibouti 30

Dong Jun 32

Don Pramudwinai 101–102

Doshi, Rush 59

Doval, Ajit 81

DRAGONBRIDGE (disinformation campaign) *113*, 116–117

Duterte, Rodrigo 114

Duterte, Sara 114

E

East China Sea 16, 30–31, 39–40, 57, 67

Enhanced Defense Cooperation Agreement (EDCA) (Philippines and United States) 22, 40

European Union 6, 41, 96, 100
- military and naval exercises 39

F

F-22 aircraft 127, 129

F-35 aircraft 134–135

F/A-18F aircraft *118*, 135

Facebook 114, *118*

Flynn, Charles A. 28–29

France *6*, 34, 41, *66*, 79, 85, 135
    military and naval exercises 16, *21, 23, 24,* 34, *80*

Future Combat Air System programme 34

G

G7 97

Galwan Valley *see* Chinese–Indian border skirmishes (2020–2021)

Garuda Shield (exercise) 22

General Atomics 134

Germany 135
    military and naval exercises 16, *21*

Global Combat Air Programme (GCAP) (Italy, Japan and United Kingdom) 38, 135–136

Global Declaration on Information Integrity Online (2023) 110

Gulf, the 75, 79, 87

H

Hainan Island incident (2001) 57

humanitarian assistance and disaster relief (HADR) 15–16, 18, 22–26, *24*, 29, 31, 39

I

India 7, 9, 11, 31, 33, 59, *60*, 61, *83, 85, 86,* 88, 93, 101, 104, *118, 120,* 121
    defence spending 74
    Indian Army 79, 84
    Indian Navy 37, 77, 79, 84–85, 87
    lines of credit (LoCs) 73, 79, 82
    military and naval exercises 17, 22, *23, 24,* 73–74, 79, *80,* 87, 88 *see also Malabar* (exercise); *Singapore–India Maritime Bilateral Exercise* (SIMBEX)

Indian Ocean 11, 16, 31–32, 38, 40, 73, 75, 78–79, 81–82, 85–88, 93 *see also* Colombo Security Concave

Indonesia *6*, 11, 13, *17, 23,* 59, *60,* 61–63, *66,* 79, 81–82, 85–86, 98–100, 102, *118, 120,* 120
    military and naval exercises 18, 22, 26, *27, 80*

Iran 40

Iraq War (2003–11) 28

Israel *21*, 40

Italy 135
    military and naval exercises 39

J

J-10 aircraft *54,* 126–127, *131,* 131–132

J-16 aircraft *54–55,* 126–127, *131,* 132–133, 137

J-20 aircraft 126–127, *131,* 132–133, 137

Japan *6,* 7, 10–11, *17,* 41, 52, *54,* 57, 59, *60,* 61, 63–65, *65, 66,* 67, 68, 74, 77, 79, 81, 88, 110, 117, *118, 120,* 120–121, 135–136, *135*
    Japan Air Self-Defense Force 134–135
    Maritime Self Defense Force 37, 41
    military and naval exercises 18, *23, 24,* 26, 29, 38, 39, *80*

Japan–China Maritime and Aerial Communication Mechanism 52

Joint Staff Dialogue Mechanism (2017) (United States and China) 56

K

Kakadu (exercise) 34

KF-21 aircraft 136

Korea Aerospace Industries 135–136

Kumar, Radhakrishnan 80

L

Laos *6, 21,* 22, *23, 24, 66,* 100–101, 120

Latheef, Hussain Mohamed 78

Liaoning aircraft carrier 53, *54*

Libya 40

Linyi (People's Liberation Army Navy) *32,* 33

Li Shangfu 58

Lockheed Martin 127, 129, 134

M

Malabar (exercise) 26, 77

Malacca Straits Patrol (MSP) (Indonesia, Malaysia, Singapore and Thailand) *6,* 9, 62, *66*

Malaysia *6,* 7, 11, *21,* 59, *60,* 62–63, *66,* 79, 99–100, *118,* 119–121, *120*
    military and naval exercises 17, *21,* 22, *23, 24, 27, 80*

Maldives, the 78–79, *80,* 81–82, *83,* 85, 87

Marcos, Imee 114

Mauritius 78, 81–82, *83,* 87

MBDA 136

Memorandum of Understanding of Notification of Major Military Activities Confidence-Building Measures Mechanism (2014) (United States and China) 56

Memorandum of Understanding on the Rules of Behavior for the Safety of Air and Maritime Encounters (2014) (United States and China) 56

Meta 117, 121

Meteor missiles 130, 136

Military Balance (2024) 137

Military Maritime Consultative Agreement (MMCA) (United States and China) 53, 58–59

Min Aung Hlaing 98–99, 101

Modi, Narendra 74–76, 79, 82

Mozambique 87

Myanmar 6, 9, 10, 12, *21, 23, 24*, 67, 80, 83, 95, 97, *101*, 104, 111
    2021 coup 9, 93–94, 96–97
    2024 ceasefire deal 99, 103–104
    Dry Zone 95–96, 103
    ethnic armed organisations (EAOs) 94–95, 97, 100–103
    K3C (Kachin Independence Organization (KIO), Karen National Union (KNU), Karenni National Progressive Party (KNPP) and Chin National Front (CNF)) 94–96
    Kachin Independence Army (KIA) 103
    local defence forces (LDFs) 94–95, 97
    Myanmar National Democratic Alliance Army (MNDAA) 95, 103
    National Unity Government (NUG) 95–97, 99, 100–101, 104
    Operation 1027 96, 103–104
    People's Defence Forces (PDFs) 94–97, 103
    Shan State 95, *95, 97*, 103–104
    State Administration Council (SAC) (junta) 93–97, 100–101, 104
    Three Brotherhood Alliance (Arakan Army (AA) and Ta'ang National Liberation Army (TNLA)) 95–96, 103

N

Nepal *21, 22, 23, 24*, 80, *83*, 121

New Generation Fighter (France, Germany and Spain) 135

New Zealand *21, 23, 24, 66*, 81, 110, *120*

North Korea 6, 7, 25, 52, 63–64, 66–68

Northrop Grumman 134

O

Obama, Barack 53

Oman *80*, 81

Operation Pathways (US Army programme) 29

Operation Team-Work (exercise) 25

P

Pacific Partnership (mission) 26

Pacific Skies 24 (exercise) 34

Pakistan 6, 13, 40, *66*, 76, 87, 130
    military and naval exercises 16, *21*, 22, *23*, 24, *24, 32*, 33
    Pakistan Navy (PN) 33

Paolo Thaon di Revel-class frigates 38

Pelosi, Nancy 52, 59, 61, 115–116

Philippines 6, 7, 10–12, *54–55, 57*, 59, 61–65, *66*, 80, 82, *83*, 100, 109, 112, *113*, 115, *118, 120*
    BRP *Sierra Madre* 114
    military and naval exercises *17, 21*, 22, *23, 24*, 40

Pitch Black (exercise) 34, 38

PL-12 missiles 131, *131*, 137

PL-15 missiles 129, 130, *131*, 132, 136–137

PL-16 missiles 132

PL-17 missiles *131*, 133, 137

Pompeo, Mike 114

Prayuth Chan-ocha 101

Q

Qatar 79, *80*

Qin Gang 58

Quadrilateral Security Dialogue (Quad) 9, 74–75, 77, 81

R

R-77 missiles 131, 136

Raytheon 130, 133–135

Red Cross 102

Retno Marsudi 98, 102

Rim of the Pacific (RIMPAC) (exercise) *21*, 38, 39

Russia 33, 40, 52, 62, 63–64, *66*, 67, *80*, 81–82, 104, 126, 130–131, 136
    military and naval exercises *17, 23, 24, 26*, 31

S

Saif (Pakistan Navy) 33

Saudi Arabia 79, *80*
    military and naval exercises 24, 40

Sea Guardian (exercise) 24, *32*, 33

Senkaku/Diaoyu islands 67

Seychelles, the 78, *80*, 81–82, *83*, 87

Shah Jahan (Pakistan Navy) *32*, 33

Shangri-La Dialogue 13, 58

Shapps, Grant 40

Sihasak Phuangketkeow 102

Singapore 6, *37*, 59, *60*, 61–62, 79, 81, 85, 99–100, *118*, 120, *120*
    military and naval exercises *17, 21*, 22, *23*, 24, 26, *27, 80*

Singapore–India Maritime Bilateral Exercise (SIMBEX) 85

Singh, Rajnath 79

Six-Party Talks (China, Japan, North Korea, Russia, South Korea and United States) 52, 63, 66–68

South China Sea 6, 7, 11, 16, 25, 28, 30–31, 39–41, 53, 57, 59, 61–63, 66, 67, 68, 112–114, *113*, 133
    Scarborough Shoal stand-off (2012) 113

Southeast Asia 11, 26, 52, 66–68, 75, 79, 82, 85, 87–88, 100 *see also* Association of Southeast Asian Networks (ASEAN)

Southeast Asia Treaty Organization (SEATO) 25

South Korea 6, 7, 10–11, *17*, 28, 52, *60*, *66*, 63–64, 68, 110, *118*, 120, *120*, 135
    military and naval exercises *23*, *24*, 26, *27*, *80*

Spain 135
    military and naval exercises 34

Spratly Islands 68

Sri Lanka 6, *23*, *24*, 78, *80*, 81–82, *83*, 87

Su-27SK aircraft 130

Sukhoi 130

T

Taiwan 6, *24*, 12, 25, 28–29, 39, 52, 57, 59, *60*, 61, 88, 109, 112, *113*, 114, 117, *118*, *120*, 128, 132, 136
    2024 presidential election 12, 115–116

Taiwan Strait 7, 11, *37*, 41, 65, 115

Talisman Sabre (exercise) 26, 28, 34

Tanzania 87

Telegram 117, *118*

Thailand 6, 9, 11–12, *17*, 25, 59, *60*, 62, 81–82, 85–86, 93, 99, 100–102, *101*, 104, *118*, *120*
    military and naval exercises *21*, 22, *23*, *24*, 25–26, *27*, *80*

Tornado aircraft 34

Trilateral Cooperative Arrangement (TCA) (2016) (Indonesia, Malaysia and the Philippines) 62, *66*

Trump, Donald 6, 57

Tsai Ing-wen 116

Twitter *see* X

Typhoon aircraft 34

U

Ukraine war (2022–present) 13, 33, 64, 67, 109, 121, 126

United Arab Emirates 79, *80*, 85

United Kingdom 6, *23*, *24*, 41, 135–136
    Carrier Strike Group *36–37*, 41
    military and naval exercises 16, *21*, *23*, *24*, 41, *80*

United Nations 97, 102, 104
    United Nations Convention on the Law of the Sea (UNCLOS) 51, 58, 61, 65

United States 6, 7, 10, 13, 33, 41, *57*, *65*, *66*, 68, 74, 77, 85, 88, 96, 99–100, 109–110, *113*, 114–115, 117, 121, 125–126, 129, 132, 135–137
    arms sales 76
    Department of Defense 126
    Indo-Pacific Command 26, 28
    Joint Pacific Multinational Readiness Center 40
    military and naval exercises 15–16, *17*, 18, 20, *21*, 22–23, *23*, *24*, *27*, 29, 34, 40–41, *80*
    Next-Generation Air Dominance (NGAD) 128–129, 134, 136
    Pentagon 26, 39, 52–53, 56–57
    United States Air Force (USAF) *54–55*, 56, 128–129, 135
    United States Navy *37*, 53, 56, 129, 133

US–India Initiative on Critical and Emerging Technology (iCET) 76

V

Vietnam 6, 7, 11, 59, 61–63, *66*, 79, *80*, 81–82, *83*, 85, 100, *120*, 121
    military and naval exercises *17*, *21*, *23*, *24*, 39

Vietnam War 25

W

Wei Fenghe 58, *113*

WhatsApp 117, *118*

Wormuth, Christine 28

Wu, Joseph 116

X

X 115, 117, *118*, 121

Xi Jinping 7, 31, 53, 59, 67, 75

Y

Yama Sakura (exercise) 39

Yemen 40
    Houthis 40–41

YouTube 116, 121